Republic of Shame

Republic of Shame

Stories from Ireland's Institutions for 'Fallen Women'

CAELAINN HOGAN

PENGUIN
IRELAND

PENGUIN IRELAND

UK | USA | Canada | Ireland | Australia
India | New Zealand | South Africa

Penguin Ireland is part of the Penguin Random House group of companies
whose addresses can be found at global.penguinrandomhouse.com.

First published 2019

001

Copyright © Caelainn Hogan, 2019

The moral right of the author has been asserted

Set in 12/14.75 pt Dante MT Std
Typeset by Jouve (UK), Milton Keynes
Printed and bound in Great Britain by Clays Ltd, Elcograf S.p.A.

A CIP catalogue record for this book is available from the British Library

ISBN: 978-1-844-88445-2

www.greenpenguin.co.uk

MIX
Paper from
responsible sources
FSC® C018179

Penguin Random House is committed to a
sustainable future for our business, our readers
and our planet. This book is made from Forest
Stewardship Council® certified paper.

Contents

Tea in the Provincial House

In the bleak first hours of a new year, the park across from the house where I grew up was empty and wild in the darkness. There had been an unholy family row, a sour beginning, and my mother had suggested we go and walk it off. The dogs dived ahead, and as we strolled through the wet grass at the strangest of hours, possibilities blossomed in the biting air and we could breathe again.

The paths and fields of The Rockies – as locals call Rockfield Park – were so familiar that my feet walked them without my mind having to pay any attention. As students in the navy uniforms of Guardian Angels', the primary school that borders the park, we had potato and spoon races in the fields. On the steps that lead into the park from the school, we would often pass young people sitting hunched together, wreathed in cigarette smoke, cans occasionally crackling in their fists. Soon enough it was my friends on the steps and crouched under the monkey puzzle tree, drinking naggins in the damp summers, kissing boys in the grass. The local priest, Father Gaughan, was often to be seen sashaying through the park in his dramatic black soutane and white collar. In darkness, the scent of foxes behind the park walls drove our mongrel terrier mad.

As my mother, my younger brother and I walked, we could see a high wall on the flank of the park. Set into the wall were a narrow gate and a little electronic keypad; mounted on a pole behind the wall was a CCTV camera. Through the bars of the gate, we could spy a stately blush-pink building surrounded by manicured slopes and gardens. I knew vaguely that 'the nuns' lived in there, but I couldn't have said what order they belonged to or what they did. I don't remember ever seeing any of them. And, although I had passed it many times, I had never noticed the name on the pillars of the main gate, facing the busy road on the other side of the park: 'Daughters of Charity'.

A few years after that New Year walk with my mother, I found myself strolling up the winding lane that leads to that blush-pink building, on my way for tea with the provincial head of the Daughters of Charity. In the preceding months, I had learned a few things about this part of Dublin, Blackrock, and about the Daughters. I knew, for instance, that the order had purchased part of the Rockfield Estate a few years after the establishment of the Irish Free State. I knew too that the Daughters had for many decades operated St Patrick's Home on the Navan Road in Cabra: the largest 'mother-and-baby home' in Ireland, a place where women pregnant out of wedlock went to give birth in secret.

And we all knew, by then, about the findings of Catherine Corless, a local historian in Tuam, Co. Galway. Her research on the mother-and-baby home run by the Bon Secours Sisters from 1925 to 1961 in Tuam had determined that there were nearly 800 children who had died while inmates of the institution but for whom no burial records could be found. Corless hypothesized that at least some of those children had been buried in what seemed to be a sewage tank, in the grounds of the institution. Her findings made international news in 2014, and the State established a Commission of Investigation into the mother-and-baby homes the following year.

The women of the religious orders, once held in reverence, were now widely seen as cruel, and bitter about their waning influence. Despite this, or perhaps because of it, I worried about what I was wearing, whether I would look respectable to Sister Goretti Butler in jeans and boots. The buzzer by the door of the main house made a dull ringing inside, while I peered at the lawns and gardens behind the wall that I had only ever glimpsed through the bars of the narrow gate.

Sister Goretti came to the door alone and ushered me into a cosy room to the side, with faded blue armchairs and a wooden cross on a lace-covered table. She disappeared for a minute and then hurried in with a tray of tea and biscuits, settling herself beside me, dressed in a simple cardigan and a long skirt. It felt like visiting a grandparent.

I had first met Goretti earlier that month, in the church across from my house. She had been part of a procession celebrating four centuries of the Vincentian order in a packed church, carrying a Bible aloft towards the altar. Now she sat beside me, the gold of a Communion box glinting behind her, a lone flourish in the simple room. I dipped a biscuit and wondered if Goretti would attempt to measure the degree to which my Catholicism had lapsed.

I was determined to get one thing out in the open: my mother and father had been unmarried when I was born, and my father's parents didn't speak to them for a while because of it. I didn't mention the two abortions my mum chose to have before she gave birth to me. For her part, my mother had never mentioned the abortions to me until, amidst the whir of debate generated by the Repeal campaign, I asked. The inside of my mother's left forearm is covered in flower tattoos and she doesn't go to Mass. She was never afraid to stand out or to tell a stranger about her life. But even though I'd helped her put up posters supporting Repeal, she had been worried I would judge her.

She had the first abortion as a teenager growing up in the US. The Planned Parenthood clinic calmly presented the options and respected her decision. Her mother, not really knowing what else to do, brought her sweets afterwards. The second time was in the mid-1980s, after she'd moved to Ireland and not long before she met my father. She didn't feel ready to become a mother, and so she travelled to England for an abortion. She had to fly home to Dublin the same day and go straight to work waitressing tables in a nightclub. My father, worried about what people might say, didn't want me to write about it at first. There's still shame.

I was born in November 1988, fully breach, my legs snapping out with such force that my hips were dislocated. If I'd been born just a year earlier, I would have been an illegitimate child under Irish law.

The Status of Children Act, passed in 1987, abolished the legal concept of illegitimacy.

After my mother became pregnant with me, my father suggested that they get married. She agreed – but she wouldn't walk down the aisle for that reason alone, and at her insistence they were not married until after I was born. My mother was four or five months pregnant on the day when they showed my father's parents her engagement ring and broke the news that she was having a baby. My father's mother struggled with the idea. She went to Mass every Sunday, but I don't remember her being extreme about religion. She was, it seems, mainly worried about what the neighbours would think. At one point, in shock, she told my parents it was the worst thing that had ever happened to her, and that she would never be able to show her face again. When I was born, though, she doted on me.

That was not my granny's first brush with that kind of shame. The man she married, my paternal grandfather, was an only child raised by a single mother. When his family announced their engagement in the newspaper, they wrote that his father was deceased. In fact, my grandfather told me late in his life that his father, a baker, was probably alive at the time. He insisted that his parents had been married – he had the document – and that either his mother had kicked his father out or his father had walked away. But the Ireland of that time was not a place where such events could be acknowledged.

A few years ago, when I began asking people about their experiences with the institutions for 'fallen women', my brother's godmother told me about how her own mother, Angela, had been chased back into her house from the front garden by the local priest because she hadn't been 'churched' after having a miscarriage. I had no idea what she meant; my generation has no fluency in the language of that Ireland. Up until the 1970s, a married Catholic woman who had given birth was expected to go to church to thank God for the 'gift' of her child and receive a blessing from the priest, who would lead her to the altar then and bless her again. Until she had done so, she was considered unclean, and some Catholic women felt they could not prepare food or go to Mass – or, apparently, stand at their own front gate – before receiving the blessing.

A charming woman who always answered the door immaculately dressed, with her make-up done and silver hair in perfect curls, Angela lived near the mother-and-baby home run by the Daughters of Charity on the Navan Road. When she moved to the area in the 1950s with her husband, people in the area were well aware of the institution, and stories circulated about the treatment of the unmarried pregnant women who entered. But even for a married woman, procreative sex and pregnancy were seen as shameful things. 'Just because you had a baby, you committed a sin,' she told me. 'You made an appointment with the priest to be churched and your sin was gone.'

The culture of shame was not restricted to sex and reproduction. Two of Angela's sons, her first and third born, died when they were very young due to spina bifida. 'No one ever spoke about it,' she told me.

The rate of cultural change in Ireland during my lifetime has been disorientingly rapid. The referendum that led to divorce being legalized was held the day after my seventh birthday. As teenagers we joked about the 'shopping trips' we'd have to take to London if we ended up pregnant. In secondary school we studied *An Triail*, Máiréad Ní Ghráda's 1964 play about an unmarried mother who kills her own baby girl, terrified the child might endure the same suffering she had as a shamed woman. To us, growing up in boom-time Ireland, such events seemed as distant as myth.

We were wrong about that.

Sister Goretti told me that her sister-in-law had recently asked her how she could get up in the morning and face the condemnation of the religious orders, spouting from every newspaper, radio and telly. Her answer seemed to imply that I should consider this too: the difficulty of being a religious Sister in a world that seems hostile to her very being. She was less keen to discuss the substance of the allegations against the religious orders. 'There were things done wrong in the past and things done wrong in all walks of life,' Sister Goretti said.

She reminded me that the people who worked for the religious orders were brothers and sisters and nieces of 'ordinary people', as she put it: 'They weren't born in outer space or anything.' Her own nieces were out travelling the world, one a solicitor, another a civil engineer. If she spent time thinking of the hostility towards the Church, she would get nothing done, so she tried to focus on the order's mission. 'We don't call people poor any more, but that's what the community was set up for,' she said: to help poor people.

I thought about the extensive gardens that surrounded us, the walls, the grandeur of the stately house we sat in, drinking our tea.

On a blustery Tuesday after the June bank holiday in 2017, I went to a demonstration outside the Dáil by people who had spent time in the institutions. They called themselves survivors. There were only maybe ten people, trying to light red candles despite the weather, their home-made signs blowing over in the wind. There was a man in a blue T-shirt that read 'illegitimate child'. Two women had come from Cork to be there, one a mother who had grown up in Catholic institutions and then given birth in a mother-and-baby home. 'I want to find my child,' one woman told me. 'It has been thirty-nine years.' She had become pregnant at eighteen after meeting a man at a dance, and was kicked out of her home by her family. At St Patrick's on the Navan Road, she told me, she was put to work and treated like dirt. She told me about a 'reject ward' for children with disabilities who were not to be adopted. A man who lived in New York but grew up with an adoptive family in Sligo told me how he had traced his mother through searching baptism records and death notices. Another man who spent four years in St Patrick's on the Navan Road described learning from his records that he had nearly died from malnutrition there, had been the subject of vaccine trials, and had been given the last rites on two occasions. 'They told my birth mother I had died,' he told the small crowd.

Attending memorials and protests, I became acquainted with a community of activist survivors. One of them, Terri Harrison, had set up a secret support group in the 1990s for women who gave birth in the institutions. These women talked for the first time amongst themselves of their experiences at the hands of the nuns: the abuse, the neglect, the way they were denied medical care and coerced into giving up their children. Once I started working on this book, and mentioning it to people, it came to seem that everyone I knew had a friend, an aunt, a cousin, a classmate or a neighbour who had been sent to one of the institutions, or who had been born in one of them. This was not a subculture; this was a mainstream set of experiences, hidden in plain sight.

In the time leading up to my meeting with Sister Goretti, I started talking to people who knew things about the institutions, in hope of getting a bit closer to understanding their origins, logic, methods and consequences. How did women end up in the homes and laundries? How did we justify the system of institutionalizing vulnerable or stigmatized people over so many decades? To what extent was this system of homes and laundries interlinked with the formation of our national identity? How did it shape the Irish family? Was Tuam an anomaly, or were high mortality rates and secret burials the norm? Did no person within the religious orders or the Church speak out against the way women and children were treated? Did ordinary citizens never question the system?

The moral judgement – that the institutions and the culture that produced them were cruel, controlling and misogynist – was the easy part. The hard part, from the vantage point of the present, was to enter into the mindset and methods of the nuns who created and operated the institutions, the churchmen and politicians who supported them, the public servants who compiled reports about them, the doctors, priests and social workers who referred women to them, the families that sent their daughters to them, and the women and children who spent time in them.

Thousands of women and girls passed through the doors of St Patrick's, the Daughters of Charity's mother-and-baby home on the

Navan Road. From 1924 to 1930, a reported 662 children died there, nearly two per week. The remains of more than 400 dead children from St Patrick's were donated for medical research between 1940 and 1965, without the knowledge of their mothers. Hundreds of live babies were sent from St Patrick's to adoptive American parents, often in exchange for donations to the order.

Sister Goretti joined the Daughters of Charity in 1970 and worked briefly on the Navan Road – not in the mother-and-baby home, but in a different institution on the site for 'severely retarded' people. She remembered it as a 'lovely place', and she told me she had never visited the institution for unmarried mothers. Sisters within the order were advised not to set foot inside the home, she said, in case they stumbled upon a neighbour or a member of the parish having a clandestine child. The health board paid all the wages, and she saw the nuns as essentially State employees. 'What the Church was doing was making a response to families that were in difficulties,' she said. 'It was a safe place for people to go. That was it, really. It was a safe place. And the problem was solved, but it wasn't solved really.'

Sister Goretti's analysis of the reasons why such institutions were needed had two parts. When she was growing up in Tipperary in the 1950s and '60s, she told me, an unmarried woman having a baby wouldn't have been accepted. 'I don't think my brothers would like it at this stage either, to tell you the truth, if one of their daughters . . . They'd probably put up with it, but do you know what I mean?' Later, though, she framed the problem as economic. 'They wanted to keep the babies but they weren't in the position, they couldn't work,' Goretti said of the single women who entered the homes. She suggested that people blamed the Church because it's an easier target than their own families, or even themselves. The Church, and the Sisters of her order, had provided a sanctuary for women shunned by society.

One of the decisions the government would have to make was whether or not to exhume the bodies of children found in Tuam. 'I don't know what happened down there really,' Sister Goretti said.

'It must have been a shock for all of them.' By way of explaining what seems to have been an extremely high death rate at the institution, she suggested that more children died in those days due to lack of vaccinations. 'Children became much healthier after that,' she said. 'That's why I'm saying it's very hard to judge today.'

I mentioned that, regardless of how the children had died, people were shocked when it was reported that they had been buried in a septic tank.

'That wasn't right,' she said, shaking her head. 'I mean there's no . . . You can't say that was right. You can't. That wasn't right.'

It was close to Christmas 2017 the next time I met with Sister Goretti, and she was busy writing thank-you letters to members of the order's many boards. 'I was surprised by how many there are,' she told me. Religious orders, operating in tandem with the State, are still part of the bedrock of social services in Ireland. The Daughters of Charity also operate a number of foreign missions, and Goretti was preparing for her annual trip to Kenya. Three young Kenyan women were ready to make their vows.

In Ireland, there was a trickle of women entering the enclosed orders, but no one was joining the active orders any more. Still, Goretti talked enthusiastically about the Daughters of Charity's ongoing work, particularly with anti-trafficking campaigns. It was a modern issue that they were eagerly trying to get students and young people involved in tackling. I thought of reminding her that her order and others had been accused of trafficking babies to America for adoption, but I didn't.

Gerry Adams had recently stepped down as President of Sinn Féin, and Goretti noted how other parties were always dredging up the past sins of the republicans; the obvious parallel with her own position hummed in the air between us. We talked of the fallout from decades of clerical scandals. When Mass was popular, she stressed, there was a sense of community, even the simple contact of the sign of peace, shaking hands with the people around you, a fleeting moment of physical connection.

I told Sister Goretti about a graffiti image of the Pope near my apartment in the city centre. The Pope was wearing a Repeal jumper. Goretti saw a connection between abortion and the homes. 'We're talking about mother-and-baby homes and children not being wanted back forty, fifty, sixty years ago,' she said. 'But the way I see it, at the minute, it's actually the same children that are going to be aborted now. They're still unwanted in a different way.'

When I asked her if there was anyone within the order who could speak about working in St Patrick's, she told me a Sister Maeve was the expert, but had just recently passed away at the age of ninety-eight. She had been a social worker involved with pioneering Ireland's modern fostering services. It turned out she had worked alongside the father of a friend of mine, who told me that sometime in the 1980s they had been mentored by the well-known PR consultant Terry Prone on how best to promote fostering to the public, with the aim of deinstitutionalization.

I wondered why she hadn't suggested I talk to Sister Maeve during our first meeting. She had still been alive then, and Sister Goretti said that her mind was perfect until the end. 'It's kind of unfair because none of the people who are around now were there,' she told me. 'Anybody who was working there is nearly dead.'

Goretti explained that the Daughters of Charity felt a split in loyalty between the people in the community and those within their religious order, but they were trying to focus on the present. Blaming the nuns today for what happened before would be like blaming me for something my granddad did, she said. She depicted the Ireland of the past as a poor, hardscrabble island, with families unable to bear the burden of an unmarried woman and her child. She spoke of poverty and shame as an overpowering mixture that drove parents to kick out their daughters if they became pregnant. 'It was hard,' she said. 'It was hard because of the shame.'

But where did the shame come from?

2.

The Milk Kitchen

Just a few hundred metres from the Daughters of Charity's Provincial House, set back from a road called Temple Hill on the slope leading down to Dublin Bay, stands a stately old Georgian manor. Today, Neptune House is surrounded by a ring of freshly built houses, a gated community with fancy cars in the drives. As a teenager, before the new estate was built, I walked past Neptune House in my navy-blue uniform five days a week on the way to get the train to school, but I didn't know its name or what used to go on there.

Neptune House had a long and colourful history. It had been home to the earl known as Copper-Faced Jack. It had been used as a shelter by British troops sent to put down the Easter Rising. But I wanted to know more about what went on there from the time the first baby was admitted to the so-called infant hospital run by religious Sisters, in October 1930, until it was identified for closure by the Minister for Health in 1986.

A narrative of the early decades of St Patrick's Guild can be pieced together from records held in the Dublin diocesan archives. In 1910, a Miss Lizzie Hawthorn Carr, who ran a Protestant children's home in Dublin, approached her next-door neighbour, Mary Cruice, and asked her to take on the case of a young Catholic woman and her child. Cruice, who had no experience in this area, was astonished at the lack of Catholic organizations providing for 'unwanted babies', and she moved quickly to found St Patrick's Guild. A priest in the inner city and Countess Plunkett became allies, as did a man who had influence with the St Vincent de Paul Society. Cases poured in.

In 1917, St Patrick's Guild secured its own office at 50 Middle Abbey Street. The following year, the local government board awarded them a yearly grant.

The Guild produced annual reports in flimsy black-and-white pamphlets. The covers bore the motto 'Save the Child' and an illustration of St Patrick in his robes, crook in hand. Appeals for donations promised: 'Save the Children and you save the Nation'; 'The work is national, it is Irish, it is Catholic.' On the back covers of the pamphlets, readers were encouraged to sponsor a cot. For £5, you could name a cot in memory of a deceased friend. For £25 you could support a cot for a year. For £250 you could endow a cot in perpetuity, thus making a 'constant appeal to Almighty God to shower graces and blessings on you'. Following the death of Mrs Margaret Rowe, a committee member and benefactor of the Guild, the 'St Mary Magdalen cot' was endowed.

Some of the pamphlets contained black-and-white photos of babies and toddlers in white socks and shoes, surrounded by illustrations of roses, advertising their qualities and the fact they were 'for adoption'. A girl called Winnie was 'one of our favourites – a lovely child of six', available to be adopted. So was Joseph, 'a bonny boy of two'. Suitable couples were encouraged to apply.

In 1919, Mary Cruice set up a 'baby's home' in Mountjoy Square that also trained nursery nurses. After Ireland won its independence, the issue of women pregnant out of wedlock emerged as a national concern. There was also the worry, dating back to the nineteenth century, that children would fall under the influence of Protestant proselytizing organizations. Any case where a woman or child's faith was in danger was referred by the Guild to the Catholic Protection and Rescue Society.

The mission of the Guild, as stated in one of the pamphlets, was to assist unmarried mothers 'whose previous characters give promise of redemption', and both mothers and children whose religion might be in danger if they were not provided help. It wanted to secure the baptism of infants as Catholics and board children out with respectable families. The Guild arranged adoptions, provided lodgings and procured employment for women, and 'occasionally' arranged marriages. 'While the Guild extends the arm of protection it does not in any way lend itself to becoming a cloak or a refuge which might be abused,' the pamphlet stated, helping only unmarried mothers who 'owe their unhappy plight to credulity, folly, or impulse rather than to any inherent wickedness.'

A document sent to the Archbishop of Dublin showed that between 1923 and 1926 the Guild took in more than 500 cases, at least one from each of the 32 counties, with 28 cases 'taken from England'. Since 1910, Cruice claimed to have 'dealt with not less than between 5,000 to 6,000 cases', including some from England, Scotland, America and one from France. 'They were of every class, from the professional man's daughter to the peasant's,' she wrote. 'Some were highly educated, others were grossly ignorant and in most cases very ignorant of their religion.' She described half of them as 'a little abnormal'. But more than half 'turned out satisfactorily – many of them got married.' A quarter 'fell a second time'. The women were expected to pay for the upkeep of their children. Cases that she couldn't take on were passed to other institutions, the local authority or parish priests.

Numbered 'specimen cases' were published in the pamphlets, with sensational titles such as the 'Erring Wife Case', the 'Cripple Case' and the 'Destitute Case'. No. 2059 was a 'most refined superior girl', betrayed under a promise of marriage, who became 'passionately attached to her baby'. When the father said he'd marry her if she gave up the child, she refused and was maintaining the baby out of her own earnings. One baby – case no. 1859, born to a 'young girl of decent parentage' – was adopted by a couple 'on holiday from the Colonies' only for it to turn out by chance that the man adopting the child was the little boy's biological grand-uncle. The Guild described it as a 'fairy tale'. A girl in an important government position was led astray by a man unable to marry her and was on 'the brink of self-destruction' before the Guild became involved.

Case no. 1733 differed from the ordinary because 'sympathies lay mainly with the man', who was married but had been 'entangled' with a girl who threatened to ruin his home. Case no. 483 was a young, unmarried pregnant woman who went to Liverpool to 'avoid publicity' and while there came under the care of a Catholic rescue society that made sure she and her baby were brought back to Dublin. But she was in love with the father of her child, a married man, and she tried to leave the country with him and the baby. 'Providence intervened,' Cruice wrote: the woman's plans somehow became known to the Guild and she was intercepted. Rescue societies clearly relied on a network of informants. 'Immediate action was taken and her plans frustrated,' it was recorded. 'She is, of course, kept under close observation.'

In 1923, forty-one children under the care of the Guild died, seventeen of them from 'marasmus', or malnutrition. A Dr Reddin, who visited the Guild's institutions to do check-ups on the children, wrote that 'our babies are of such a class as to be predestined to disease' and that he considered the mortality rates satisfactory in light of this. The babies that weren't sick he described as 'birds of passage on the way to foster-parents'.

In 1929, the Guild purchased Neptune House and established St Patrick's Infant and Dietetic Hospital there. This is the institution that would come to be familiarly known as 'Temple Hill'. Despite its claim to be a hospital, it accommodated babies not because they were sick but because they were awaiting adoption. The babies were mostly born to unmarried mothers who had been referred from public hospitals, nursing homes or mother-and-baby homes. The first baby was admitted in October 1930. There was a matron, resident 'lady doctors', two trained and state-registered nursing sisters, a staff nurse and a certified housekeeper employed there, as well as eighteen trainee nurses.

During the 1930s, Miss Cruice described Temple Hill as catering to 'expectant mothers of the better class, genuine first offenders, of previous good character' who represented different sections of society including nurses, teachers, 'daughters of respectable farmers and sometimes professional men'. She worried that in mother-and-baby homes 'first offenders' interacted with women who had become pregnant multiple times outside of wedlock. She had statistics from a priest in London that indicated the number of Irish girls 'going there in trouble' was decreasing, and she ascribed this to the new homes in Bessborough and Roscrea, and to the Tuam home admitting prenatal cases.

In 1938, Cruice sent a letter to Archbishop Byrne telling him that the number of 'unmarried mothers' applying to the Guild for help was increasing. She enclosed details of cases from the Dublin Archdiocese. Most of the cases came with a recommendation from a local priest. In one case, a cook was introduced to the Parish Priest of Blackrock so he could persuade her to enter St Patrick's on the Navan Road. Many of the women were domestic servants, and some of them had been made pregnant by their employer. Typists, cleaners, factory workers, dressmakers and a sweet confectioner were also listed. Fathers figured mainly by their absence: 'Putative father not contributing' or 'Putative father refused help.' The 'general remarks' told difficult stories in a few words. A 23-year-old 'became pregnant' while living with relatives in Limerick. 'Putative father is uncle of girl,' the sheet read. He was not named, and there was no reference to the gardaí being informed.

Around 1937 the Guild closed the Mountjoy Square residence and opened St Gerard's, a mother-and-baby home named for the patron saint of expectant mothers, in a building called Lowville on Herbert Avenue in the wealthy Dublin suburb of Merrion. The archbishop had in his records a copy of a 1938 letter from residents of Herbert Avenue, complaining to an estate agent about unmarried mothers on display in their neighbourhood. They remarked that the use of Lowville as 'a Maternity Home for unmarried mothers' was unfortunate and had they been allowed a say they would have 'instantly protested' against an 'unwanted intrusion' on their area. 'One would imagine that this Home would attempt to use a decent concealment about its activities,' they wrote. But the mothers were seen outside in the avenue, 'not always with reticence', and men were seen 'to meet and greet these women'. There was concern about the proximity of the local riding school and its groomsmen. 'The atmosphere generated by this Home, and by the absence of decent concealment that should characterise it, has produced in the respectable persons of the avenue a very uneasy conviction that the neighbourhood has lost its former character of desirability,' the local residents wrote.

A Miss Jennings of the National Society for the Prevention of Cruelty to Children also wrote to the archbishop about the St Gerard's inmates. 'Women even in advanced stages of pregnancy go into neighbouring shops, walk up and down the avenue and meet undesirable men who loiter at the gates of the residents on the avenue,' she wrote. 'It is true to say that there is an element of shamelessness in the freedom with which these girls and women publicly comport themselves.' Perhaps at least in part because of such objections, St Gerard's lasted only a few years as a mother-and-baby home.

Miss Jennings' letter also contained details of the fees facing the women. If they could pay three guineas, they spent their confinement at St Gerard's; otherwise they went to Holles Street maternity hospital. 'They then return with their babies and Miss Cruice either obtains a foster-mother or keeps the child herself,' she wrote. The mother, or another person responsible, would pay £90 if the baby was a boy and £80 if it was a girl, and £40 of this was paid out to a foster mother over two years. If Miss Cruice kept the baby, the mother paid 30 shillings a month 'till the sum agreed upon has been paid' or until the child was three and could be 'committed to an industrial school'.

Mary Cruice had attempted to transfer the running of St Patrick's Guild over to the Archdiocese as early as 1927. But it was not until 1943 that she eventually handed over control – to the Sisters of Charity.

The archives indicate that a key issue for the Guild, after the Sisters of Charity took it over, was foreign adoptions. Within the Church, there was concern not that there was no legal basis for adoption (as there wasn't until 1953), nor that Irish children were being adopted abroad, but that the adoptive families might not in every case be Catholic. In 1950, a Sister Joseph Byrne wrote to assure the Archbishop of Dublin, John Charles McQuaid, that the Guild was being careful to investigate the Catholic faith of adopters in the US. The reply from the Archbishop's Palace asked that the Sisters 'kindly obtain an explicit affidavit in each case that the adopters will educate the children in Catholic schools and submit letter to me before allowing children to go.'

In 1951, after articles were published raising concerns about the 'export' of Irish children to the US, a correspondence ensued between Archbishop McQuaid's secretary, Father Chris Mangan, and solicitors for St Patrick's Guild. At first it was deemed not to be 'prudent' to reply, because any reply would have to refer to 'the main complaint therein of children being sent to America'. They decided they wanted the *Irish Times* to apologize for what it had written on the subject, and drafted the text of an apology.

In the 1960s, after construction of a new annexe, Temple Hill was able to house close to a hundred babies. A lot of women and children were coming and going; and yet my father, who grew up just up the road, knew nothing about the institution. A family friend, who worked as a local garda for a decade from the mid-seventies, told me that he thought it was a convent.

The documents in the diocesan archives gave a remarkable insight into the institutional history of St Patrick's Guild and Temple Hill, and into the thinking of the people who oversaw the institutions. But they held few clues as to what it was actually like inside. At one point I stumbled across an article about Niall Fortune, the founder of the fast-food chain Eddie Rocket's, which quoted him speaking about the worst job he ever had to do. As a teenager, he said, he worked at Temple Hill, where his aunt – Sister Joseph Fortune – was a nun. He said, 'For three months, I worked in the laundry and washed what seemed like thousands of nappies every day. I managed to sell the job to a friend when something better came along.'

I called him up. He told me that it was the mid-seventies when he worked at Temple Hill. He remembered a big laundry with kegs full of nappies, where he worked with another woman and a very old nun. He remembered the wards being bright and airy and the place well run. He wondered whether the nurses were 'real nurses', or maybe mothers of the babies who were working there while their children were in care. Every now and then, he recalled, a car would come into the drive and bring a child away. He didn't think much of it at the time.

Across online chat boards and Facebook groups, I found adoptees who wanted to know more about the place where they spent the first few months or years of their lives. Who cared for them, and were they ever held or loved? They formed a community bonded by a shared lack of knowledge. There were also posts by former nursery nurses and the relatives of women who had trained and worked there.

While the mother-and-baby homes were mostly run by religious Sisters, Temple Hill depended on a constantly changing team of young laywomen, who cared for the babies and trained as nurses. These young women saw the inner workings of the institution every day. I came across a Facebook post from one such woman, who had moved from Cobh to train at Temple Hill in 1979, aged eighteen. On Good Friday in 2017, the last officially dry one in Ireland, I met Jennifer Sadurski in a café upstairs in Arnotts department store in the centre of Dublin, one level above the women's clothes and lingerie.

As we talked, Jennifer took from her bag a crisp white envelope, from which she pulled a thin stack of colour photos and laid them out on the table between us. She allowed me to slowly go through them. These were stolen moments from inside the 'infant hospital'.

The prints were small, and they were fuzzy. The snapshots were taken clandestinely on night shifts, when the nun, the matron and the older staff nurses were all in bed. Teenaged faces grinned out from the prints, the trainee nurses dressed up in pointed white headdresses and high-collared white dresses. They posed for each other in awkward and dramatic stances, clearly egging each other on, suspended on the verge of laughter or sometimes caught in an explosive fit of giggles. Against a backdrop of pink-flowered wall-paper, perched on a deep window sill, one young nurse balanced on one foot, the white wooden shutters open, her other leg flung out behind her as if performing in a cabaret, holding on to the curtain drawstring like Tarzan. Below her, another young nurse in a frumpy dark cardigan smirked guiltily at the camera, while pointing to a large 'NO SMOKING' sign below the feet of a religious statue. Another shows Jennifer herself sitting with one leg up on a counter top in the kitchen, a defiant wide-mouthed smile on her face, as she demonstrated how to jump over the steel island to reach the cup-board where the biscuits were kept. A nun soon cottoned on and locked it. The food they were given was difficult to stomach, she remembered. It was a good way to keep slim.

Then there were the armfuls of babies. Jennifer and another nurse sat inside a large metal cot, one of a row, with the white paint peeling off the metal bars; the nurses' legs hung over the bars, and they were cradling two children each in their laps. The babies, near-ing toddler age, were dressed in what look like T-shirts, with pastel cardigans on top. One child was opening its mouth to chuckle, and Jennifer was gently pinching the cheeks of another. The cots seem large enough to accommodate more than one baby.

At that time, Jennifer told me, she had 'no clue' the mother-and-baby homes existed. Her parents would never have discussed such things with her. When she started at Temple Hill, she said, 'I didn't realize what these babies were doing there, up for adoption because their mother couldn't keep them.' The trainee nurses would discuss it among themselves, guessing at the possible reasons so many seem-ingly healthy newborn babies would come to the hospital without their mothers.

Eventually the penny dropped. Jennifer enjoyed her work caring for the children, but she hated working in the milk kitchen, two rooms separated by a hatch at the front of the building. The staff nurse, in gloves and bonnet, would mix formula and prepare the bottles there. The trainees would scrub the huge pots they boiled the milk in. When Jennifer was on duty in the milk kitchen, it was her responsibility to answer the front door. Women of all ages, many even younger than her, turned up with babies in their arms – they were often in tears, sometimes accompanied by ashen-faced parents or nervous friends – to hand over their children to the nuns.

'It was heartbreaking,' Jennifer told me. 'I broke down crying, especially for the girls with their parents, who were brought to the door and physically made to hand over the baby.'

Jennifer would bring the women and their babies into a room and wait for the nun to come down and deal with them. She never heard what was discussed. There was a feeling that gnawed at her, something unfair about the whole procedure. She felt that the mothers were having a choice made for them. A young woman came to the door once with her parents. Her father was very tall. He reminded Jennifer of a garda. Another woman, who looked to be in her early twenties, arrived with a friend. 'We weren't allowed to engage in conversation,' Jennifer said. 'I had to show them to the room with the nun. They were usually expected.'

The Coombe hospital would deliver babies to Temple Hill with ID tags on. Jennifer remembers one such baby, a girl born prematurely. When the trainee nurses went to wash her, they discovered that her name and date of birth had been scrawled in red ink on her back. They felt the nurses who had sent her must be heartless to write on her body in that way. Jennifer still remembered the girl's name. She turned out to be a healthy baby and was later adopted. But the image of the baby's branded back still haunted Jennifer. It would not have happened, she felt, if the baby had not been born out of wedlock.

In the corner of a café in Blanchardstown shopping centre, tucked down the back of a shop packed with picture frames, trinkets and crafting materials, I met another woman who had trained to be a nurse at Temple Hill. Catherine Garton sat waiting at a table with a bag full of hand-drawn maps and photos. She trained from 1974 to

1976 and was just twenty years old when she became certified. The cherry blossoms were beginning to open up like clouds of pink confetti in the air when she walked out of Temple Hill for the last time, in the half-light, after her final shift of night duty.

Now nearing her mid-sixties, she spoke in a voice that was sweet but could turn sharply on you. It sounded fitting for a nurse. Like Jennifer Sadurski, Cathy had brought photos with her. In one shot she wore a nurse's hat, poked up into twin peaks on the top of her head, almost like cat's ears.

When she finished school, Cathy began studying dress design. Her father told her there was no future in such a frivolous trade. She loved children, so he told her she should be a nurse. What he said was usually law.

The Saturday night before her training started at Temple Hill, she went to a dance: she was mad for the dances. The singer Red Hurley, with his shock of red hair, would sometimes come and perform in a white linen suit. She couldn't remember who played on that particular night; all she remembered was the man that would become her husband. He invited her to a dance the following night, but she couldn't go, because she was starting work at Temple Hill on the Monday morning. The job was live-in, and it was the first time she had ever been away from home. When she arrived, the matron in charge brought her to her room and gave her a uniform and a veil. She was to present herself for breakfast at 8 a.m.

In the morning, she followed the other young women filing into the reception area. They were laughing and that put her at ease. The air was thick with the smell of talcum powder and there was the soft sound of babies chuckling to themselves in the wards. Many of the girls she worked with complained about the strictness of the nuns. But as the eldest girl in her family she was used to burdening chores. She threw herself into caring for the children. A cuddle or a song could seem to change their whole world and that made the work feel rewarding. 'Adults can be cold and sterile,' she said. 'But children just accept you.' She knew nothing about why the babies were there, all she knew was that there were many of them. She didn't ask for much more information.

A Sister Francis Lombard ran Temple Hill during Cathy's time, working with a matron and the staff nurses. She died in 2015, and Cathy told me to read her obituary on the Sisters of Charity's website. It described a woman who loved music, horses and the British royal family; a niece used to send her pictures clipped from *Hello!* magazine. She was born in 1928 in Cork and had three sisters, all of whom became members of religious orders. She entered the Sisters of Charity in February 1947, just before she turned nineteen, and earned her habit and the name Teresa Aloysius by August. She served 'short spells' in Donnybrook, St Vincent's Hospital and Cork, among other places, before spending two years training in nursery management. She worked in Temple Hill from 1958 until 1987. 'Her ministry included the care of infants prior to their adoption and the management of a Training School for Nursery Nurses,' the obituary stated. 'These Nursery Nurses were much sought after by families and nurseries.'

'I have no time for them,' Cathy said of the nuns. 'I was educated by them, trained with them, worked with them, I didn't meet a decent one.' Her head shook as she said the words. 'Not one.' Then she corrected herself. There was one exception, a nun she was fond of at school. She was the only religious Sister that Cathy thought of as a normal human being. 'They lacked that connection,' she said. 'I don't know whether it was beaten out of them or whether they never had it.'

She placed a sheet of A4 paper on the table: a photocopy of a floor plan, drawn by hand from her memory of how the wards at Temple Hill were laid out, with the name of each room carefully marked. Neptune House, which she called 'the convent', was where Sister Francis Lombard lived. There were other nuns there too, she assumed. When you came into the drive, Neptune House was on the left-hand side, and straight in front was the L-shaped annexe building, built in the 1960s. This two-storey, flat-roofed annexe was the building in which she and the other young trainees lived and where the baby wards were located.

The first ward she worked in was St Mary's, where the youngest babies were sent. Cathy pointed out that there was an adjoining door to the convent, so the nuns could pass through. On the other side of the building, parallel to St Mary's, was St Joseph's ward, which was for the oldest babies in Temple Hill. In this ward there was a set of double doors that opened into the convent and also served as an entrance to the chapel. 'In my time, the children went out from there,' she said. A staff nurse would come and tell them to make a particular baby ready. Cathy would get a yellow Babygro and a yellow blanket, and a bottle would be made up. The child would be carried out through the double doors to the plush rooms of the convent, where the adoptive parents would be waiting. In Cathy's time, no outsiders were allowed into the hospital area where the wards were, except for mothers visiting their babies, who were ushered into a parlour on the ground floor. The turnover was quick in her days there, the demand for adoptions so high that Cathy had the impression that the babies were 'preordered' by couples on a waiting list.

Cathy told me that in her conversations in recent years with adoptees, the first question they often asked was how they were cared for and what the place was actually like. They had heard of babies wearing dirty clothes and of dark, cold rooms crowded wall-to-wall with cots. Cathy was adamant that these stories were inaccurate. She could criticize the nuns for many things, but during her time at Temple Hill the children were beautifully dressed and they had the best of everything. They were put in little cotton gowns until they were six weeks old, and then in bright little Baby-gros. If the Babygros got tatty or spoiled, they were thrown away. The bed linens were of good quality and the wards were decorated in Berger paints, a fancy new company that specialized in daring new shades at the time: beautiful pinks and lavenders and yellows. The place she described seemed a different world to the hospital that Jennifer Sadurski worked in just a few years later, where clothes and Babygros were donated and the nurses competed with each other to get the best clothes for their babies. The toddlers in her photos wore T-shirts that didn't seem to quite fit.

With a pen, Cathy went from ward to ward on the floor plan she had drawn. On the ground floor of the annexe, there was the staff dining room, and then three steps going up to St Joseph's ward, where the double doors swung into the convent. This ward was for babies from around nine months old until they were walking. There were ten cots, though only nine of them housed babies; the tenth was kept free for changing. St Joseph's ward had a parquet floor, which the trainee nurses had to wash and polish, down on hands and knees. The floor leading into the convent needed to shine. Some of the nurses put cloths on their feet and polished the floor by sliding up and down.

Along a main hall there was the nurses' station, the milk kitchen and the parlour. A corridor led across from this main hall to a big wide room where the toddlers would play. There were doors opening on to a small garden from this playroom, where sometimes the children could spend time in sunlight. On the ground floor there was also the matron's office, a laundry room and two wards for toddlers, where children were kept from the age they could walk until around three years. The toddler wards had ten cots apiece. There was also a sluice room, where the nurses would rinse dirty nappies and plastic pants and sometimes potty-train the children. Some of the children who stayed longer at Temple Hill may have been there because of health problems, Cathy guessed, but she thought it was mostly for other reasons. 'Maybe mammy didn't sign the form' allowing adoption, she suggested. 'Or maybe mammy was paying for them to stay there until she got herself sorted.' There were also quite a few babies who were 'given out' only to be returned to Temple Hill.

Stairs led up to the first floor and St Bernadette's ward, which had ten cots for babies aged six to nine months. Then there was St Agnes's ward, with four cots for younger babies. Represented by the lamb, Agnes was venerated for being violently martyred at the tender age of twelve or thirteen, a beautiful young woman from a wealthy family who refused repeated marriage requests. She was wedded to the Lord and He wanted her untouched. Some said she was dragged through the streets naked to a brothel to be punished, but her hair grew miraculously to cover her body and the men who tried to rape her went suddenly blind. She was fastened to a stake, but the flames would not burn her, so she was beheaded. The faithful mopped up her blood with cloths. She died a virgin-martyr and became a patron saint to whom young women prayed in hope of learning the name of their future husband.

Around the corner was St Camillus's ward, which had the same set-up as St Agnes's ward. Across the hall was St Gabriel's ward, with four cots for newborns. These three wards were known as the 'private' wards, though Cathy wasn't sure why. They were smaller than the other wards and the turnover was quicker. Across from the private wards was St Teresa's, with ten cots for babies between nine weeks and six months. St Teresa of Avila was a nun who experienced a transcendent silence and pain during an illness, as well as epiphanies about original sin, and later practised mortifications of the flesh. For years she endured visions of Jesus Christ thrusting a spear through her heart, leaving her on fire with love for him, moaning with an agony that she could not get enough of, a masochistic ecstasy. When she died she welcomed the longed-for meeting with her saintly spouse. The Church kept her right foot and part of her jaw in Rome, gave Spain her left eye and her right hand. Franco kept the hand for himself until his own death. Paris got a finger.

Every ward had a 'bath book' recording the washings, any blemishes or problems, charting each baby's temperature to monitor sore throats or minor symptoms of conjunctivitis. Nurses in later years kept these books and sent them to Cathy. She said there were admittance slips, with the mother's name, the hospital, nursing home or institution the child had been sent from, and a note as to whether the child was baptized or not.

Every morning the children were weighed. One little boy, whom Cathy looked after from the day he arrived in St Agnes's ward, weighed only a pound and a half when he was born. Sister Francis Lombard came in one morning and, according to Cathy, looked down at the baby. 'Oh, look at this little rat,' she said. Cathy asked the Sister not to say that. 'We're fond of him, are we?' Sister Francis asked. The next day, Cathy was moved to a different ward. 'He was tiny, but he wasn't a rat,' she told me, shaking her head.

To complete their training, the nurses worked in every section, starting in the ward for the days-old babies, often following an age cohort through the wards. They cleaned floors and did night duty. Her favourite ward was St Mary's, the first ward she worked in, where the babies were tiny and required close care. St Mary's ward was in a sort of attic. It had seven cots for babies from birth to six weeks. She spent a few months there before moving on to St Bernadette's, then to St Joseph's and then the milk kitchen.

The shifts in the milk kitchen disturbed Cathy, as they did Jennifer. Huge containers of unpasteurized milk for the babies would be brought fresh from farms to be stored and treated. It was transferred from the vats in which it arrived into giant pots in which it was then boiled. After that, supplements were stirred in. Cathy stood for hours, carefully stirring the creamy liquid to boiling point, counting each circumnavigation of the spoon so she knew when to begin stirring in the opposite direction. It took forever to bubble, but once it did, it could burn in a moment and the whole pot would be spoiled. It was almost silent in the room, apart from the scrape of the spoon against the pot and the glugging sound of the swirling milk.

Sometimes, though, the silence was broken by the sound of a doorbell.

Some young women came alone. Others were with a social worker, or with their mother or aunt, or with a friend. Only rarely were they accompanied by a man.

'They never came crying,' Cathy told me. 'But they always left crying.'

Some were there to visit their baby. They would nervously hand Cathy a card with a name written on it, trying not to look her in the eye. She would guide them to the parlour, a small room with two chairs, where they were left to wait as she went to find the baby. At the nurses' station she handed over the slip of paper. The baby was brought to the parlour and the mother granted between forty-five minutes and an hour to spend. (A number of mothers who had babies in Temple Hill told me they were allowed only half an hour.) Cathy figured these were mothers who were still hoping to take their baby home; or maybe they were coming to see them one last time before signing the papers for adoption.

She remembered seeing one young couple through the window while she was up in St Joseph's ward, both of them strikingly tall and wearing matching cashmere jackets. They held hands as they walked to the front door. Cathy assumed they must be adoptive parents, dressed in those coats. After a while, though, she saw them again through the window as they left. The woman was limp, struggling to walk, as if she had been gutted. 'Those things don't leave you,' she told me quietly.

In the mid-seventies, dance halls were still the rage. The Vietnam War was ending, Queen were singing 'Bohemian Rhapsody', and in Ireland young nurses were stealing away from an institution run by nuns to go to dances. Cathy would put her hair up in rollers the day before, and tuck it all underneath the veil as best she could; but the lumpy rollers would inevitably escape and hang down as she worked. It drove Sister Francis mad. 'I had a life she never had,' Cathy told me by way of explaining the Sister's response. 'They were put in convents when they were very young so they had no idea.'

By 10 p.m., the doors would be locked. The girls would rent rooms in a bed and breakfast in the city and spend the night there, slinking back early the next day. Sister Francis would stare them out of it. Pregnancies that resulted from trysts on those stolen nights were hidden away. Cathy remembered one nurse who was isolated in a room for a little while. They were told that she was sick. No one was permitted to visit her. 'But we snuck up one night and she told us she was pregnant,' Cathy said.

After Cathy completed her training she was employed by a prominent family. The family treated her unfairly, though, and she found herself looking for work again. Through Sister Francis, she found work in Madonna House, an orphanage in Blackrock also run by the Sisters of Charity. (In 1999, Mary Raftery would bring to light accounts of sexual and physical abuse at Madonna House in her seminal RTÉ series *States of Fear.*) Cathy was often put on night duty. After six months she got so sick she began to lose her hair. The orphanage was attached to Linden House, a nursing home also run by the order, where de Valera died. Mother Joseph, who used to run Temple Hill, was in charge for a while; then a Sister Dennis took over.

'She had a ledger inside the door of Linden and the girls came with their three pounds a week,' Cathy said. By girls, she meant mothers with babies at Temple Hill, who she understood were coming to pay for the upkeep of their babies. Sister Dennis would open the ledger and mark off the payments. When Cathy asked what the payment was for, she was told, 'People have to pay their debts.'

Social workers have since told Cathy about what happened if a woman fell behind in her payments. 'They'd turn up at her house in a black taxi in full regalia, the nuns,' Cathy said. 'And shame her into paying it or shame her family into paying it.'

3.

In the Diocesan Archive

The beliefs and stigmas that underpinned the mother-and-baby homes and the Magdalen laundries all existed in Ireland long before the creation of the independent Irish state. The institutional infrastructure, too, dates back centuries. None of the building blocks of the shame-industrial complex was intrinsically Irish or intrinsically Catholic. But independent Catholic Ireland brought them to a sort of dark perfection.

In seventeenth-century France, the Daughters of Charity – Sister Goretti's order – operated a home for foundlings: babies abandoned on the streets of Paris.

More than a century before the Famine, a Foundling Hospital was set up on the grounds of the House of Industry in Dublin, with the main purpose of saving illegitimate children from abandonment or infanticide. In 1730, after the institution became exclusively devoted to foundlings, a revolving cradle was fitted in the walls of the hospital, a device into which a baby could be placed from the outside and brought within the walls without anyone being identified.

The Foundling Hospital continued in operation until 1835. In an 1876 pamphlet entitled 'A Brief History of the Ancient Foundling Hospital of Dublin', edited by a civil servant called William Dudley Wodsworth, the former 'Inspector of Invalid Foundlings' reported on his conversations with the 'few remaining individuals' with first-hand experience of the institution, and he was 'much struck by the feeling of painful wonderment and anxiety existing with many of them as to whom their parents might possibly have been'. Thousands of foundlings were sent out 'at nurse', before being hired or 'farmed' out to Protestant families to work until the boys were twenty-four and the girls twenty-one years old. Although the aim of the hospital was to prevent the death and 'actual murder' of illegitimate children, the death rate of children in the institution and 'at nurse' was extremely high. In the decade ending in March 1760, half of more than 7,000 babies admitted died in the institution, and 52 children were unaccounted for. The bodies were disposed of in an 'indecent and improper manner', put naked into a hole eight or ten at a time and treated with lime.

Lady Arabella Denny, who had devoted time and money to the Foundling Hospital, went on to establish the Magdalen Asylum for Penitent Females in Leeson Street, Dublin, in 1767: Ireland's first such institution. Like many of the other early Magdalen asylums in Ireland, it was a Protestant establishment. Many laundries started as halfway houses run by lay people at a time when the State's own approach was to incarcerate the vulnerable, poor or morally contagious. In the aftermath of Catholic Emancipation and the Great Famine, Catholic orders opened a number of Magdalen asylums, and there were twelve of these Catholic-run institutions by the turn of the twentieth century.

The Sisters of the Sacred Hearts of Jesus and Mary, a French order with a mother house in Britain, ran one of the first religious 'homes' in London for women pregnant out of wedlock, set up by the Westminster Archdiocese in 1890 and called St Pelagia's. Their mission was the spiritual reform of these women, who remained there for a year. Their babies were sent to a nursery run by the nuns until fostered or admitted to a Catholic orphanage. The Sacred Hearts Sisters would go on to run three different mother-and-baby institutions in Ireland.

Another crucial building block in the shame-industrial complex was the United Kingdom's Poor Law system, and the network of workhouses established under it. Daniel O'Connell warned in 1839 that 'Ireland is too poor for a poor law.' Poverty was worse in Ireland than almost anywhere else in Europe, with millions struggling for basic survival. But some in the Catholic hierarchy believed the Poor Law could empower the Church at a parish level to compel people to support their ageing parents or their deserted children. The country was carved up into more than a hundred Poor Law unions, and each union had its own workhouse and board of guardians.

Around the turn of the twentieth century, the workhouse at Pelletstown on the Navan Road was converted into an institution for women pregnant out of wedlock, though it also accommodated the sick children of married couples who couldn't look after them. A public institution under the stewardship of the Dublin Board of Guardians, which would eventually become the Eastern Health Board, it was run by Sister Goretti's order, the Daughters of Charity, who renamed the institution St Patrick's. It would eventually be certified by the State to cater for 149 mothers and 560 babies.

The Catholic Protection and Rescue Society was established in 1913 with a mission 'to protect the faith of baptized Catholics in Ireland from proselytizing influences and to rescue baptized Catholics who have already fallen under them'. It would specialize in bringing Irish women who were pregnant in Britain back to Ireland to give birth, in order to ensure a Catholic family adopted their child.

Bethany Home was a Protestant mother-and-baby home established in 1921 by the merger of two Protestant rescue societies, the Dublin Midnight Mission and Dublin Prison Gate Mission. It was located initially at Blackhall Place in the north inner city and later moved to Orwell Road in Rathgar. The home was reported not to differentiate between first or multiple 'offenders', as the women were known. Local courts used the institution as a 'remand centre' and inmates included women incarcerated on criminal charges such as infanticide. Women and children were also brought through the Protestant rescue societies. Between 1925 and 1949, more than 200 children died at the home, and were buried in unmarked graves in Mt Jerome Cemetery.

The years immediately following Irish independence saw the rapid development of mother-and-baby homes – often in former workhouses or in stately homes purchased from the retreating Protestant gentry. According to Sister Rosemary Clerkin's history of the Sisters of the Sacred Hearts of Jesus and Mary, the founder of the Catholic Women's Aid Society, a Mrs Neville, was trudging around the countryside trying to find Catholic families willing to employ unmarried mothers and give homes to their babies. The local county council paid a shilling a week for the boarded-out children, but they had no legal status within that family. Mrs Neville encouraged the Sacred Hearts to open up a home for unmarried mothers in Cork. The Westminster Archdiocese purchased an estate of 210 acres at Bessborough, overlooking the River Lee. In February 1922, the institution was opened and the Department of Health referred children from the local workhouse. Within two years of the institution's opening, the Bishop of Cork suggested expectant mothers should be admitted. These women were put to work on the estate's farmland, which produced fruit, vegetables, butter and cheese. A maternity unit was built in an old stable complex on the grounds. Like the immaculate Blessed Virgin, the inmates would give birth in what was once a manger.

In 1931, the first Mass was said in the institution the Sacred Hearts called Sean Ross Abbey, on an estate purchased from a minor aristocrat in Roscrea, Co. Tipperary. It was certified to accommodate 152 mothers and 200 children. Many of the women who came to Sean Ross Abbey to have their children in secret would have looked out through a specially designed stained-glass window in the chapel and read the inscription: 'If God is for us, who can be against us.' In 1934 the Sacred Hearts opened a third home at Castlepollard in Co. Westmeath, at the request of the Local Government Board. A grant from the Sweepstakes funded a new nursery unit. The order installed a commercial laundry on site, where the women worked. The Sacred Hearts' institutions were often described as 'private', which they were in the sense that the State had no direct role in opening or running them. But the distinction was misleading, given that all mother-and-baby homes received capitation payments from the State. Just as it is impossible to imagine the institutions taking the form they did without the involvement of the religious orders, it is impossible to imagine them becoming so extensive in the absence of State funding and support.

Like St Patrick's on the Navan Road, the mother-and-baby home at Tuam had its origins as a workhouse, established by the local Poor Law union around 1840 and designed to accommodate 800 inmates. On one day during the Great Famine, the *Tuam Herald* reported, at least 2,000 'unfortunates' were lined up in front of the workhouse on the Dublin Road waiting to be granted admission. The local graveyard was overpopulated with the dead, to the extent that medical officers reporting to the Board of Guardians of the workhouse warned that it threatened the health of the entire town. Both British soldiers and Free State soldiers occupied the workhouse during the war for independence. In 1923, six Anti-Treaty men were executed against the workhouse wall, followed by another two men later that year. The bodies of the 'Tuam Martyrs' were buried on the grounds.

In October 1925, it was decided that the 'destitute and orphaned children' at Glenamaddy workhouse would be moved to the workhouse building in Tuam, though this was delayed as Free State soldiers were still based there and parts of the building were overgrown with weeds. In 1934, through a public grant and Sweepstakes money, a maternity wing was created and babies began to be delivered.

In 1927, Frank Duff – founder of the Legion of Mary – established a hostel on the site of the old North Union workhouse in Dublin. Three years later, he opened a segregated section, 'Regina Coeli', for women pregnant out of wedlock. The women were expected to pay a small sum of money and most went to the nearby Coombe hospital to give birth. The hostel had capacity for more than a hundred mothers and a hundred children. A rotating group of 'care mothers' looked after babies at the hostel, and Duff often used his network of businesses to secure employment for the mothers once they were ready to leave. The Regina Coeli hostel was perhaps a more community-based and less punishing solution than the religious-run institutions, although its model did not differ greatly from theirs. After a government inspection found dire conditions at the hostel, it received a Sweepstakes grant for improvements. It remains operating as a shelter for women today.

*

When I contacted some of the religious orders, seeking access to their archives for the purpose of this book, I generally received the same sorts of answers that other researchers have got. The Sisters of Mercy, which ran Magdalen laundries, would not grant me any access to their records unless I was acting on behalf of women searching for their own personal details. The Sisters of the Sacred Hearts of Jesus and Mary had an historian working on their behalf, helping with their submission to the Commission of Investigation, and said they did not want to engage with journalists or independent researchers before the investigation was finished.

Father Francis Mitchell, Diocesan Secretary for the Archdiocese of Tuam, told me that they had no resident archivist I could speak with. In any case, he said, the Archdiocese 'had a very minor role in regard to the forty-plus Houses of Religious' – i.e. the religious orders, including the Sisters of Bon Secours, who ran the Tuam home. 'There is nothing, therefore, in our archives on the Tuam Home apart from a few letters of a peripheral nature from the owners of the Home, namely Galway County Council.' The letters, which he said dated from 1952 and 1957, referred to proposals to improve and, later, to abandon the home. When I wrote back to say that I would like to see those letters, I was told no one had been given access since the Commission's investigation began, except for the Commission itself. Mitchell ignored my request for an interview with Archbishop Neary, whom I had met in Knock the year before. When I asked Mitchell if he would speak to me himself, he sent me back a five-word email: 'No! I don't do interviews.'

I was told by freedom of information officers, researchers and diocesan archivists that it was common for bishops and religious orders to destroy records either by burning them or by using professional shredding services. But the archives of the Archdiocese of Dublin were a distinct exception, operating with what appeared to be genuine transparency. Their archivist, Noelle Dowling, was well respected. Their archives were housed within a massive building on the estate of the Clonliffe diocesan college, not far from Croke Park.

One day I was sitting there, before large boxes of papers dating from the reign of Archbishop McQuaid (1940 to 1972), when the current Archbishop, Diarmuid Martin, strolled into the room in his long black robe and made some quiet request of the archivist. I introduced myself, telling him I'd been in touch with his PR person a number of times, seeking an interview. He mumbled something about the Commission of Investigation not being finished yet and strolled out again.

Having been told by an historian that there might be records for Sean Ross Abbey in the archives of the Diocese of Killaloe, I took the train to Ennis. From the station, I walked past a laundry van outside the massive parish centre near the main church and through the picturesque old streets, past the pillar with Daniel O'Connell perched on top, and on to the housing estate that Google Maps had directed me to, once part of the bishop's lands. It turned out the archives were housed in what might have been a stable or shed to the side of a grand old mansion where the bishop lived.

A friendly woman of whom I asked directions gave me a lift in her car to the gates of the property. She asked me what I was here for, and I told her I was writing about the mother-and-baby homes.

'Good,' she said. 'It's about time.' She didn't say much more, but there was an unspoken resoluteness. I wondered who in her life might have been affected by these places.

Father Ger Nash, a man with slightly receding dark hair and an air of genuine hospitality, met me at the door and led me straight into a kitchen in the back. Women were sitting at a table, chatting over home-made cheesecake and tea. A Polish family had made a tray of the stuff for the bishop, and one of the women would end up wrapping the last slab in tin foil for me to take home. I met the archivist, a tall man wearing an orange puffer gilet and glasses, who was introduced to me as Joe. The bishop was out for the day doing confirmations.

Over a phone call, and in his email, Father Nash, the Diocesan

Secretary, had said that because the Commission of Investigation was still doing its work, they weren't sure they could show me anything. I explained that I had visited the diocesan archives in Dublin, which surely were subject to the inquiry also, and that I would be happy to come and meet him in any case.

Father Nash and Joe brought me out to a converted outbuilding, which housed an archive room. Joe pulled two grey boxes from a lower shelf and told me they were filled with records and correspondence relating to Sean Ross Abbey. He explained that there were also letters to the diocese from adoptees or mothers looking for information as well as marriage notifications and other personal documents. People still contacted them every year seeking personal records. I mentioned that I had on my phone the details of a woman adopted to the US from Sean Ross who was looking for her records: a PDF with her identification and permission for me to make searches on her behalf. Could I maybe send it to them and find her baptismal record while I was there?

Father Nash explained that under the terms of the adoption legislation it would not be possible to send records or identifying details; they could only confirm details the adoptee already had. If she wanted records containing details about her mother's identity, she would have to apply through Tusla – the State's Child and Family Agency – or another approved organization.

'Who are we protecting here?' Joe asked rhetorically.

Joe then took me on a tour of the main house. He pointed out the bishop's personal office and admired a room with green wallpaper, an old chandelier and impressive white stucco. Upstairs we passed a type of walk-in closet with shelves full of assorted books, including a book on sexual morality. On a high shelf I saw a cardboard box with a label referring to child protection. In the rooms used as the diocesan offices, Joe led me to a metal filing cabinet and extracted two old ledgers of baptismal registrations from the bottom shelf. I could see that some entries had been updated when the children had completed their Communion or gotten married. I was told there were really no general records about the institutions, apart from a letter or two that the Sisters would have had to send to the local bishop, advising him they were setting up a home in his parish. I explained to Joe that that was exactly the sort of documentation I was looking for.

We went downstairs again and had a long chat in the reception room with Father Nash, surrounded by framed photos of leaders of Irish revolutionaries and politicians, including two separate portraits of Michael Collins. I alone was served a tray of tea and sandwiches.

Father Nash spoke candidly about the Church's past and Ireland's history of institutionalism, about how the religious orders 'lost their founding charism' when they began putting vulnerable people into institutions 'on an industrial scale'. We talked about how abuse still happens nowadays in institutional settings. Joe spoke of a current generation that didn't want to see complexities and about a tendency to blame a few scapegoats, whereas talking openly about where responsibility lies would implicate many more people. He spoke of how much we owed Mary Robinson for her work as the 'bête noire of the Church' and opening doors for women's rights as a lawyer and senator.

Father Nash said that in trying to understand the past, we were 'exploring a land we don't know'.

I asked him about the role of priests in referring women to the institutions.

'I think the priest in the local parish would have been hugely powerful,' he said: whether preaching from the altar or consulting privately, the priest would have had great influence over the decisions taken by families. He spoke hypothetically about a family whose seventeen-year-old daughter was pregnant. 'They don't care if the Church or State takes care of that, as long as it's not their problem,' he said. 'Every section of society was glad somebody was dealing with it, I'd say knitted together in a circle that suited everybody except for the victims.'

*

After lunch, Joe brought me back to the archive room and set me up with boxes of files from 1904 to 1955, the span of Bishop Michael Fogarty's reign. He took out some of the files that were non-identifying, such as correspondence from St Patrick's Guild and letters from the government departments. 'They called them offenders,' he remarked, clearly disapproving of this language. He then told me he would leave me alone for an hour.

After he left there was silence and the whir of an air-cooling system.

Not knowing how long I would have to go through the records, I took photos of each page on my phone, the battery low, rushing back and forth from the plug and trying to juice it up just enough to go back and photograph more. When Father Nash ducked in at one point to say goodbye, I was startled by the sound, being so engrossed in trying to take note of everything.

There were requests for donations from the Rotunda Girls' Aid Society, a rescue society in Dublin's north inner city. The society offered its assistance 'only to those of a first offence'. Orphaned and illegitimate babies were 'saved' from a life of hardship and placed with acceptable Catholic families. The Society continued to broker adoptions for decades after it became legal.

Within their 1923 appeal pamphlet promoting their services, they included a letter written by a mother who had returned home after going away, ostensibly for a medical operation. 'Oh, if she had only known what kind of operation it was,' she says of her own mother. 'I could not tell her that I too am a mother; that while I smile, and try to be cheerful, my heart is breaking with longing for my baby boy.' She had given him up a week before, and described it as an eternity. 'I try to bear the separation as part of my punishment for the cruel wrong of bringing him into the world, but the one pure love of my life is stronger than I, and my heart cries out for my boy day and night.' She asks the Society to pray for her. 'You who have lived a good life cannot understand what I feel.' It was very strange: this woman's pain was being used to promote such services.

In 1930, letters were received from the Sisters of the Sacred Hearts of Jesus and Mary in Chigwell, discussing the purchasing of 600 acres in Roscrea for what would become Sean Ross Abbey. This was more land than they strictly needed for the institution they planned to open, but it was necessary to ensure they were well hidden away from prying eyes. The Superior General stated that the aim was to establish a home for 'the unmarried mothers in Ireland' and she asked the bishop to 'sanction the place being used as a Home for feeble-minded women of the same class'. In a following letter she had to clarify that when she said 'feeble-minded women of the same class' she meant women 'who had fallen and were so weak in mind and will, that it might be necessary to retain them in the Home in order to prevent another fall'.

Three years later, the local health board wrote to the bishop seeking his advice regarding the care of unmarried mothers. 'The Board at present sends first offenders to Sean Ross Abbey,' the letter stated, referring to the local health boards. 'As far as possible, the mothers are retained there for a period of two years.' The children were retained or boarded out until the age of fifteen and then 'hired out' or apprenticed. There were an average of fifty 'first offenders' yearly and the board had to pay ten shillings a head per week for maintenance. The author of the letter signed off as an 'obedient servant' to the bishop, asking for the bishop to 'favour' the health board with his views and to nominate a committee of parish priests who could advise on the issue.

In his reply, the bishop noted that the nuns endeavoured to get the young women employment after they left Sean Ross Abbey and seemed to have some success. 'This is true at least of inmates of a certain class,' he clarified.

The bishop then divided the women into three classes. There were a great number of women who 'will never be able to take care of themselves and are easy victims to the wicked', for whom the 'one form of protection' would be to 'collect them into institutions under the care of nuns'. As long as they remained in institutions 'they are quiet, happy and inoffensive'. The second class of offenders was the 'naturally decent' girls who had fallen through accident. This class was 'dealt with by the nuns' at Sean Ross, some of them getting jobs and marrying. 'The third class is that of women of a wild and vicious nature who are a harmful influence wherever they prevail,' he stated. 'Some are taken as Penitents into houses under the care of the Good Shepherd nuns and remain there.'

The next year, the Department, evidently satisfied with the bishop's assessment, laid out requirements for a new maternity hospital on the grounds of Sean Ross Abbey and agreed the capitation payment they would provide.

In some handwritten notes in a copybook within a file marked 'Roscrea Monastery' there were references to 'seculars abroad' getting information about a charge brought against a brother, rumours of a 'monk and his woman' in Roscrea that had reached Nenagh, with barmaids gossiping that a religious brother had a baby with a married woman. While women were being hidden away in homes, religious brothers were allegedly getting them pregnant.

Within the files, there was a handwritten list of names and the donations paid to the Catholic Protection and Rescue Society. It seemed the Society was in serious debt, and 'many souls' had been lost to the Church because of it. A letter from Mary Cruice of St Patrick's Guild sent 'particulars' of applications by women from the diocese over six months in 1939; her letter was signed 'your obedient child'. The initials of each woman were noted, as well as parish, occupation, general remarks and the decision of the Guild. One woman had been recommended by a Catholic curate and went home after confinement, having been admitted to St Gerard's, and the Guild 'accepted custody'. A domestic servant was described as 'a case for Sean Ross Abbey'. I wondered if women were assessed according to their perceived moral or labour value.

A document listed the number of women admitted to Sean Ross between 1950 and 1965, as well as the number of babies born, baptized and adopted. In 1950 there were 149 mothers present and 134 children. Admissions peaked in 1962, following the closure of the Tuam home and the transfer of many of its inmates: 179 children were born in or transferred to the home in that year.

In documents regarding the rules of adoption, a snapshot was included of the reality for women giving birth in secret. Women were terrified of being talked about in the town once their pregnancy was showing. 'We have many examples on record where a patient had to be admitted to her own District Hospital at night and had to be hidden from the staff until she was transferred here a few hours after,' the report stated. 'Every girl here is under an assumed name.' It listed school teachers, general and mental nurses, physiotherapists, bank clerks, typists, shop and post office assistants, hairdressers, domestics and schoolgirls from sixteen to eighteen years, 'from very nice families, in fact from every walk of life'.

When Joe came back, I asked him if I could see material relating to a more recent bishop, Michael Anthony Harty, who served from 1967 until his death in 1994.

In 1969, the year Sean Ross Abbey closed, Bishop Harty received a letter from a Sister Hildegarde, explaining that baptismal certificates were being transferred to the parish to be kept secure. There were also reports from 1971 for the Catholic Protection and Rescue Society, booklets with a glossy white-and-orange cover design, and an illustration of children meeting a glowing Jesus. Their acknowledgements indicated the degree to which Church and State worked together: the hierarchy, clergy and laity; the Ministers for Health and Foreign Affairs; the chief executive officers of the health board, the religious communities in the mother-and-baby homes and the Adoption Board. The Society boasted of having arranged more than 200 adoptions and having 'repatriated' 33 pregnant Irish girls from England the year before.

A newspaper clipping from 1970 about unmarried mothers and adoption, evidently saved by the bishop, spoke of the 'hard luck' of children given to 'itinerant families, or to elderly neurotic couples'.

It quoted an air hostess talking about the children taken to America: 'It reeked of commercialism, as though the air-borne babies were being sold.'

What did the bishop think, reading those words? Was he pleased that, on his watch, such adoptions were no longer being brokered by the nuns at Sean Ross Abbey? Or did he worry that the closure of such an institution signalled the weakening of the stigma against sex and pregnancy out of wedlock?

I ran out of time before I found any document that suggested an answer.

4.

'Everyone knew it was there'

My first visit to Tuam was badly timed: it was the August bank holi-day, and most people were busy with family, or away. But on the way down, phoning from the passenger seat as my boyfriend drove, I managed to reach a woman called Teresa Killeen-Kelly. She told me to meet her upstairs at an Indian restaurant on the high street, where we could get served late.

Teresa joined us at the table, a middle-aged woman with striking black hair and a voice like wet gravel. My boyfriend sat across the table, tucking into a bright yellow lamb pasanda. I snatched bites of poppadom while scribbling down notes as Teresa told me about what she called the Tuam Home Babies Graveyard Committee.

Since she was a child, Teresa had known there was a grave where the big H-block buildings of the mother-and-baby home in Tuam used to stand. In the 1970s, some boys had found human bones, which were quickly covered up. 'Everyone knew it was there,' she told me. 'It was just normal. People kept it tidy. But did we know how many? No.'

In 2012, a Tuam woman called Catherine Corless published an article in the *Journal of the Old Tuam Society* in which she reported her finding that some 800 children had died in the Tuam home. After Corless began collecting the children's death certificates, she approached Teresa and they discussed setting up the Graveyard Committee, which sought to erect a memorial to the children who had died in the institution.

As mothers and grandmothers, both women felt a deep need to see the children who died named and remembered. All of the mem-bers of the committee agreed on that. But when it became clear that most of the children did not have burial records, and Corless hypothesized that they'd been buried in a mass grave, the committee members did not all agree on what should become of whatever remains were buried behind the old home. Teresa, for her part, did not want them dug up. 'The babies were born here, they died here and they'll stay here,' she told me. That was that.

There were other sections of the old property still under suspicion, she explained, including a grassy lump of ground beside the playground, a small hill that children liked to roll down. I tried to picture it, having only seen photos of the place in the news or on TV. By now, she told me, she was accustomed to people like me turning up in her town and thinking they would find something new.

It was August 2017. More than three years had passed since Alison O'Reilly of the *Irish Mail on Sunday* reported Catherine Corless's findings.

When the story broke around the world, I was working as an intern on the health and science desk at the *Washington Post*. A story about the number of deaths was written by an incredibly sharp young reporter, Terrence McCoy, who spoke to Corless over the phone. 'The bones are still there,' she told him. The headline of the *Post* article mistakenly said that 800 bodies had been 'found' at the site, though this was quickly corrected. Other reports had made the same mistake. There was a swift backlash, and even claims that the entire story was a hoax. Lengthy corrections and discussions of those corrections were published, though few challenged the archival research done by Corless. Terry Prone, whose PR firm acted for the Bon Secours order, wrote a now infamous email to a French documentary journalist, responding to a request for an interview with Sister Marie Ryan. The 'O my God – mass grave in West of Ireland' story, as Prone called it, 'surprised the hell out of everybody, not least the Sisters of Bon Secours in Ireland, none of whom had ever worked in Tuam and most of whom had never heard of it.' She told the journalist, 'If you come here, you'll find no mass grave, no evidence that children were ever so buried.'

In a statement at the time, the Archbishop of Tuam, Michael Neary, said he was shocked, horrified and saddened to learn of the 'magnitude of the numbers of children buried'. He claimed that his Archdiocese had no records relating to the burial of children at the home and had played no role in its operation. 'I can only begin to imagine the huge emotional wrench which the mothers suffered in giving up their babies for adoption or by witnessing their death,' he said. Their 'pain and brokenness' was 'beyond our capacity to understand'. He welcomed an inquiry. The Bon Secours Sisters had a 'clear moral imperative', he said, to 'act upon their responsibilities in the interest of the common good'. One of his predecessors, Dr Thomas Gilmartin, in the revolutionary year of 1916, had said: 'The future of the country is bound up with the dignity and the purity of the women of Ireland.' Now the country's future was bound up with what lay buried beneath a patch of ground in the corner of a Tuam housing estate.

In 2015, the government established a Commission of Investigation into Mother and Baby Homes and Certain Related Matters. In November 2016, a test excavation of the burial site in Tuam began. In March 2017, it was announced that two large structures had been revealed, one of which appeared to be a large sewage containment system, filled with rubble and debris and covered with soil. The second was a long structure divided into twenty chambers, and this structure too appeared to be for the containment or treatment of sewage. In these chambers, 'significant quantities of human remains' were discovered. A number of bones were retrieved for analysis. Age at death ranged from approximately thirty-five foetal weeks to between two and three years old. The radiocarbon testing dated the bones from the period the mother-and-baby home was in operation: 1925 to 1961. 'The Commission is shocked by this discovery and is continuing its investigation into who was responsible for the disposal of human remains in this way,' the press release stated.

The Taoiseach, Enda Kenny, called the discovery a 'chamber of horrors'. He also noted that no nuns 'broke into our homes to kidnap our children. We gave them up to what we convinced ourselves was the nuns' care. We gave them up to spare them the savagery of gossip' and because of Irish people's 'perverse, morbid relationship with what you call respectability'. He noted the double standards that let men off the hook, as though women 'had the amazing capacity to self-impregnate'. And he admitted that the 'situation' of there being bodies buried on the Tuam site had been known about since 1972.

Teresa Killeen-Kelly told me that the Graveyard Committee was initially only interested in petitioning the government to put up a plaque or statue of some sort acknowledging those buried on the site. The Bon Secours Sisters had offered them €2,000 towards their campaign. Teresa believed that if a monument had gone up when they first asked for it, before the full extent of infant mortality and the unmarked grave at the home were exposed, the matter might have been put to bed and the site never fully investigated.

Her mother, now in her eighties, had lived her whole life in Tuam. When the home was in operation, she said, you wouldn't have been able to ask questions or to see inside the place, unless you were sent there yourself. There were vast distances from her mother's generation, when nothing was spoken about, to Teresa's generation trying to put together lists of names of the dead, to her daughters' generation now growing up in a town marked by the discovery. 'My own girls ask, how did ye let that happen?'

When I walked around the next morning, in the daylight, the town was bigger than I'd expected. Outside the Supermac's, P. J. Haverty waited in his car to take me to the burial site. A kind-faced man in a pastel-coloured sweater, with white hair and the burnished skin of a farmer or gardener, he launched into his story right away.

He was born in the home and stayed there until the age of six. As we drove, he described being marched to school by the nuns in pairs, ten minutes before all of the 'legitimate' children arrived. At the end of the day, the home children would be marched back ten minutes later.

His mother, Eileen, was twenty-seven when she gave birth to

him, in 1951. The local priest arrived to his grandparents' house on a bicycle to instruct them what to do: once her pregnancy started to show, she had to be sent to the home. Haverty stayed there until the nuns fostered him out to a farming family. 'You're one of them things,' people would tell him, growing up. 'A bastard. A queer.' The foster family was extremely religious, holding Mass for neighbours in their own house, with confessions in the sitting room. His foster father's sister had wanted to send him back, believing him to be a stain on the family.

We drove around the town and then to the Dublin Road housing estate, where the home once stood. The road leading to the estate was lined with institutions, from the national schools with saints' names to the old residence of the Christian Brothers, now the grounds for a non-denominational school and a men's shed. I was told there was also a seminary somewhere, tucked in behind hedges. A dismal building housed the local branch offices of Tusla, the Child and Family Agency, which now held the records for the mother-and-baby homes.

At the entrance of the Dublin Road estate, a part of the old wall that once surrounded the institution jutted out. In the midst of a maze of narrow, house-lined streets, we came to a tarmacked playground and basketball court. A kid was idly balancing a ball on a hurley, and a young girl with pigtails played near the swing set. In the far corner, the burial site was boarded up, hidden from view after the test excavation.

It was drizzling and grey, so we talked for a while inside the car, looking out over the playground, before we pulled ourselves out into the damp air and walked around the playground, past the back gardens and sheds of the houses, to the patch of land in the far corner. Through a round hole in the wooden board I could see the statue of the Virgin Mary in the far corner and the dark gravel raked over the disturbed ground, with spray paint marking certain locations on the surface, presumably left by the technical team.

Stuck to the outside of the board were pieces of A4 paper, laminated but not impervious to the rain. Lists of names were typed out in neat rows: the hundreds of small children recorded to have died at the home, suspected to be buried under that patch of earth. Sodden teddy bears and angel figurines were lined up in front of the boards and tucked into crannies or balanced on the edges of walls nearby. The back gardens of several houses reached right up to the path, and one bordered the burial ground itself.

The only distinct memory P.J. had of the home was rocking himself to sleep at night. He told me that he still did that sometimes. He was locked inside the dormitory bedroom at night with twelve other boys. They sometimes had to urinate on the floor. A few years ago, P.J. met a man who had also grown up at the home, who said the priest used to come in and sexually abuse the boys at night.

On one occasion, as an adult, P.J. told a woman that he had been born at the home. She told him her father had once hidden a woman who escaped from one of the laundries in his attic. The gardaí came by and warned her father that there was a girl on the loose and she was very dangerous, but he kept her in the house until it was safe and then she escaped to England. On another occasion, he was at the hairdresser's and discovered that a man he had known for years also grew up in the home.

When P.J. finally reunited with his mother, after years searching for her, she told him that she had worked as a cleaner at the Grove Hospital, down the road from the home, also run by the Bon Secours Sisters. For five and a half years, she walked every week from the hospital to the home, knocking on the door to beg the nuns to hand over her son. They told her she wasn't fit to be his mother. In truth, P.J. believes, the problem was that she was too poor: 'If my mother had a hundred pounds, she could have bought me,' he said. When he was sent to the foster family, Eileen emigrated to London, knowing there was no chance now of getting him back. She told P.J. that she had prayed every day to the Virgin Mary that he was healthy and alive, safe with another family somewhere. P.J. knew his foster mother had prayed to Padre Pio that he would find his birth mother. For these two women, he still goes to Mass, though he has little faith in the institution of the Church any more.

'Our Lord was crucified and so were the women of this country, the unmarried women of this country,' he told me. 'The nuns had power, it was all about money and it was all about power.' All he wanted was an apology, to be able to go to his mum's grave and tell her he'd got her an apology, from the Church and from the State: 'To know she wasn't a sinner, that she would have made a good mother, that she did love me and did want me, she told me that herself.'

After speaking to P. J. Haverty, I went by myself back to the estate. A man in his early thirties maybe, with a green shamrock tattooed on his neck, had heard me talking to some neighbours, and followed me over. Daniel was born on the estate but knew nothing about the children's remains until the recent revelations.

'You would never think you'd be out here running around and it's a graveyard really,' he said. 'It's hard to be religious after that.'

He motioned towards the main cemetery, just beyond the houses across the road. The proximity of consecrated ground seemed to add to the insult.

'What were they hiding?' he wondered aloud. 'I don't think God was here.'

The heart of Tuam beats between two cathedrals, huge slate-grey buildings, one Protestant and the other Catholic. On the Sunday of that August bank holiday in 2017, I ended up in the wrong one. There were only a handful of people inside the cavernous building and I was musing about how people had abandoned Mass because nuns had buried children in a septic tank. But when the service ended and people were invited for tea and sandwiches, it finally clicked.

I ended up chatting for a few minutes to the cathedral groundskeeper, who happened to be a Catholic. He told me there were two nuns still alive who had worked in the home that he knew of: one of them had Alzheimer's but the other, at ninety-seven, was apparently in decent health. The groundskeeper had known the doctor who used to deliver babies at the home but he said only the nuns knew what really went on behind the walls.

By the time I rushed up the road to the Catholic cathedral, wanting to see how many people still went to church in a town rocked by such a discovery, Mass had just finished, and a traffic jam inching out of the car park gave me my answer.

The priest was busy with a rehearsal for a baptism. A gaggle of young women, glammed up in short dresses and heels, were making their way down the aisle.

Two biddies in a back pew were tutting so hard their voices echoed.

'That's a bloody tape, sounds like a cat,' one said, referring to the bells.

'The women have gone to hell,' said the other. 'The lads deserve a medal. I never saw the like of it, a dress out to here, when the flap went up to here.'

Her accomplice hummed in agreement. 'Women have let women down badly, women are a lot worse than men.'

In December 2017, a technical report on the Tuam burial site was published by the government. It laid out options for what to do next, now that the existence of a mass grave had been confirmed. Many people were calling for a full excavation of the site, and families with relatives who died in the institution were eager to start DNA testing as soon as possible.

In January 2018, the government announced that the public would be asked to have a say on the 'appropriate courses of actions'. Notices were printed in national and local papers that there were to be four public consultation meetings: the first in Dublin, then three in Tuam. The five options were listed online. Respondents could identify themselves as a former resident of the home, a relative of a former resident, a local resident of the estate and the roads surrounding the burial site, or as a member of the public. They were asked to place an X in the box beside their preferred option.

1. Memorialisation
2. Exhumation of known human remains

3. Forensic excavation and recovery of known human remains

4. Forensic excavation and recovery of known human remains with further evaluation/excavation of other areas of interest

5. Forensic excavation of the total available area

I went to Tuam to attend the second public meeting on the fate of the mass grave. The landscape was still patched with ice after a vicious cold snap that had shut down roads and left shelves around the country void of sliced pan.

Before getting on the bus, I spoke to Catherine Corless on the phone. She told me that she believed a full forensic exhumation was required to get to the truth about how the children had been buried, how many there were, and how they had died. On the radio programme that I listened to on the bus, a priest called in to support Mary McAleese, the former President of Ireland, who had called the Catholic Church the 'primary carrier of the virus of misogyny'. The priest said his parish had put out a tweet acknowledging the work of local women. 'We work with the heart,' he said. 'But there is also an institutional Church, a Church I feel very distant from.' He thought too many in the Church remained locked away in ivory towers. 'We are at a point where we must be brave.'

The bus stopped in the car park of the Catholic cathedral. To one side of the cathedral are the old buildings of St Jarlath's College and the Bishop's Palace, to the other the convent of the Mercy Sisters and the convent of the Presentation Sisters. In the top corner is a nuns' burial ground, with nearly a hundred rows of shiny black metal crosses laid out in exact lines on an immaculate cream gravel surface.

Inside the door of the cathedral, a laminated A4 sign reminded the faithful: 'A baby in the womb is God's creation.' The referendum on abortion was just a few months away. 'Cherish the mother and the baby,' the sign read.

On my way through the town I passed a shop window packed with giant cellophane-wrapped Easter eggs, those chocolate symbols of fertility. The dim-lit bar and restaurant of the Corralea Court Hotel was mostly empty. Up the stairs in the first-floor conference room, at two in the afternoon, there were around sixteen chairs in a circle on what looked like a wooden dance floor. The cushioning on the chairs matched the royal blue of the carpet around the edge, patterned with gold stars. On a table to the side, there were large old maps of the area. One was a technical drawing from 1979 of the layout of the estate being built by Galway County Council at Dublin Road. At the centre of the rows of houses, 'old children's burial ground' was written in brackets in the far corner. Directly underneath this was written: 'proposed playground'. You could see from the plan how the back garden of one of the houses ran right down to the edge of the burial site. No official plaque or monument was ever erected by the council to mark what, since at least as long ago as 1979, had been accepted in their own drawings as a place where the bodies of children were buried.

The walls were beige, and softly glowing Christmas lights were inexplicably strung across a table. We could have been a recovery meeting or a local committee planning a raffle. The two women facilitating the meeting sat at the top of the circle. A member of Galway County Council sat to their left. Two members of the expert technical group sat outside the ring to their right, near a projector screen. A local photographer worried around the edges of the room and gently asked if he could take a photo from the back. The request was denied. We wrote our names on pink labels and stuck them to our shirts and jumpers. To keep order during the meeting, a grey lump of felt they called the 'talking stone' would be passed around. You could only speak if you held the stone. We all nodded obediently. A few latecomers took up empty places. Everyone was asked to talk, one by one, about their feelings. Although it was a public meeting, the facilitators specified that no names were to be shared outside the room.

One man described Tuam as 'ground zero' and was adamant that the bodies must be exhumed. 'If I have to go up with a shovel myself and start it, I will,' he said. 'Dig those bodies up, every one of them, all over the country. Give the children some dignity. They're someone's children.' If they were dug up, DNA tested and logged, and even one woman who came back searching for her child was able to get an answer, it would be worth it.

A woman pointed out that Masses had been held at the burial site for years before Catherine Corless's findings were reported. As a child she recalled the cans of Coke and packs of Tayto they would be given while the adults were busy saying prayers. The people of the estate had maintained the area for forty years with care and respect, she stressed, yet when the news broke it was described to the world as some neglected patch of dirt. The Graveyard Committee and the people who lived around the site had tended to the burial ground when no one else did, and felt protective of it, with people from outside campaigning for decisions that would literally affect what happened in their back gardens. The woman didn't want the children's remains dug up.

An older woman who had lived in Tuam all her life said she remembered the children walking to school from the home. She wanted a memorial erected in their honour, but worried that 'digging them up and trying to find out what baby is what baby' would go on forever. She was not the only person who had such concerns.

Some surmised that the majority of the remains that were found would never be linked to family members, and there was a worry about what would happen to the unclaimed bones. There was also some local disquiet relating to the fate of a different mass grave recently discovered in Tuam. In 2012, human remains had been found during the installation of a new water main on the edge of the Dublin Road estate: 15 adult men, 11 adult women, 3 adolescents, 17 juveniles and 2 infants, according to an excavation report published in 2014. One infant had been buried at the feet of two adults. Eighteen grave pits were identified. Nails and the orientation of the bodies suggested that the bodies had been buried in coffins. The remains were located just inside the old walls of the workhouse and likely belonged to Famine victims. Residents of the estate said that the remains were still in boxes in a university lab or morgue somewhere, and they were uncomfortable with the idea that bodies had been disturbed and then not given a proper burial.

Now, some people were worried that the remains of the children might meet the same fate. There were a few who were publicly calling for exhumation in hope of being able to identify relatives. Anna Corrigan had discovered only after the death of her mother that she had two brothers who had been born in the Bon Secours home; now she wanted to know if they'd been buried there. Peter Mulryan was born in the home and boarded out, made to work on a farm: a brutal life. His mother was sent to a Magdalen laundry in Galway, where she spent the rest of her life. Later, he reunited with her, but she never told him that he had a sister who had died in the Tuam home. It was Catherine Corless who found Marian Mulryan's name and shared it with him. There were others, too, who did not speak publicly but who wanted to find out if relatives were buried there.

'I've no right to tell a survivor you cannot identify where your brother or sister is,' said a woman who lived on the estate. 'We have no right to vote on this.' She hoped the skeletons of the children would not be left 'in a cesspit with just a plaque'.

Another woman got up quietly to leave – and then started speaking with urgent conviction. 'I have no right to tell Joe Soap, "Yeah, your sister might have been buried there, but we don't know, she might have been sold in America."' Her voice was strained, her eyes wide. 'Just because the death certs are there, who's to say they weren't falsified.' It was known that children had been adopted from the Tuam home; this woman was voicing the theory that, in order to conceal the extent of such adoptions, the Bon Secours Sisters had reported the deaths of children who had in fact been given to families in the US. It was known that birth certificates were sometimes falsified in order for families to claim adopted children as their own, erasing any evidence of their origins; could death certificates have been falsified for a similar purpose?

The woman then returned to the fate of the remains buried behind the old home. She asked the people in the room, who would bury any child of their own like that? As much as she wanted to let them rest in peace, they should be dug up. 'I've seen grown men in front of me, old men, crying,' she said. 'Crying because they didn't know where their sister was buried.' She had never spoken up like this in her entire life, she told the room.

After she had left, and we had heard a rather impenetrable speech from an employee of Galway County Council, the experts took the room through 'a whirlwind, whistle-stop' tour of the logistics of the various options. The remains were 'commingled': bones had become mixed together as the bodies decomposed. The chambers within the old sewerage system were very deep and very narrow. The patch of ground where the memorial garden was now located would be a tight squeeze for big machinery to manoeuvre in.

We were told that individualizing remains was different from legally verifying them. With a plane crash, there was a list of passengers and it was just a case of matching them up with their families. In this case, by contrast, the institution had closed in 1961; even the most recent of the remains had been there for over half a century; records linking children to mothers were patchy; and the majority of the mothers – probably the vast majority – were no longer alive. DNA would be gathered and a database built up, but it would be up to surviving relatives to come forward in order to match DNA to a name.

The majority of the remains discovered in the test excavation were of infants, many just days old. The children were close in age range, so separating by eye would be difficult. Juveniles had more bones than adults, and their bones were more prone to decay. Water may have been seeping in or flowing through the tanks for decades. During her visit to the test excavation, the State Pathologist, Dr Marie Cassidy, had described 'disarticulated, dark-coloured and fragmented' bones in a 'haphazard arrangement with no indication of having been encoffined or laid out'. The experts explained that there was a risk DNA extraction could destroy many of the bones.

The beep of the projector slide signalled the end of the presentation, and the chirpy voice of the facilitator returned. 'So, that's a lot of information,' she chimed.

Chairs scraped as people rearranged themselves wordlessly. One woman asked, what happened if the bones were tested and no one came forward to claim them? The members of the technical group had no clear answer to this.

I asked if there was a rough estimate for how long identification would take. The archaeologist said that the process of identifying the victims of the Grenfell Tower fire took between three and four months for around seventy people, and that they were still collecting 'tiny, tiny specks' at Ground Zero after 9/11. He admitted these examples weren't really comparable. 'Make what you want of that,' he said. A mass grave of the commingled remains of hundreds of small children, it was clear, was uncharted territory.

One woman asked if she could clear up a matter that she felt was widely misunderstood: that not all the children who died in the institution were necessarily buried on the grounds. When the list of names was being prepared for a memorial, two people contacted the Graveyard Committee to tell them that their child was not buried behind the Tuam home. The speaker denounced the idea that 796 babies had been buried behind the home as hype and media shenanigans. For that many children to be buried, she said, bones would have been popping up all over people's gardens, when they put down vegetable patches or planted flowers.

Some people who lived locally took offence at strangers coming from all over, to leave things around the site. 'Maggots running out of the teddy bears,' one woman said. 'You can't leave that rubbish there.'

If the neighbours cleaned up the area, they were accused of callously removing offerings. 'People here in Tuam have no voice,' another woman said. 'We have not been able to open our mouths for the last three years.'

At the end, the facilitators asked which option everyone would prefer. It made people uncomfortable.

One woman reminded the room that the babies' remains were in septic tanks: 'Definitely excavate.'

Another felt it was pointless, since the souls were already in heaven: 'We're all complaining about flesh and bones.'

Some felt the process had been rushed, others wanted it over and done with. 'We're up to here with it.'

Another woman argued the only way the town would get closure would be to find out what was buried there. She grew up beside an informal children's burial ground, or *cillín*, that her family still maintained. 'Those children who were buried in the still of the night and in the darkness and silence, in a shoebox carried at dusk, were given more dignity and love in their burials than those children that were here in Tuam,' she said. These were mostly unbaptized or stillborn babies. There were countless informal graves like this around the country, known about and sometimes tended to by local people.

A few months later, the report on the public consultation process was published. The 799 people who had made submissions were almost perfectly split between those who favoured memorialization (49 per cent) and those who favoured exhumation and DNA analysis (48 per cent). Residents of the estate mostly wanted non-disturbance of the remains; former residents of the institution wanted full forensic excavation. Submissions came from the UK, Germany, Belgium, Canada and the US. Three people were identified as both former residents of the home and current residents of the estate.

The report noted that people on the estate felt intimidated by the media, by constant door-knocking, cameras in their faces, and once even a drone flying overhead. Because of a new 'gruesome' type of tourist, some said they felt unsafe letting their kids spend time in the playground alone.

The voices of the Bon Secours congregation were completely absent. When invited to take part, they stated that any decision regarding the remains should be made by former residents of the home and their relatives and friends, and that it would be 'inappropriate for the Congregation to influence it in any way'. The report concluded that the reasons the Sisters who ran the home acted as they did was 'as yet an untold story'.

5

Penitents

At the top of Shandon Street, up a narrow lane overlooking Cork city, the black gates of the convent are eternally in bloom: ornately wrought flowers make the bars strangely more forbidding. The convent itself is a vast and imposing red-brick building on a rise of ground, surrounded by thick walls of rough purplish-red stone.

The Magdalen laundry at Peacock Lane was established by lay-men in 1809 'for the protection and reformation of penitent females of dissolute habits, who now contribute to their own maintenance by honest industry', according to Samuel Lewis's 1837 *Topographical Dictionary of Ireland*. The Sisters of Charity took it over in 1845 and established the convent, the looming building atop the hill, where the nuns would reside. By 1914, more than a thousand children attended schools on the grounds of the convent, and the primary school still operates there today. For many decades, children were educated and fallen women were incarcerated in the same religious complex. There was capacity for 110 women in the laundry. As late as 1986, there were still around sixty women there.

On the right-hand side of the convent there was an old extension or annexe, now used as a nursing home. The first thing that caught my eye, after I was buzzed inside, was a quilt draped over a black couch in the reception area: a riot of yolk yellow, sherbet pink, baby blue and other bright colours.

Sitting in a wheelchair in the middle of the room was Mary Gaffney. There were rollers in her hair, with neat furrows of scalp visible in between, and a little woven pouch hanging from her neck for her old Nokia phone. She looked up at me through crimson-rimmed spectacles. I would learn that she often spent the day there knitting, chatting away with the receptionist, making her quilts and donating them to cancer patients. It was a few weeks after her seventy-third birthday. Mary had lived her entire life in institutions run by nuns, but still she was bringing colour into the world.

State inspections of the care centre found that needs of residents were not being met; that an allegation of abuse had not been reported or appropriately investigated; that necessary medical treatments were not facilitated. The inspectors had also received allegations of 'financial irregularities'. By 2017, when I first visited Mary, the Health Services Executive (HSE) had taken over the running of the facility from the nuns. The Sisters of Charity had said they intended to sell the property, meaning the women in care would be forced to move. They no longer saw the nuns, who lived on the other side of the convent.

In a small visiting room, with just enough space for the two of us to sit opposite each other, Mary told me about her recent trip to Lourdes, five days of 'praying and things'. It had rained almost constantly, and the grotto flooded. I asked her was the food nice at least, and she told me without hesitation that it was 'desperate'. We laughed about that.

The past is difficult territory for Mary. She was born in 1945, in St Patrick's on the Navan Road. 'I never met my mother,' she told me. 'I wasn't allowed to see her.' She was sent briefly to the Glenmaroon school for children with special needs run by the Daughters of Charity, but was never taught properly to read or write. At some point, still a child, she returned to the mother-and-baby home and was put to work minding babies in the wards. She scrubbed floors and endlessly cleaned. Her only break was visiting a former classmate, whose mother said she knew Mary's mother and who tried to reconnect them. But it was forbidden by one of the nuns: 'Sister Dympna would not let me see my mum.' Mary's mother went to England, and Mary was never told about the existence of any other form of family. 'They wouldn't tell you nothing, girl.'

One day, with a few other girls, she was sent away on a train to Cork and put to work at Peacock Lane. 'Slaved,' she said. 'God, they were nasty enough, girl, I didn't care for them when I was working with them. Hard work, girl.' The working day started at 8 a.m. She worked in the laundry then, washing and scrubbing away until the evening. In their free time, the girls would knit: a nun taught her how. The jumpers they made were sold in a shop, and the inmates got some pocket money for that.

At one point, Mary asked me if I'd always worn my hair long. I told her it grows quickly. She said she always wanted long hair, but she was never allowed. I felt embarrassed about my long hair, when she could never have it; about showing her photos of my family's dogs, when she, a dog lover, never had a pet; and for mentioning my mother as we chatted. It was gutting to contemplate the scale and the ordinariness of the things she had been denied.

In the late 1990s, when Mary was about to undergo major surgery, the Sisters set out to locate her relatives. It crossed my mind that they wanted to find a family member who would cover the cost of burial. Two Sisters went to Dublin and tracked down an aunt, who opened the door and was minded to hurry them away until they told her they had a girl in St Vincent's Convent in Cork who was their flesh and blood. Mary remembered her aunt coming to Cork to visit her. 'That was my first time to meet my family,' she said.

I asked her did she forgive the Sisters?

No, she told me, she did not.

The Magdalen rescue movement used Mary Magdalen the same way cheap hair salons use photos of celebrities: as an idealized role model to advertise their business. The pervasive image of Mary Magdalen as the forgiven whore was spun in the sixteenth century by Pope Gregory the Great, who conflated three different people: Mary of Bethany; the unnamed sinful woman who washed the Lord's feet in penitence and dried them with her hair; and Mary Magdalen herself, one of Christ's followers. In 1969, the Church acknowledged the mistake. In 2016, Pope Francis redefined Mary

Magdalen by decree as Apostle of the Apostles, first witness to the resurrection, and declared a feast day in her honour.

We know far less than we ought to about the workings of the Magdalen laundries in independent Ireland, in large part because the religious orders that operated them have generally refused to open their archives to scholars. Historians – notably Frances Finnegan, Maria Luddy and James M. Smith – have done valuable work in spite of this obstacle, as have journalists, notably the late Mary Raftery. The Justice for Magdalenes organization has compiled oral histories and advocated effectively for the rights of survivors. But the inaccessibility of the archives is a serious problem.

One scholar who did gain access to a key archive was Jacinta Prunty, a Holy Faith Sister and historian. In 2017, Prunty published a history of the Sisters of Our Lady of Charity of Refuge in Ireland, and while I was working on this book people within the Church often urged me to read it.

Prunty has a number of interesting things to report. The first Magdalen laundry run by the Sisters of Our Lady of Charity of Refuge in Ireland was St Mary's Asylum, which had been founded in a house on Drumcondra Road in Dublin by an often drunken and gambling priest. All Sisters of the order vowed to work towards 'the restoration and reformation of souls'. Any hardship was preferable to putting the eternal soul in jeopardy. The soul was God's property.

The Sisters of Our Lady of Charity of Refuge opened the first reformatory school certified for girls in Ireland in 1858, on the grounds of High Park in Drumcondra. They then opened so-called training centres, to integrate the girls who had been institutionalized. Specific institutions were intended for girls who were 'sexually involved', Prunty writes, acknowledging that girls were 'held to be culpable for what would, in the 21st century, be termed child sexual abuse'.

Meetings were held between the Department of Education, judges, guards and Archbishop McQuaid to discuss what should be done about the 'immoral conduct of girls'. Girls who had sex, even those who had been raped, were seen as an 'evil influence' on other children. The Department specifically asked the Sisters to set up a reformatory for girls 'whose moral life is in danger', eager to solve the problem of girls between twelve and seventeen who, in their words, 'a) have had sexual intercourse or b) are living in circumstances which may reasonably be expected to lead to their downfall'.

St Anne's reformatory was opened in 1944, in Kilmacud, as, in the words of McQuaid, 'a house of detention for juveniles committed for immoral charges'. A representative of the Department of Local Government and Public Health was quoted in Prunty's book as saying 'girls addicted to sexual immorality are more or less mental' and should be committed to psychiatric institutions.

In May 1967, the records Prunty had access to showed that there were 134 women between the ages of seventeen and seventy-one living as penitents in the order's laundry in Seán MacDermott Street, Dublin. More than two thirds of the inmates had been there for six years or more; around twenty of them had been in the laundry for upwards of thirty years or more; five had been there for nearly half a century. Half of the women in Seán MacDermott Street laundry in May 1967, for whom a reason for admission was known, had been transferred from a mother-and-baby home. Obituaries in the Sisters' records for Magdalen women boasted of a 'remarkable penitent', a 'great sufferer'.

In February 2013, the Taoiseach stood in the Dáil on the occasion of the publication of a report by the committee of inquiry chaired by Senator Martin McAleese. Speaking in front of women who once worked behind the walls of the Magdalen laundries, Enda Kenny said: 'Today we acknowledge the role of the State in your ordeal.' He spoke of what he had learned about the laundries from the McAleese report, and concluded: 'The Magdalen women might have been told they were washing away a wrong or a sin. But we know now and to our shame they were only ever scrubbing away our nation's shadow.' On behalf of the State he apologized for the hurt done to them. He told them they were 'wholly blameless'.

The McAleese inquiry found that more than a quarter of women and girls in the laundries were admitted through agents of the State, whether police, judges or social workers. At least 10,000 women were recorded as having been admitted to the laundries since the foundation of the State in 1922. This did not include the decades before, or admissions to laundries for which no records apparently survived. The total number of women who worked in the Magdalen laundries, including the years before the State inquiry's cut-off, is estimated to be around 30,000.

The inquiry found that Magdalen women washed the laundry of the State. Health authorities and hospitals used Magdalen laundries. A notebook found at High Park listed customers that included the Departments of Fisheries, Education, Health, Justice and Agriculture, as well as the national transport organization Córas Iompair Éireann. The National Library utilized the laundry, as did Áras an Uachtaráin, the Electricity Supply Board and Limerick Prison. Hospitals were big customers, and used the Magdalen laundries until 'very modern times'.

Dating back at least as far as 1926, there is evidence of government departments worrying about the fact that Magdalen women were unpaid, but this did not stop the State from using the services of these institutions. In 1954, the Department of Defence considered that 'allowing even no payment at all to the inmates of the institution doing the laundry, the cost of keep, clothing, medical attention and all the other factors in the running of the institution would more than amount to the equivalent of a fair wage'. The State used the Seán MacDermott Street laundry until the mid-nineties.

A letter from a county council to the Department of Health in 1956 described a patient being sent to High Park as 'an unmarried lady who has given birth to two or more children and whose moral rehabilitation would prevent her becoming a health and social problem'. A Minister of Health consented directly to a 'patient' being sent to High Park laundry in 1954, an unmarried mother from Castlepollard mother-and-baby home who had been 'found unsuitable for retention there'. Her baby was sixteen months old;

being committed to the laundry meant inevitable separation from her child. An internal government memo regarding the admission of two girls to a Good Shepherd laundry in Limerick specified that one of the 'mental defectives' was seventeen years old and had recently become a mother. The other girl was only fourteen.

The Justice for Magdalenes group issued a counter-report, saying it was 'deeply troubled' that the McAleese inquiry seemingly ignored 793 pages of transcribed survivor testimony that the group provided. They said the report marginalized 'the women's lived experiences in these institutions, minimizing the physical and psychological abuse suffered, while evading human rights violations'.

In 2013, when the McAleese report was published, there were 58 former Magdalen inmates – like Mary Gaffney – living in the care of religious orders. In emails between researchers for the inquiry, folders of which I was shown by a source, there was discussion of twenty former Magdalen women, aged between fifty-six and eighty-five years old, who were living in Beechlawn Nursing Home, run by the Sisters of Our Lady of Charity on the grounds of High Park. The nuns were in receipt of regular State funding for the women's care.

In 2012, a researcher working on the HSE's contribution to the McAleese report phoned the Sisters to inquire about the Magdalen women still in the nursing home. He was told no information would be provided. He then emailed the Sisters, noting for the record the telephone refusal and pointing out that the order was receiving public funding. It was clear from the emails that this researcher had travelled to far-flung hospitals and archives to search through boxes of documents, piecing together referral pathways between laundries and the homes, even coming across an old report book documenting abuse claims. I imagined him picking up the phone to ask a straightforward question on behalf of an official State inquiry, only to be told to get lost.

After worries were expressed in internal HSE emails about 'stirring up a very sensitive situation', Martin McAleese himself wrote to the Sisters, apologizing for the 'confusion and distress' caused by the researcher's request for information, and emphasizing their 'invaluable assistance'. He expressed gratitude that cooperation had been provided 'voluntarily by all the relevant Religious Orders despite the absence of any legal obligation to do so'.

Perhaps he was making an effort to maintain good relations with the Sisters, with a mind to the possibility that the orders might still contribute towards redress payments. Perhaps he just understood the weakness of his own inquiry's position, without the power to compel cooperation from the people whose cooperation was most needed. We'll probably never know whether the Sisters were genuinely 'confused', or if they were stonewalling in the belief the inquiry could not lay a finger on them or their funding.

In 2013, after the publication of the McAleese report, four religious orders issued statements expressing regret for any hurt the women may have experienced in their institutions. But they added caveats about the laundries being a product of the times, or about the nuns providing a refuge in good faith. They would not commit to making any contribution towards the State's multimillion-euro redress scheme, despite several requests by the government. The redress scheme had been devised on the basis of a review by John Quirke, a former High Court judge. Quirke spoke to 337 Magdalen women and deemed their claims of forced and unpaid labour to be credible. He also noted that the religious orders, as 'service providers', claimed to be concerned that redress paid to women still in their care facilities, some on the grounds of the laundries, could jeopardize State funding for the care institutions. The orders clearly still claimed a form of ownership over these women.

'For some unknown reason, she wasn't given up for adoption,' Mary Gaffney's cousin Mary Driver told me. 'Mary was left in the care of the nuns.'

In a pub near the seafront in Bray, Co. Wicklow, Mary Driver and I chatted over a salad and chowder. I was baptized in Bray, and my mother's parents met here. My nana spent some time in a Sisters of Charity convalescent home in Bray, when she was a teenager, and used to sneak out of the convent to meet the man who would become my granddad at the dances. After they died, we scattered their ashes from the top of Bray Head, in front of a giant wooden cross.

'I knew I had a cousin somewhere, but we weren't given any information,' Mary Driver told me. Mary Gaffney's mother, Dorothy, went to England after giving birth; Mary Driver's father gave her a lift to the ferry. It was all 'hush hush'. Much later, Mary Gaffney learned that her mother had come to visit her in St Patrick's. Her mother was forced to look at her through a glass partition.

It was in 1995, after the nuns turned up at the Dublin home of Mary Gaffney's aunt, that Mary Driver learned she had a cousin in a laundry in Cork. She went down for a weekend with her husband to meet Mary Gaffney, and has been visiting her cousin ever since.

When Mary Gaffney learned that her mother died only a year before she was reunited with her family, it hardened her heart against the nuns. 'I never forgave Sister Dympna then, I never forgave her,' she told me. Her cousins gave her a photo of her mother, which she keeps now in her room, on the old convent grounds.

Over the years, Mary Driver pieced together more details about her cousin's life. She reckons Mary Gaffney lived in St Patrick's until her mid-twenties. There was a man who would take some of the women out of Navan Road on Saturdays to do a bit of shopping for basics. (This man was still 'full of memories'; but when Mary Driver asked him to speak with me he refused the interview.) The move to Cork was pitched as an exciting development. 'A couple of them were called into the office one day and were told they were going away, that they were getting a new job,' Mary Driver told me. 'They were delighted with themselves.' They were then brought to Peacock Lane.

'Mary to this day would iron for Ireland, even in the wheelchair,' she laughed. 'She'd sit in the wheelchair and iron all day. That's all they were used to: scrubbing.' When she wanted money out of the bank, maybe to go on her trip to Lourdes, she had to ask a man who worked with the nuns to go to the bank. The nuns told Mary Driver the money was in a special account. 'I can't get any answers,' she told me.

Around the time the first redress payments reached the Magdalen women, when the care home was still under the charge of the Sisters of Charity, a solicitor was brought in and the women had wills drawn up. Mary Gaffney had never learned to read. Mary Driver wrote to a Sister Paulina to express concern, and was told an advocate would be there. 'At the end of the day, please God, she'll be able to spend every penny of it,' Mary Driver said. 'What she has is her own money that she earned through sweat, blood and tears.' Then she looked up from the chowder and wondered aloud if there was any possibility that her cousin had donated the money back to the nuns. That was the first thought she'd had when she realized her cousin was receiving a significant amount of money, not just a token sum she could get her hair done with.

When I asked Mary Gaffney once about the nuns selling the building, she told me not to worry, she was going to spend every penny of her money. 'They won't get very much off me,' she said.

There were moments like that, when she spoke, that I felt the breath catching in my throat and I wanted to tell her I'm sorry. But pity does no one any good.

6.

The Adoptee and the Sisters

On a cold January day, Karl O'Kelly stood at a Dublin bus stop peering up the street through rectangular glasses, on the lookout for the 39A. He was dressed entirely in beige, his parka buttoned up to his chin, trousers wrinkled over the tops of his deck shoes. A plastic shopping bag from Dunnes Stores, also beige, dangled in his hand; it was empty save for a single laminated piece of paper, a treasured possession he had for some time been carrying around the country, to graveyards and memorials for survivors of the mother-and-baby homes. Two aged photos, given to him by a nun, were pasted on to the laminated page. One was a shot of a nun, all in white, her habit like the wings of an origami bird, her face lost in its shadow. The photo below was of a towering red-brick building with a wide glass conservatory. This was St Patrick's mother-and-baby home, the place where Karl was born. He was bringing me to the site on the Navan Road where the building once stood, a pilgrimage he made regularly.

As the bus trundled its way out of the city, Karl told me the story of his birth. He came into the world on 17 May 1964. It was ten past eleven on a Sunday, which means that he took his first breath at the same time as many thousands of people around the country were mumbling their prayers at Mass. The story of his birth and his search for the woman responsible was one that he repeated to anyone who would listen. 'My mam called me Joseph Anthony Ryan,' he would tell strangers he met on the street.

Karl suffered oxygen deprivation during his birth, he told me, and this sometimes caused him to struggle with words. As a child, he attended St Augustine's School, in Blackrock, for children with special needs. Over the past decade he had doggedly searched for his birth mother, gathering records and tracking down phone numbers. For the children adopted from mother-and-baby homes, now adults, the search for information about their first few months or years of life was often a protracted and frustrating treasure hunt. Those who had completed the search knew the unofficial clues and secret markers: the mother's maiden surname matching the baby's in the official birth register; a birth certificate lacking the name of a father and with a stranger as witness; the address of an institution as place of birth.

Years before, social workers had provided Karl with some basic information about his origins, but they were not permitted to give any details that might identify his mother. Adopted people in Scotland have had the right to their birth records since 1930, in England and Wales since 1976, and in Northern Ireland since 1987. A Supreme Court case in Ireland in 1998 weighed the rights of two adopted people wanting access to their birth information against the rights of their mothers, one of whom preferred to keep her identity secret. The court ruled that the mother's right to privacy outweighed the child's right to know her identity. Since then, all legislative efforts to expand adoptees' access to information within the bounds established by the Supreme Court ruling have been unsuccessful. And even within the narrow boundaries of what is legal, adoptees seeking information via the government agency Tusla, which holds most adoption records of the mother-and-baby homes, frequently must wait two to three years.

Karl had a letter from a social worker in 2013, providing non-identifying information from his adoption file. It said that a week after his birth he was admitted to hospital for a 'dietary upset'; he was there for more than a month before being returned to St Patrick's. Ten days later, he was placed with adoptive parents. The letter also included his birth mother's first name. She was twenty-one and from Co. Limerick, admitted to the home around a month before giving birth. She signed the consent for his adoption a month and five days after he was born and left St Patrick's the following day, returning to her family home. She didn't sign the final consent to adoption until January the next year, while in London. The adoption order was finalized in March. Karl couldn't remember all the details of what happened, but evidently the social worker tried to trace his birth mother but got no positive response from her, and his case was closed.

With help from a 'search angel', a woman who informally assisted people with tracing, Karl got hold of records through other channels. He showed them to me, all carefully filed. 'Infant appears healthy' the record of his mother's labour noted. 'Cried well.' There was a photocopy of a small square of paper with his date of birth written on it, along with the crucial piece of information: his birth mother's full name, which would ordinarily be redacted. The 'state of the child' was listed as 'illegitimate'. He was baptized a Catholic at St Patrick's. There were two different names used on different records: Joseph Anthony Ryan and Domhnall Kennedy Ryan. He was desperate to know why there were two names and which was the name his mother wanted him to have.

He searched his mother's name online and eventually found a phone number. 'You don't know me from Adam,' he told the woman who answered. 'But my name is Karl and I was born in a mother-and-baby home.' The woman told him that the name of the woman he was looking for matched that of her sister-in-law and gave him another number to call.

When Karl reached the woman – I'll call her Fiona – he asked her if she was sitting down. 'She said hello. I said hello. I said did you ever have a baby boy in a mother-and-baby home?'

The line went silent for a few agonizing minutes. 'Never ring me again,' she told him, hanging up.

After several weeks, he called again. Fiona told Karl he had nearly given her a stroke.

'How did I come to be on this globe?' he asked her.

The response was again a long silence.

He asked if she had christened him Domhnall.

Silence followed again.

Everyone told Karl the silence must be an acknowledgement that she was indeed his mother.

They began texting back and forth. Fiona sent him a birthday card and a Christmas card. In what was probably her first card to Karl, she explained that it felt strange to be writing to him, but that she hoped he had a good and happy life with a loving family. 'When you were born, I called you Anthony as I had great devotion to St Anthony,' she wrote. 'I'm so sad to learn you had lack of oxygen to your brain, what can I say, that was a very sad and stressful time. To be an unmarried girl in those days was almost a crime. Thank God you sound to be a loving and caring person with great faith. Thank you for praying for me.'

One of the other cards Karl received had '10 simple things to remember' on the front and a goofy line drawing of a little girl with dots for eyes and wild hair. Number one on the list of ten things was: 'Love is why we are here.' Inside, Fiona enclosed a photo of herself. She wrote that the photo had been taken about a year earlier, before she had trouble with her hip. 'Please God I shall have a new hip soon and be pain free.' It was signed 'God Bless You' with her name at the bottom. She also sent a creased black-and-white photo that she said was of him as a child.

None of her cards explained what happened when she became pregnant, her time in St Patrick's, or whether it was her choice for Karl to be adopted. But in one of their phone calls, Fiona told him the story of how he had been conceived. While working as a nurse in Dublin, she said, she had been raped on the way back from a dance hall.

Karl was raised by a woman called Peggy. He took me to visit her at the house where the two of them still lived, in the Dublin suburb of Terenure. The couch in their living room was lined with a misfit gang of old teddy bears, its cushioned seats weighed down with stacks of magazines. Framed photos hung along the walls and crowded around the telly, stationed next to an old-fashioned gas heater. A tiny woman over eighty years of age, Peggy was spry and full of chat. She gently scolded Karl for eating all her biscuits, as he towered over her in a *Ghostbusters* T-shirt. In a sing-song voice, with dancing hands, she spoke about the trials that her family had faced over the years, in the same matter-of-fact way that she spoke about the joys.

She had experienced multiple miscarriages and given up hope of having her own child. When she admitted this to a local priest, he advised her that there was another way. She knew nothing about the institutions where women gave birth in secret until she adopted her own son from St Patrick's. She described going with her husband to the red-brick building on the Navan Road to collect Karl. A nun took them into a private room, but the door was left slightly ajar. She caught a glimpse of a young pregnant woman in the hallway and knew instinctively that it was something she wasn't meant to see.

When Karl was two years old, she took him for a check-up. The doctor, who had worked in St Patrick's and knew Karl as a baby, asked her why she hadn't given him back. It was explained to her for the first time that Karl likely had a disability, caused by oxygen deprivation during his birth. The doctor told Peggy that she could still return him to the nuns if she wished. She refused.

After adopting Karl, she gave birth to two sons. It felt like a miraculous gift, a sign from God that she had been right not to give Karl back like the doctor suggested. Karl's brothers were born with muscular dystrophy and they died as young men. Her husband later died, leaving just her and Karl.

It is common for adoptees to wait until their adoptive parents are dead to initiate a search for birth parents. Some worry that such a search would be insulting to the people who raised them. But Peggy always encouraged Karl to find his birth mother. When Fiona sent Karl the photo of herself, Peggy put it in a big, fancy frame and set it on the mantelpiece of their best room. She brought me in especially to see it when I visited them.

A while after the initial contacts, Karl's calls and texts to Fiona began to go unanswered. She eventually told Karl never to ring her again. I listened to Peggy trying to place herself in the other woman's shoes, to understand how difficult it would have been to be pregnant as an unmarried woman, let alone as a result of rape, or to engage with a son after decades of separation. But she also wondered how the woman could deny Karl the opportunity to meet her. Only recently, Peggy had found out that someone she knew had had a daughter out of wedlock in a mother-and-baby home and had since reunited with her. They had formed a good bond, met in person and spoke regularly over the phone.

When I asked Peggy if I could speak to this woman, she told me her relative would still be fiercely private about it and that she wouldn't dare to even suggest it.

As we travelled together on the bus, Karl told me that he now doubted that Fiona was his birth mother. 'Last time I rang her, I said do you miss me? And she said no.'

He knew that women were sometimes signed into the institutions under pseudonyms. His birth certificate had Fiona's name on it, but then again the name was a common one. I reminded him that the woman he contacted had sent him cards and the photo of herself, that they texted and spoke on the phone. But maybe it was easier to embrace doubt than to face up to the heartbreaking feeling of rejection. He rubbed a gold band on his finger, his adoptive father's wedding ring. His mind was churning over the evidence he had accumulated over the years. 'Karl, will you ever leave me in peace?' Fiona had told him during their last phone call. But he still kept calling.

The bus stopped on the Navan Road, pulling up to the kerb opposite the low wall of the Kempton Estate, built on the extensive plot where St Patrick's mother-and-baby home once stood. There was no surviving trace of the original building, demolished decades ago; not even a plaque to indicate what was once there.

'I love coming up here because I was born here,' Karl told me.

I thought about my own indifference to the location and circumstances of my own birth. I never made any special visits to the National Maternity Hospital in Holles Street, where I was born. Sometimes I had to go for an appointment regarding a cervical smear test. The poky colposcopy clinic was next to a shop selling balloons and stuffed animals for newly arrived babies. I always thought it was cruel to require women worried about cervical cancer to wait in a maternity hospital. But the hospital's status as my own birthplace held no power for me. It wasn't an anchor to a mother I never knew; a place to stand where I know she once stood.

Karl had a grim vision of the institution in which he was born. He imagined his mother and his infant self sequestered behind impenetrable walls, with iron gates pried open only to let the shamed women in and the cars of the families collecting babies for adoption out. We surveyed the entrance to the housing estate. Karl was desperate to pinpoint where the mother-and-baby home once stood, where the woman who gave birth to him saw his face for the last time, but there was no way of knowing for sure.

He loped off into the estate, swinging his arms, greeting every passer-by, showing them the laminated page, telling them this was the place of his birth. His thinning grey hair stood up in a peak, like a shark's fin, trembling as he walked. One woman stopped and chatted with him. Her mother had lived on the Navan Road most of her life. Karl told her his theory that there were babies buried in unmarked graves on the grounds there.

A middle-aged man with a walking stick and wearing mucky hiking boots remembered as a child seeing girls with prams. He thought unmarried mothers were sent to work in a nearby tin box factory. This land was once the countryside, he reminded us, not a city suburb. Farmers used to drive cattle past here on the way to the markets. A memorial on a roundabout up from the estate was dedicated to a slain IRA member. On the anniversary of the young lad's death every year, men in berets would come and march around the patch of ground. Karl said they should have put up a memorial for the women who came to this place, where he and so many others had been born.

Just weeks earlier, it had been reported that an orphanage run by the Daughters of Charity in Scotland, called Smyllum Park, was under investigation after it was found that some 400 children might be buried on the grounds. But other than local speculation, there was no evidence to support Karl's suspicions of a mass grave here. Children who died at St Patrick's were buried in Glasnevin Cemetery, and the bodies of hundreds of children were also donated for medical research without mothers' consent. Karl led me to a low wall between a lumpy grass field and the main road, against which was an improvised shrine of teddy bears and greeting cards, sodden and forlorn, half buried in a mulch of brown leaves. This is where Karl and others believed children might be buried, and they had left trinkets for what they considered their lost cribmates.

As we made our way back towards the entrance, an elderly couple emerged from a red-brick gatehouse, a surviving remnant of the St Patrick's complex. They were bundled up against the cold, setting off for a walk with their dogs. Peter, who had a wispy halo of white hair, told us they had lived there for nearly fifty years. He used to work as a maintenance man inside the home. Peter pointed out to Karl where the building he was born in once stood, showing him how to match the trees in his photo with the ones that still stood. Then he launched into a defence of the nuns who ran the institution. 'Don't mind all this talk about Magdalens, that's rubbish, it's money-orientated,' he said. I gathered he was suggesting that people who made accusations against the religious orders were only after compensation. 'They were the best in the world, I worked there.' A woman called Sister Bernadette had been in charge, a 'lovely woman', but she was long dead. 'They used to send letters over to England and get them signed off,' he said, presumably talking about the adoption papers women like Karl's mother signed after moving away. 'They got them jobs and everything.'

Karl told the couple he was adopted at seven weeks. 'You wouldn't remember it, so,' Peter responded quickly. Kay, with a fur hat and drawn-on eyebrows, asked Karl if he was happy. It was a question that adopted people were often plied with. Did their alternative lives work out? Karl told them that his dad had died of a heart attack and that his two adoptive brothers had died of muscular dystrophy. 'Wasted off their bones,' he said. 'So it's just my adopted ma and me.'

They told Karl he should go talk to a Sister who had worked as a midwife at the home and now lived with other nuns on Henrietta Street in the north inner city. Karl was determined to go that very evening and knock on their door.

★

Girls just off school in bright white socks and plaid skirts filled the seats of the bus back into town. On my phone, a news bulletin popped up about a plan to build apartments on the site of a Magdalen laundry in Cork. There was also news that Dublin City Council was selling the site of the Magdalen laundry on Seán MacDermott Street to a developer who wanted to build a hotel. Karl talked about the bullet marks in the pillars and stone of the General Post Office, dating from the Easter Rising; people still came to run their fingers along the marks, touching history. But the place where he was born had no scrap left for him to go and put a hand on. It was the same with many of the other institutions where women were secreted away. They felt erased from the history of the country. The lands were being sold off, built over and forgotten.

Henrietta Street is one of the most beautiful streets in the city, a short cobbled ascent flanked by towering Georgian mansions. The Daughters of Charity owned three of these buildings, two of which housed community support services for people living in the inner city. We stood on the step of number 10 and rang the doorbell. A minuscule woman in a powder-blue cardigan with a grey headband over her white hair answered the door cautiously. We mentioned the Sister's name we'd been given, and she let us in. She directed us to a high-ceilinged front room, with aquamarine upholstered chairs, a fireplace with an elaborate grate, a piano, and an old telly on a wheeled wooden stand. Through the wall could be heard the chatter of voices, a gathering of some sorts. There were roses in a vase on the table and a book on Impressionist garden paintings. 'They give you coffee and biscuits, the nuns,' Karl told me.

We waited a while for the Sister whose name we'd been given to emerge through the door. An eighty-year-old woman, tall and solid, her hair short and white, she peered out calmly behind large spectacles at us, betraying only the slightest suspicion as to why two strangers had turned up unexpectedly on her doorstep. She sat down in an armchair between us, worrying a button on the navy cardigan she wore, with fleshy, pink-dappled fingers, her eyes moving from Karl to me, back and forth. Karl explained to her he was adopted from St Patrick's and that he was looking for more insight into the place where he was born.

She asked me to use a pseudonym – Sister Éabha – because she was an old woman and didn't want trouble. She worked as a mid-wife at St Patrick's for a decade, from 1966 to 1976. Most of the other Sisters and doctors she worked with at the time were dead now, including an ex-master of the Coombe maternity hospital, who had been a visiting gynaecologist at the institution and was 'very devoted'.

Secrecy at the home was paramount, she said: the mothers 'didn't want anyone to know'.

There was one young mother who came in a week before she gave birth. 'She had two corsets tied on her,' Sister Éabha said, in order to conceal her bump. The woman had been living at home with her family and would leave for work every morning with her father, who gave her a lift. She held out until the very last, telling nobody, unable to figure out an alibi for longer than a week. One evening, her mother mentioned that her ankles were looking swollen and she knew she had to leave. I thought of stories I'd heard about women whose labours were induced in the homes, because the excuses they'd given for going away were flimsy and they had to get home quickly.

'The baby had club feet,' Sister Éabha remembered. 'She did damage to the baby.' I wondered whether corseting during pregnancy could actually cause club feet. Sister Éabha remembered the woman was inconsolable at having to leave her child and at the same time terrified of being found out. The child was held back from adoption because of the club feet.

Sister Éabha recalled that most of the women ended up at St Patrick's after being kicked out by their families. Parents from Dublin would sometimes take their daughter and the baby back home, but families from the country almost never did. The women rarely received visitors; they were there in hiding. One woman told her family she was in Norway, bringing atlases and maps with her to the institution, writing pages and pages of letters to her parents, describing the journeys she was taking and the landscape and the people. It drove Sister Éabha into a panic and she urged the woman to write very little or she would be caught. But the woman maintained the pretence and left after giving birth, finding a temporary job in a department store. Her son was adopted. Later, Sister Éabha came across the woman's name on the list of victims killed in the Dublin bombings of 1974. 'I often wonder where her son is,' she said. 'Making up all those stories, I'll never forget it. I'd say it was all revealed after death.' I tried to imagine the aftermath of the bombing: grieving parents packing away their daughter's things and finding a photo of a baby or an entry in a diary, realizing there was a grandchild they never knew existed.

After her ten years at St Patrick's, Sister Éabha left to be a missionary in Nigeria. She didn't want to work as a midwife there. 'I saw all the difficulties that can happen,' she said. 'I couldn't do it any more.'

Karl asked if she could explain why his brain had been deprived of oxygen in childbirth, and she walked him gingerly through some of the possibilities. Karl told Éabha that he wasn't supposed to be adopted, because of his condition. 'It's good that you were,' she told him.

The Sisters in charge of the adoptions were very exacting about the condition of the babies who were going to be adopted: 'They had to be perfect going off.' This was a time in Ireland when children were sometimes put in institutions for having cleft palates, so any perceived physical flaw or disability could have made a child unadoptable. As we sat there, it was clear that Karl would not have been considered perfect by this standard when he was adopted. He said it himself: they must have made a mistake.

Sister Éabha had two nieces adopted through the Catholic Protection and Rescue Society. She remembered her sister being in a terrible state as she waited for the adoption papers to be signed, having already become attached to the baby.

Later, when one of her nieces wished to trace her birth mother, Sister Éabha had sent her to Sister Maeve. After five years searching, her niece received a letter from her birth mother and they met at the office of the CPRS in South Anne Street in Dublin. The birth mother had told only her husband and one of her four children about the baby she had given up for adoption, and continued to keep her secret even after they met. 'She hadn't the courage,' Sister Éabha said. 'It's a very hard thing to tell.'

Karl told her the story of contacting his own birth mother, and Sister Éabha asked if she was married. It was something that I had heard women in the religious orders and people in the Church emphasize before. Marriage was the happy ending, and if a woman ended up married it was taken to indicate that the institutions had done their job. They would say, 'She went on to marry and have children,' as if that had always been the ultimate goal, to ensure a respectable family could be achieved. Karl told Sister Éabha that his birth mother had not got married.

Karl asked Sister Éabha what St Patrick's looked like in her time. She described a low wall and beds of flowers outside. There were big verandahs where they would wheel the babies to get some sunshine. 'There isn't a scrate of it left,' she said. After it had been demolished, she had taken her own niece out there to see where she had been born. 'It's to know who you are, isn't it?' she said. She knew a local couple who had adopted a child, she told us, a beautiful girl with curly hair. They had gone all the way to a mother-and-baby home in Cork to get her. Why had they gone so far when they lived on the grounds of the biggest mother-and-baby home in the country? 'I suppose it was the secrecy of it, really,' she said. 'The birth mother might find out where the baby is, interfering and all that.'

After an hour of talking, we were invited into a different room for tea and cake. In contrast to the grandeur of the front rooms, the room where the Sisters ate had the feel of a nursing-home canteen. Around fifteen women, the youngest probably in their seventies, sat at tables of four and five, collecting their dinners on brown wooden trays from a counter where a man was serving the food. The Sisters came one by one to our table to welcome Karl, flat silver crosses lying against their chests and simple gold wedding bands on their fingers, showing they were married to Christ. They asked if he was enjoying his tea, demanded that he have more sandwiches, cooed over him like a visiting grandchild.

I asked about the hostility many nuns felt from the public. A woman sitting at our table, thin-lipped and nose wrinkling, didn't mince her words. 'They blame us for everything!' she said, leaning in close. 'They want money.' She repeated the accusation bitterly, picking at brown soda bread, smeared with butter and crumbled into pieces. She dipped the fragments into a boiled egg, bird-like, and fished them out. Without the religious orders, to her mind, there would be no public services of any kind. Without the Church, the people on this island might as well have been left in the primordial slime. 'There would be no schools, there would be no hospitals, you name it,' she said, listing off siblings who had been educated by Christian Brothers or Sisters of Mercy. She decried the fact that churches were mostly empty at Mass time. 'Father forgive them for they know not what they do,' she said, shaking her head.

A month after we met Sister Éabha, Karl brought me to the General Registration Office near Dublin Castle, where shelves of red-and-black bound volumes held the details of almost every birth officially registered in Ireland.

Karl decided to look up the women with his birth mother's name in the ledgers of the years of birth that matched her age. A mother's birth certificate would give her family address, which might be a way of finding her. Karl already had a birth certificate for the woman he had contacted. Now he found two more women with his mother's (quite common) name, born in Limerick around the right time, and asked the clerk to print out their birth certificates. He felt as though he was starting his search all over again.

A few weeks later, Karl bundled his way up the path to the Daughters of Charity's provincial house in Blackrock. Bluebells had sprouted up all of a sudden along the lane and birdsong filled the grounds, sequestered away from the fumes and traffic of the main road and walled off from the public park. Sister Helen, who had short-cropped white hair and stocking-clad toes poking out through navy sandals, led us into the room to the left. Easter hampers, filled with chocolates and sherry, and a large teddy bear sat on the shelves, near to a golden tabernacle, the ornate box that held the thin Eucharist wafers, the bodies of Christ.

Karl sat in a chair opposite Sister Helen, the table laden with coffee cups, plates of biscuits and a basket of scones. Sister Helen spoke earnestly, starting almost every sentence with 'But Karl' and 'Now Karl' and 'So Karl'. He handed her the two birth certificates for the women with his birth mother's name. She peered at the documents, confused, because she had met Karl before and thought he was already in contact with his birth mother.

When his mother signed him over for adoption, Sister Helen explained, she promised never to attempt to contact him or interfere with his life. There was a clause relating to this in the adoption orders that mothers had to put their signature on. 'She signed away her rights,' she said. 'If she didn't sign, she could have been knocking on the door all the time or coming back to the adoptive parents saying I want my baby back, blah, blah, blah.' The agreement was protection for him, she told Karl, and protection for herself. 'She would have been a very sad, lonely, hurt woman, having to do that,' she suggested, trying to capture how it would feel to promise never to attempt to see your child again. 'It was an immediate answer to a problem.'

Karl joked about how a social worker once 'bit the nose off' his adoptive mother for encouraging him to search for his birth mother himself. Sister Helen told him they couldn't possibly know the circumstances his birth mother had been in, whether her parents knew, whether they threw her out. Though the records kept by the religious orders and adoption societies often included details about the circumstances of mothers, anything identifying was not supposed to be shared. The institutions had operated on the assumption that pregnancy out of wedlock was a secret to be concealed, a scandal that mothers automatically felt the need to hide.

I felt that Sister Helen was imposing this idea on a woman she didn't know anything about, unless she was being deliberately vague. At the same time, it was a reality that women did keep these pregnancies a secret, and perhaps the nuns felt eternally bound to a privacy the institutions had promised, enabling a new life. 'Any of us have no right to add pain to pain and invade her space,' she said. 'That's the pain of life.' His birth mother, she said, had 'buried that pain'.

She told Karl about an older woman who had been reunited with her son. The son came to Ireland from abroad with his own children and grandchildren, an 'army of them', going to visit her little house. 'The neighbours knew she was a single lady with no children,' Sister Helen said. 'That woman wouldn't have been telling any neighbour that this was her son that she had sixty years ago.' The woman knew her son was coming to visit and made up a story to tell the neighbours, that he was some more distant relative. Karl remembered calling Fiona one time, and her frantic hisses down the phone: 'I'm at Mass, I'm at Mass.'

I asked if Sister Helen could still mediate reunions between an adoptee and a mother. She explained that as the institutions shut down, their records were handed over to the State to manage, tens of thousands of files. The work of tracing and reuniting people separated through adoption then fell to social workers. The surprising result of this, in some cases, was that the State ended up being more controlling over what information was given out than the nuns. But the orders and the social workers are all bound by the same legislation: if a mother does not want contact with an adopted child, or vice versa, then anyone trying to assist with a formal trace has their hands tied.

'Supposing your poor mother doesn't really want to make contact? Can we, any of us, can we respect that?' Helen asked.

The pain doesn't go away, Karl told her. Between the slurps of coffee, the sun glowing through the old curtain, his voice started to waver and break. There was a bewilderment rising slowly from the pit of his stomach.

Of all the people whose lives were touched by the institutions, the mothers who choose not to meet their children or who do so in secret seem the hardest to write about. Few of these women are talking to journalists like me. They had dealt with a crisis pregnancy in the face of huge stigma, and in a climate in which the vast majority of babies born out of wedlock were adopted: 97 per cent in 1967, according to the Adoption Board. Some of them had signed consent forms in which they undertook never to contact the child. I read Caitríona Palmer's book about her relationship with her birth mother, who was willing to meet her but only in secret: an unimaginably difficult experience so honestly and insightfully told. That is perhaps the closest that any journalist or memoirist has brought us to understanding the way these mothers feel – and even Palmer does not claim to fully comprehend it.

'It's like a jigsaw puzzle, you can't find the piece,' Karl said.

'But if the piece had fallen on the hearth of the fire and was partly burned, or singed,' Sister Helen asked him, 'would it be any use?'

Was she implying that the mother was the damaged piece of the puzzle?

Sister Helen went on to say that everyone had some piece missing. Being adopted wasn't something to be ashamed of. He was still loved and precious in the eyes of God. Karl shrank in the chair, knowing that he was going to come out of this room without any answers.

He said to Helen something he had previously said to me: 'Once I said to her, do you miss me? And she said no.'

'But Karl, why would she miss you? She never lived with you.'

'She had me.'

'The mother that you go home to this evening, that is your mammy,' she said. 'She didn't give birth to you, but she raised you and nurtured you and made you the person you are.'

Focus on what you do have, she told him, not on the piece of the jigsaw that is missing. Sister Helen also advised Karl that if he did ever meet his birth mother, he should do so in a neutral place, where no one who knew either of them would see, so they wouldn't have to make up lies about who he really was.

7.

'Proof of the mother's shame'

The Irish State facilitated and funded the growth of the mother-and-baby homes and Magdalen laundries. It viewed illegitimacy and sexual activity out of wedlock as grave social problems, and it outsourced the job of dealing with them to the religious orders.

It was not ignorant of the terrible conditions in the institutions, or of the high mortality rates there. But reading documents in State archives, Oireachtas debates, memoirs, and the published work of historians, what struck me was how the State failed to protect vulnerable women and children, despite knowing how bad things were. While there was some official concern for the welfare of the inmates of institutions, the desire to reinforce societal norms regarding premarital sex and childbirth out of wedlock proved by far the stronger political force. Poor conditions and high mortality rates were seen as regrettable, but not regrettable enough to compel the State to change the system.

One in every three illegitimate children born alive was dying within a year of birth, according to a 1924 report by the Registrar-General, quoted in the Dáil. These children were dying at five times the rate of other children. Why was their death rate so high? 'It is high for many reasons, but there is one to which we wish specially to refer,' the report stated. 'The illegitimate child, being the proof of the mother's shame is, in most cases, sought to be hidden at all costs.' The mother or her family would often leave the child at a hospital or institution, or with foster parents to whom they would pay a lump sum or ongoing maintenance. But even in a foster home, the child was at heightened risk. 'If a lump sum is paid or

84

if the periodical payments lapse, the child becomes an encumbrance on the foster mother, who has no interest in keeping it alive.'

In 1926, the high mortality rate among 'illegitimate infants' was described in a Dáil debate as an 'unfavourable feature' that the Department of Local Government and Public Health wanted to tackle, particularly in counties where loss of life was 'abnormally heavy'. But morality was a more urgent concern than mortality. During the same debate, the chairman of a county health board apologized for introducing the 'unpleasant subject' of unmarried mothers, but warned there were large numbers of 'these people' in the county homes. He described first offenders 'herded together' with 'professional' women who had 'reared a family' in the institution. 'The more innocent girls have very little hope of reformation.' He wanted to know if an institution would be set up in Dublin 'into which those unfortunate people can be taken'. He wanted them 'classified' into categories of offender and to be given work to do. Taxpayers would be willing to pay for that, he felt.

The Commission on the Relief of the Destitute Sick and Poor, which began taking testimonies and inspecting workhouses or 'county homes' in 1925, recommended in 1927 that these institutions were not the place for unmarried mothers, children or 'mental defectives'. The Commission found that, as of March 1926, there were 629 unmarried mothers 'classed as first offenders' in county homes and the remaining Dublin workhouse, along with 391 women 'who had fallen more than once'.

The treatment of the 'first offenders' needed to be about 'moral upbuilding', and the Commission recommended that Boards of Health give 'almost complete discretion' in the matter of dealing with this category of women to the rescue societies and voluntary organizations: in other words, the nuns. The multiple offenders and unredeemable women were described as 'residue'. While the report acknowledged that the State had no power to detain a woman in a Poor Law institution, 'even when it is clearly necessary for her protection', it suggested unmarried women applying for assistance agree to remain for a period not exceeding one year, in the case of a first offence, and two years for a second time. 'On third or subsequent admissions the Board should have power to retain for such period as they think fit, having considered the recommendation of the Superior or Matron of the Home,' it stated. An aim of detention was to segregate what they considered 'degraded cases', women who had 'become sources of evil, danger, and expense to the community'. No woman was to be discharged if she could not prove herself able to provide for her child or children. It was a Superior or Matron's duty to try to place them in suitable positions outside the institution.

In 1929, a series of debates in the Dáil focused on what to do with the large number of unmarried mothers in county homes, including 'chronic' and 'professional' cases 'rearing families at the expense of the ratepayers'. There were calls for a 'central institution' where first offenders could be 'kept together, graded and provided with employment'.

In the following year, the Dáil passed the Illegitimate Children (Affiliation Orders) Act, which made it easier – at least in theory – for unmarried mothers to secure financial support from the child's father. This was, in its way, progressive legislation, but the debates on the bill made it clear that it was rooted in a culture of shame. The Minister for Local Government and Public Assistance described how, after the birth of a child, the unwed mother was an 'outcast' whose 'disgrace has become public'. The main point of contention in the debate over the bill was whether women should be required to appear in open court, or whether they might be allowed to bring a case against an alleged father without the risk of their name appearing in the papers. The people considered best suited to judge the psychology of unmarried mothers were priests and nuns. Some TDs were very worried that the legislation would play into the hands of women from 'an illegitimate stock . . . who are bred in the art of blackmail'.

A Jesuit priest called Richard Devane, who supported the legislation (and who had, in a different context, expressed the desire that the Irish people be as Catholic 'as the Germans are Nazi'), conducted an informal survey of the institutions. In 'Convent A' there were 160 'penitents', none of whom, it was believed, would 'expose herself' to public legal proceedings; but the majority would seek maintenance for their illegitimate children if cases could be brought in private. In Convent B, with 107 penitents: 'some respectable farmers' daughters would be glad of a private court with redress.' In Convent C, with 140 penitents, it was stated that no girl would subject herself or her family to such exposure.

A snapshot of the expert view of sexual morality in the Irish Free State was provided by the report of the Carrigan Committee, delivered to the Minister for Justice in 1931 (but never published because its findings were deemed too sensitive). The committee consisted of lay people, law enforcement and clergy (including Father Devane) who were involved in the 'protection' of women and children. Testimony was heard from women who ran the Magdalen Asylum in Leeson Street and St Patrick's Guild, and from Frank Duff of the Legion of Mary, among others. The committee was specifically tasked with advising on the reform of legislation regarding juvenile prostitution and abuses to public decency, but its findings ranged somewhat more widely. The report described a country rife with sexual assault and abuse of young people, a court system that could not offer any justice when it came to sexual crimes, and a Church obsessed with the evils of contraception, joyriding in motorcars and sinful dance halls.

Illegitimacy was a central preoccupation of the report: 'The official statistics are sufficient to show that illegitimacy is an evil which, contrary to past experience of history, has begun to grow and spread latterly in the country.' The official recorded illegitimacy rate in the Free State was 3.2 per cent in 1929, but the actual figure was believed to be much higher. As of the end of 1928, nearly a thousand unmarried mothers were 'maintained' through the workhouse or 'county home' system. The fact that unmarried mothers were institutionalized alongside 'the decent poor and sick' was deemed 'objectionable'. It had been necessary for the Poor Law bodies in Dublin, Clare and

Galway to provide 'auxiliary institutions for unmarried mothers', and the Catholic Protection and Rescue Society and St Patrick's Guild were dealing with hundreds of applications. References were made to the voluntary agencies in Britain that dealt with Irish unwed mothers, from the Catholic Police Courts Mission in Manchester to the Crusade of Rescue in Westminster. The number of cases was increasing yearly. The report recommended the establishment of reform institutions for 'girl offenders' who would be kept apart from others.

A section of the report was devoted to the moral danger of contraceptives, which were described as a way of 'avoiding the consequences of sexual indulgence among the unmarried'. Clergymen attested that contraceptives were being sold openly in cities, towns, villages and the remotest parts of the island, arriving by post and advertised publicly with price lists.

Less than a quarter of sexual crimes against minors were prosecuted, due in part to the desire of parents to spare their children the ordeal of being subjected to cross-examination in public court. Dance halls, picture houses and joy drives, 'availed of by male prowlers', were responsible for bringing 'ignorant' girls to ruin. The report did not speak of abuses going on within the homes of families, in the homes of neighbours, or indeed in the houses of God.

There was no basis for legal adoption in Ireland until 1953. Searching through newspaper reports from the early decades of the independent state, I found stories of married couples being brought to court in Dublin for making illicit payments to maternity home matrons and midwives for de-facto adoptions. In 1931, next to a listing on the price of cows, there was a report in the *Irish Times* about two women charged in Dublin Circuit Criminal Court with obtaining money on false pretences in arranging the adoption of children. They charged fees of £15 or £20, forged a document in which a mother ostensibly renounced her rights to her child, and arranged a false name for an adopted child so that it could not be traced.

In 1934, legislation was passed imposing new regulations on

privately run maternity homes, in an effort to reduce mortality rates and to crack down on illegal adoptions. The law caused the closure of a number of smaller maternity homes, leaving unmarried mothers more likely to be dependent on the bigger religious-run institutions, where death rates remained high despite the regulation. In 1939, while debating a bill relating to the protection of children by local authorities, an independent TD called Joseph Hannigan spoke out about the tendency to 'place children in institutions rather than in suitable homes'. He concluded that those responsible were 'more concerned with the interests of the institution and keeping up the numbers of children in these institutions' than with the welfare of the children themselves.

That same year, the inspector for boarded-out children in the Department of Local Government and Public Health, Alice Litster, compiled a 'Report on Unmarried Mothers in Ireland'. It described how deaths in these institutions are generally caused by an epidemic of some kind, which spreads quickly among the children and 'wipes out the weaklings'. The nurseries were overcrowded. In Tuam, an experiment was apparently being made with smaller nurseries, and in the new building at Sean Ross Abbey, no more than thirty would be in a nursery room.

'The chance of survival of an illegitimate infant born in the slums and placed with a foster-mother in the slums a few days after birth is greater than that of an infant born in one of our special homes for unmarried mothers,' Litster wrote, noting that in theory the child born in an institution ought to have an advantage. 'I have grave doubts of the wisdom of continuing to urge Boards of Health and Public Assistance to send patients to the special homes so long as no attempt is made to explore the causes of the abnormally high death rate.' The illegitimacy rate was rising and more children would inevitably be sent to these institutions. 'We cannot prevent the birth of these infants,' she said. 'We should be able to prevent their death.'

The dominant figure of the Catholic Church in mid-century Ireland, John Charles McQuaid, was Archbishop of Dublin from 1940 to

1972. Not satisfied with the already dominant position of the Church in Irish education, healthcare and social services, McQuaid conducted an often fierce campaign to shut down non-denominational and community-led services. The most famous example of this was his successful nobbling of a scheme to provide free healthcare to mothers and children, but even much smaller initiatives came under fire from the Archbishop. A scheme run by the St John Ambulance Brigade, a non-denominational organization, to promote maternal health was sidelined, with Dublin Corporation cutting its annual funding on the grounds that it 'would not be acceptable to the Ecclesiastical Authorities'.

The State, for its part, was happy to allow Catholic dogma to drive public policy. The new constitution brought in by Éamon de Valera in 1937 conferred special status on the Catholic Church – a provision not overturned until 1972. The constitution also declared that 'by her life within the home, woman gives to the State a support without which the common good cannot be achieved', and pledged that the State would ensure 'that mothers shall not be obliged by economic necessity to engage in labour to the neglect of their duties in the home' – a provision that remains in the constitution.

In 1954, a columnist called Mary Frances Keating wrote in the *Irish Times* about the twisted fear of sex that afflicted the young people of the republic. Young people were unable to glance at each other without feeling they were doing something 'darkly wrong'. Young women were more afraid of being 'named' as the kind of girl who would let a boy accompany her than of the actual dangers of walking alone at night. Men were called fools for getting 'hooked' into marriage. 'Youths are led to believe that girls are nothing less than manifestations of Satan,' Keating wrote. 'Women are there to entice and destroy them.' Men shunned marriage but were still getting unmarried women pregnant. 'In Ireland, illegitimate births are frequently concealed, and young unmarried mothers are usually hurried out of the country,' she wrote, 'with a 10 pound note and the parental injunction not to show their faces at home again.'

The year after Keating's column was published, the *Irish Times* reported that Dunboyne Castle had been purchased by the Good Shepherd nuns as a home for unmarried mothers. The shame-industrial complex was still growing.

James Deeny served as the Chief Medical Advisor to the Department of Health from 1944 to 1950. In his 1989 memoir, *To Cure and to Care*, he wrote of helping to design the doomed mother-and-child healthcare scheme, and of his work in 1943 investigating infant mortality in Belfast, where one out of eight babies died before their first year. He found the dead children's names and went to the houses of the families. 'It was extraordinary how clear people were about the circumstances relating to each death,' he wrote. 'Mothers remember every detail.'

Deeny was investigating infant deaths in Cork when he traced the high rate to 'a home for unmarried mothers' outside the city. The year before he visited Bessborough, 180 babies were born in the institution and more than 100 had died. Reading his account of the 'lovely old house', which seemed well run and 'spotlessly clean', I thought of all the people who told me that when the nuns ran the hospitals you could eat off the floors. Deeny marched around the entire building and could find nothing that seemed to explain why so many children were dying. Then he 'took a notion' and stripped the babies to examine them. 'Every baby had some purulent infection of the skin and all had green diarrhoea, carefully covered up,' he wrote. 'The deaths had been going on for years. They had done nothing about it, had accepted the situation and were quite complacent about it.'

Deeny shut the institution down, sacked the matron, and got rid of the local medical officer. Days later, in Dublin, he was visited by the nuns' 'man of affairs', followed by the Dean of Cork. The Bishop of Cork complained to the Papal Nuncio – described by Deeny as 'a former millionaire American stockbroker'. The Nuncio went to de Valera. On seeing Deeny's report, though, the Nuncio agreed with the closure. Bessborough was disinfected and a new matron and medical officer were appointed. We can only wonder if subsequent officials were as scrupulous and effective.

One of the reasons there was no legal basis for adoption in Ireland before 1953 was that the Church feared a secular adoption regime would lead to Catholic babies ending up in Protestant homes. When concerns began to be raised in the media about the 'traffic' of Irish babies to the US, Archbishop McQuaid sought – and received – assurances from St Patrick's Guild that the American adoptive parents were Catholic. McQuaid, not satisfied, drew up new requirements for approving Irish children to be sent to America for adoption, requiring prospective adopters to acquire written recommendations from Catholic charities and from their parish priest, and to supply baptismal and marriage certificates, as well as – bizarrely – proof they were not shirking natural parenthood. They had to swear an affidavit that they were Catholics and promise to rear the child as Catholic, to educate them in Catholic schools and to not give the child to anyone else.

The negative publicity about American adoptions was one of the drivers of the Adoption Act. Under the new law, all adoptions were required to be formalized through 'adoption orders' approved by a newly formed Adoption Board. The informed consent of the mother or guardian was needed. Consent could not be given until the child was six months old, nor after the child was seven years old. Only illegitimate or orphaned children could be legally adopted.

Amendments to adoption legislation introduced in 1964 allowed for the adoption of children who were 'legitimized' after their biological parents married, provided the father gave consent. Oireachtas debates on these changes were focused on secrecy and stigma. It was suggested that it would be undesirable for local authorities to inspect the homes of prospective adopters in rural areas because it was a 'delicate business in the country' and something people 'like to keep secret'. Charles Haughey, then Minister for Justice, was worried about the Adoption Act's requirement that the local authority be notified when an illegitimate child was placed with a family. He asked in the Dáil: 'Why place on record that a child is illegitimate when we are trying to ensure this fact never be disclosed?'

There were concerns about illegal adoptions through 'false registration' of children, whereby a baby was registered as the biological child of the adoptive parents. In the following year, a midwife named Mary Keating, who ran St Rita's private nursing home in Ranelagh, would be convicted in the Dublin District Court for forging birth registrations, registering the children of unmarried women as having been born to a married couple. Despite the conviction, Keating was able to continue her business for at least another decade, and these practices – known to involve priests, solicitors and doctors – continued for years after. For people like Mary Keating – and indeed for institutions like St Patrick's Guild, which was recently found to have falsely registered over 100 births – false registrations were good business in a culture where illegitimacy was so profoundly stigmatized. Falsely registered children carried no documentary trace of having been born out of wedlock, and could not be traced back to their birth mothers.

It was a Labour Party Senator from Westmeath who asked in the 1964 debate why children weren't just allowed to stay with their mothers. 'I can assure you that I would have no adoption system if I could get the mother to keep the child or the grandmother to keep the child,' Timothy McAuliffe said, going on to castigate the system of mother-and-baby homes. 'The mother becomes a sort of slave or prisoner in the home. We have homes at the moment which keep mothers for two full years, if the child is not adopted.' He wanted the institutions abolished. There was too much stigma attached to people who had illegitimate children and he implored the Minister to get rid of the system.

'I have no function in regard to that,' Haughey replied.

'These girls should be sent to maternity hospitals like every other mother,' McAuliffe told him. 'These children should have the same rights as all other children.'

*

Slowly, the climate was changing. In November 1970, a national conference was held on women pregnant outside of wedlock in Ireland, titled 'Unmarried Mothers in the Irish Community'. One of the main sponsors was Dr Peter Birch, the Catholic Bishop of Ossory. It was reported that about 70 per cent of children born to unmarried mothers would be placed for adoption despite the mother's desire to keep them, because facilities to enable them to do so did not exist.

Interviewed for a 1974 book called *The Permissive Society in Ireland*, Bishop Birch said: 'It is clear that . . . because we lacked the social, perhaps the moral responsibility, to ensure that illegitimate children from previous generations have been brought up in suitable environments, that they, lacking any warmth and love as children, become the unmarried mothers of the present day.' In 1973, the government introduced an unmarried mothers' allowance after tireless campaigning by Cherish, a group established to support single parents. There were newspaper reports of priests doing courses on how to cope with secularization and unmarried mothers.

In 1974, Senators Michael D. Higgins, John Horgan and Mary Robinson co-sponsored an Illegitimate Children (Maintenance and Succession) Bill. It proposed establishing succession rights for illegitimate children and making it easier for a mother to claim for child support from the father. Robinson argued that if both canon and common law intended the brand of illegitimacy to discourage adults from promiscuity, it was strange to go about it 'by vesting all the penalty and all the discrimination in innocent children'. As a rebuke to the decades of pathologizing unmarried mothers, Robinson argued that it was impossible to 'categorize' unmarried parents. They came from all social classes.

The bill did not pass. One objector, Senator Augustine Martin, portrayed it as a threat to the institution of the family, already under fire, and worried about there being no limit to claims of affiliation, leaving a man open to blackmail – the same argument that had been made against unmarried mothers since the inception of the state. 'There is the idea that somebody after ten or 15 years could make a claim on the property of the family, of a wife and of children, who have no idea of the existence of the child born outside wedlock to the father,' he said. 'The claim in terms of property is considerable.' Such a discovery might also cause 'spiritual injury'. He suggested 'unscrupulous women' or those 'of a certain age' who had an emotional desire 'to fulfil themselves as women' might trap a man. 'If this Bill were passed it may be dangerous, especially in the climate of strident and even vengeful feminism in which we are now living,' he said.

Also in 1974, the Minister for Justice, Patrick Cooney, introduced significant amendments to the adoption legislation. He sought to reform adoption law relating to 'private placements' and 'prevaricating mothers', who delayed in giving consent or withdrew consent at the last minute. The earliest age at which consent could be given for adoption was reduced from six months to six weeks.

In a speech at the Irish Adoption Workers' Conference in 1974, Cooney said he believed 'adoption is better for the illegitimate baby than to be cared for by its mother'. He defended this position in a Seanad debate the same year. 'Of course the reason for this is that the illegitimate child is still marked in our society and the dilemma is how to remove that mark and at the same time cater for the welfare of the child,' he said.

Robinson argued that they could not in conscience introduce a threshold of six weeks for consent 'unless we improve the position of the single mother' and give her a 'real choice', stressing that the single mother and her child must have constitutional protection as a 'family'. She did not share Cooney's satisfaction that adoption was working well in Ireland. The government provided grants for adoption societies with the expectation the money would be used to hire social workers; Robinson asked Cooney why no similar grants were being given to an organization like Cherish to help unmarried mothers keep their children.

In 1976, Cooney and Robinson were debating adoption again. Robinson argued that the concept of illegitimacy had to be abolished and called on Irish society to 'affirm strongly the right of a mother to keep her child, if she wishes to, and encourage and support her in that choice'. Cooney did not want the 'present generation of illegitimate children to be the guinea pigs in a social experiment to change attitudes'.

In 1983, a constitutional ban on abortion was passed by referendum. It was perhaps the high-water mark of the long collaboration between Church, State and society to exert control over women and reproduction. Two years later, the Minister for Health acknowledged changing attitudes about mother-and-baby homes, stating in the Dáil that only St Patrick's on the Navan Road and Bessborough in Cork 'retain babies for any appreciable length of time'.

With the unmarried mothers' allowance and workplace anti-discrimination laws coming into place, it was now more economically viable for women to keep their children. By 1980 there were more than 5,000 women receiving the unmarried mothers' allowance, and women could no longer legally lose their job as a result of pregnancy or motherhood. In 1985, new legislation allowed condoms and spermicides to be sold to people over eighteen without prescription. So while the Church's view of illegitimacy had not changed, and while the State had made no direct effort to close the institutions, a shifting legal and cultural climate brought about a dramatic decline in the number of women who felt the need to conceal their pregnancies.

Things were changing – but not nearly fast enough for some people. In 1984, a 22-year-old Garda recruit called Majella Moynihan became pregnant after having sex with another recruit. She was charged in an internal investigation with 'conduct prejudicial to discipline or likely to bring discredit on the Force'. She had to give a statement about the number of times she had sex, her pregnancy and intention to have her baby adopted. At a conduct hearing for the father of the child, she was interrogated about her sexual history. The Archbishop of Dublin was consulted, and warned that convicting her would encourage other women in her situation to seek abortions in England. Without this intervention, Moynihan was told, she would have been fired.

Also in 1984, a baby was found dead from stab wounds on a beach in Cahirciveen, Co. Kerry. Joanne Hayes, who lived some 80 km away in north Kerry, was arrested because gardaí knew she had been pregnant. She was charged with the murder of the baby on the beach, and the prosecution continued even after she explained that she had concealed the birth and death of her own baby and showed the place on the family land where her child was buried. The gardaí pursued the theory that she was the mother of *both* dead babies, and explained blood-type differences via a theory of heteropaternal superfecundation: i.e. she had been simultaneously carrying two babies fathered by different men. The prosecution was eventually thrown out by a judge, and a tribunal ruled that Hayes was not the mother of the murdered baby, but not before putting Hayes through an ordeal that the journalist Nell McCafferty described as 'medieval'.

And in that same awful year, Ann Lovett, a fifteen-year-old schoolgirl, died after giving birth alone in a Marian grotto in Granard, Co. Longford, having concealed her pregnancy.

The minutes of an Eastern Health Board meeting in 1986 document the planned closure and relocation of St Patrick's mother-and-baby home on the Navan Road. 'As a result of careful planning,' the minutes state, 'the transfer of our service for unmarried mothers from the large institutional setting in St Patrick's to a community base on the south side of the city has been quietly achieved taking account of all of the interests involved.' Eleven staff in the new institution, including nursery nurses and midwives, as well as a sister-in-charge and her assistant, would be paid for by the State.

In 1987, the year illegitimacy was legally abolished, it was reported to the Dáil that seven mother-and-baby homes had been in operation the year before, 'dealing with both women who are pregnant and women who have babies, and one infant nursing home'. Some of these were not carceral institutions but something more like halfway houses, where women had freedom to come and go.

There was a notable concentration of provision in the Dublin suburb of Donnybrook: Eglinton House, the successor institution to St Patrick's, housed 14 mothers and 8 children; Belmont flatlets, run by the Daughters of Charity, housed 11 mothers and 11 babies;

and Denny House, a successor to Lady Denny's original Magdalen asylum on Leeson Street, housed 7 mothers and babies. Miss Carr's flatlets, on Northbrook Road in nearby Ranelagh, housed 8 mothers and babies. Ard Mhuire in Dunboyne, run by the Good Shepherd Sisters, housed 30 mothers and babies. The Castle in Co. Donegal, run by the North Western Health Board, housed 8 mothers and babies. St Mura's in Fahan, Co. Donegal, run by the Sisters of Nazareth, housed 20 babies. And Bessborough, which once had capacity for about 150, was now home to 25 mothers and babies. Some of the biggest institutions – Tuam, Sean Ross Abbey, Castlepollard, and others – were no longer in operation.

In 1993, a doctor and politician named Mary Henry, who grew up near Bessborough, spoke about her memories of the institution during a debate in the Dáil over decriminalizing homosexuality. A week before, the same body had debated condoms. Henry noted that the next session would likely be about divorce, and recalled the old Brehon laws by which a woman could divorce a man, centuries ago: if he failed to support her, spread false stories about her, tricked her into marriage by sorcery, if he was impotent, or was too fat to have sex.

'When I was young, it was common in families to expel a young daughter from the family home if she became pregnant,' she said. 'An elderly nun once told me that the worst part of her work was when a girl was dumped on the doorstep and the father would tell the daughter that she would not be hearing from her family again.'

8

In the Shadow of the Stone Folly

On a bright June day, I boarded the number 202 bus in the centre of Cork. Distracted by toothache, it was a while before I realized that the woman sitting in front of me, wearing a Barbie-pink T-shirt emblazoned with the word 'Bonjour', and pink slider sandals, was someone I knew: Ann O'Gorman.

I put a hand on her shoulder, making her jump: 'Ah, love!'

Ann called everyone 'love'. The women in Dublin hawking fruit, flowers and Toblerones call everyone 'love', too, but Ann said it with a different urgency that made you feel somehow precious. I scooted in beside her. We were heading to the same place.

In her hands, Ann held a fist-sized metal sculpture, depicting a little girl with long hair lying curled up asleep in the palm of a huge hand. It was from Lourdes, a gift from a priest, to remember her daughter who died inside the walls of Bessborough. She had been to Lourdes twice herself, to the grotto where the Virgin Mary appeared to a teenaged girl. Now, though she remained a believer, she couldn't bring herself to enter a church.

After the news about the mother-and-baby homes started to break, Ann began to lose weight and to feel physically changed. 'It's doing something to me,' she told me once. 'It's breaking me down, I can feel it.' When I first met her, she was mostly silent. As the pressure on her mind became more intense, she found a voice. But she clung to the idea that none of it could change her nature. When I called her on the phone, I could usually hear her grandchildren laughing in the background.

Now, on the bus, she said, 'It wakes me up at night': the anxiety over where her first child is buried.

Ann's firstborn was a girl. A nun told her to name the baby quickly, and 'Evelyn' popped into her head. I assumed it meant little Eve, the first woman, but when I looked it up, baby-naming websites said it meant 'giver of life' or 'wished for'.

Ann was barely eighteen when she found out she was pregnant. It was 1971. The father was a married man, six years older than her, whom she'd met while working at a chipper in Limerick. At the time, she was living at home with her nine siblings. The man had a spare room in his house and he invited her to move in. To all appearances, she was living there as a lodger. That's how it began.

When her periods stopped and she realized she was pregnant, she told the father. He told her to deal with it. She didn't tell anyone else. As the eldest child, she worried that a pregnancy would be seen as a bad influence on her younger siblings. Her mother always praised her for being a good girl. She never gave cheek. She never did wrong. She remembered herself as quiet, and very naive. 'I didn't know which end a baby was to come out,' she said.

A social worker in Limerick referred her to the Sisters of the Sacred Hearts of Jesus and Mary in Cork, and drove her the two hours to Bessborough, on the eastern edge of the city. She walked up the stone steps of the convent and in through the big wooden front door, her bump only just starting to show. The nun who took down her details told her that she would have to change her name while she stayed there and that she shouldn't discuss her past with any of the other women, or ask about theirs. Una would be her house name. Her mother thought she had left Limerick for work and would cry when she called, telling her to come back. The Sisters told the other women that Ann was slow. For years afterwards she believed that of herself.

The months that she spent at Bessborough were a slow blur of work, even in the last weeks of her pregnancy. She worked in the laundry, or polishing floors, or in the labour ward with a nun as other women gave birth, terrified by the pain they were going through and knowing it would soon be her turn. There was Mass every morning before breakfast. She barely spoke to the other women she shared a dormitory with.

Some of them were even younger than her.

We disembarked on a busy thoroughfare between housing estates, in an area that used to be mainly farmland. Bessboro Road ran south from the main road through an expanse of industrial park. At least one of the Sacred Hearts Sisters who used to work in the mother-and-baby home now lived in the newly built convent up a road forking to the left. Ann had gone there once to ask the nuns about where Evelyn was buried, but they would not speak to her.

The security hut just inside the big gates at the main entrance to Bessborough looked empty. We made our way up the long narrow driveway. To the right of the drive, fields sloped away, calves and their heavy-uddered mothers slowly munching in one corner, getting fat on summer grass. To the left, behind wire fencing, were the convent gardens and a small playground. A few young women were sitting on the grass around a buggy; one was playing with a little child. There was still a type of mother-and-baby home here. The Bessborough Centre is a residential facility for vulnerable parents, some struggling with addiction, whose children might otherwise be removed by protective services. Elsewhere on the grounds was a private adoption mediation agency called Helping Hands, set up in 2005, which brokers adoptions from countries including Poland, the United States, Vietnam, Haiti and India.

At the end of the drive, the tall brick steeple of the chapel, painted white, came into view. Around the corner we passed an old glass conservatory and could see the hulking three-storey convent building. The bright red door was a shocking lick of colour against the sandy-brown facade. The front steps were flanked by two white lions, their faces turned in towards anyone approaching the door, one with its mouth open wide and its tongue lolling out.

This was not my first time with Ann at Bessborough. We had come a few months before, on one of her regular visits to the ground where she believed Evelyn might be buried. The month before that visit, the Commission of Investigation had issued a public notice stating that it was investigating 'burials of a large number of children who died while resident' at Bessborough between 1922 and 1998. They asked for anyone with personal knowledge, documentation or any other form of information regarding the burial of children there to come forward. Unlike at Tuam, where there was clear physical evidence of a mass grave, the location of an 'angel plot' – or plots – at Bessborough was uncertain. Some survivors had circulated a map, apparently dating from the 1950s, which indicated a 'Children's Burial Ground' in a field at the southern end of the estate, between the nuns' graveyard and the South Ring Road.

I visited on my own a few months after the Commission's petition for information, walking up the same lane in lashing rain, to meet Thomas Quigley, the director of the Bessborough Centre.

Quigley set a plate of biscuits down on his office table, imposing in his suit but approachable in the way he spoke. He emphasized that he was the first layperson to be director – a microbiologist by profession – but further into the conversation he mentioned that he was once a Benedictine monk at Glenstal Abbey.

When he started in his new position in 2009, he told me, 'I didn't know anything about the history of Bessborough, to be honest.' A branding exercise took place after he began as director, and they were advised by an external consultant to keep the name Bessborough. Five years later, everything changed. The Tuam story broke and the fate of the children of Bessborough came into focus as well. 'Bessborough's name becomes synonymous with dead babies, children going into care, forced adoptions,' he said. 'It is a handicap to our reputation.'

Some of the parents in the Bessborough Centre had been in the care system as children themselves, Quigley told me. Many children in State care feel as though they've been kidnapped, he noted, and their mothers feel rejected, often becoming pregnant again to make up for the loss. He described it as a 'revolving door' system. When he arrived, there were still a few women living and working in the institution who had given birth in the mother-and-baby home, which was delisted as a maternity home in 1998, and had never left.

Quigley recalled a woman who turned up at reception one day. She was trying to get to the place where she remembered burying her child, but the gate to that part of the estate was locked. He unlocked it for her and accompanied her to a spot beside the nuns' burial ground and the ruins of a stone castle folly.

'Is that a real grave?' he asked her.

'Yes, yes, he was buried there,' she assured him.

In 1994, the woman had come by train to Cork from another county, unable to tell her parents she was pregnant. She lost her baby to cot death not long after he was born.

'I couldn't go home with a dead baby or a live baby,' she told Quigley. She also said that Sister Sarto Harney, who was the director of the institution at that time, 'allowed me to bury the baby here and we had a lovely funeral'. The woman subsequently erected a wooden plaque at the site in memory of her son. Quigley told me he was shocked that such things had happened so recently: that a woman in the 1990s would have felt unable to bring the body of her dead child home.

The nuns' burial plot is located in a walled-off rectangle of ground behind the old stone folly. It is just a few metres wide, the grass sections bisected by a neat pebble path. A white-painted gate at the entrance leads into the area, which is enclosed on three sides by low walls and on the fourth by the folly. Inside the gate, to the left, are two rows of simple black crosses, barely knee height, marking more than a dozen nuns buried there.

In the shadow of the folly, facing the crosses, people visiting over the years left mementos and figurines to honour the children they believed were buried somewhere below the ground. Apart from the one mother who had described being present at the burial of her baby in the nuns' graveyard, there was little evidence that the 'angel plot' was located here. This shrine, created mainly by visiting mothers, marked not the known presence of babies' remains but rather a painful absence of information.

In the corner was a little envelope-shaped plaque, resting near the ground, in memory of a child who was born in 1942 and died a few months later. The wooden plaque for the child who was born and died in 1994 was also there. Later, I looked up that child's birth and death certificates. The photocopies confirmed that he died in Bessborough, at four weeks. The baby's death was certified by the coroner and a post-mortem was conducted: 'Sudden death of non-specific cause in infancy.'

I thought about the secret his mother might still be keeping, and the lonely pilgrimages she made to the folly.

In the late 1990s, a midwife called June Goulding published a memoir about her experiences working in Bessborough in 1951 and 1952. She described how women were expected to work for up to three years in the home; but if their family were able to pay £100 – a 'fortune' at the time – to have the baby adopted, they could leave after ten days. Goulding wrote that Cork Corporation paid the convent £1 per mother and 2s 6d per baby, per week. 'No girl could keep her baby or go home with her baby no matter what her family paid,' Goulding wrote.

She described the women doing heavy work in the laundry, clipping the grass of the grounds by hand, on their knees, and being made to tar the driveway. She recalled baptizing a stillborn baby who was buried in a 'patch of ground' that had a cement crucifix, two feet high. She depicted the nuns as callous, and tight with money, holding back on using the expensive 'cat gut' for stitches when women tore during delivery. One girl was given anaesthetic during childbirth, but only because she had paid extra. The doctor who came to administer the anaesthetic told Goulding he had failed the nun twice in her midwifery final.

Carmel Cantwell, who lives in Cork, used to help organize the annual commemoration at Bessborough. When I met her in Cork she told me the story of her mother, whom she asked me to call Bridget.

Bridget was born out of wedlock in a county home in Cashel.

Her grandparents raised her in Tipperary along with eleven other 'siblings' who were actually her uncles and aunts. She left school at thirteen, and at fourteen started work in a convent in Kilkenny, encouraged by the nuns to become a postulant. At sixteen, when she and other postulants were getting ready to be sent as missionaries to Australia, she needed her birth certificate to get a passport. The nuns told her that she would not be allowed to enter the Sisters of Charity because she was illegitimate.

A year later, at seventeen, while working as a domestic in Tipperary, Bridget became pregnant out of wedlock herself. She fled to England, where she confessed to a priest. He arranged for the Crusade of Rescue in London to send her back to Ireland. Once she stepped through the door of Bessborough, her clothes were taken from her, along with her money and her savings book, and she was put to work.

Her son, William, was born in 1960. After giving birth, Bridget became ill when the site of an injection on her buttock got infected. After three days, William too became sick. She remembered one nun accusing another of using an unsterilized needle on the baby. William was sent to St Finbarr's Hospital; then, Carmel told me, Bridget was told matter-of-factly, 'Your baby died and he's already buried.' Bridget left Bessborough within a week, put on a boat back to England. She tried to commit suicide three times.

For thirty-six years she never told anyone about her son. 'I was the first person,' said Carmel.

In 1995, Bridget went to Bessborough to ask the nuns for information. They sat her down and took out a file and told her William was buried in the nuns' cemetery. Sister Sarto then took Bridget down to the graveyard, not letting her come inside the gate, and tapped her foot against a patch of the grass. 'Your baby's buried there,' Sister Sarto said. Bridget asked if they could place a plaque, but the nun told her no, only a plain wooden cross.

Carmel remembered her mother coming back to her own home in Cork that day and collapsing in sobs on the kitchen floor. It was then that Bridget told her the whole story.

In 2014, Carmel told me, she asked Thomas Quigley if he would ask the nuns to check the burial ledger for William. She believed the nuns must have some records of burials, and there were rumours of a ledger. Quigley came back to her after consulting with the nuns and told her to check with O'Connor's funeral directors on Shandon Street, or the city archives. Carmel found the record of William's death, which listed the causes as renal abscess and septicaemia. But she could find no record of his burial. She and her mother put a small headstone over the spot Sister Sarto had indicated in the Bessborough cemetery.

On the way to the folly, Ann O'Gorman and I passed the vegetable patches and a greenhouse, around which the ground had been dug up. After a short stroll down the tree-lined path, we came to a break in the foliage and Ann gasped. In a small clearing, floating a few metres above the ground, were dozens of delicate white baby gowns. They hung from almost invisible wiring, like tethered spirits, catching the dappled light. Ann shuffled down the rest of the path in her pink sliders, past white balloons tied for the occasion, her eyes overflowing.

Nearly a hundred people were gathered in the clearing beside the little cemetery. A woman in a green-and-blue dress leapt up from her folding chair and called my name. We'd taken an Arabic class together years before. Now she told me she was adopted from Bessborough in the 1950s. A woman in a blue lace dress, named Margaret, adopted around the same time, was over from New York. Her birth mother was ninety-four years old, living in a nursing home in Cork, and had never returned to her home county because of the shame. 'She's in a terrible state,' Margaret said. 'She won't let me tell anyone.'

We sat around a circular mound of grass, scattered with clumps of daisies and dandelions, by the old folly. Some people, Ann included, believed children were buried under that mound. It was adjacent to the graveyard; there were stories of nuns telling mothers that that was where children were buried; and there was no other obvious explanation for the existence of a mound in that place. The air smelled of wild garlic.

After a minute's silence, women came to a microphone, one by one, to speak in front of the group. There was Joan McDermott, who spoke of how her son, taken from her at six weeks in the late 1960s, actively searched for her for nine of the fourteen years she was searching for him. He was given to a couple in exchange for a financial contribution, she said, but not legally adopted. She and other survivors were slowly ridding themselves of the label of 'fallen women', she said, looking out at the women in their summer dresses and sandals, surrounded by friends and family.

Noelle Brown, an actor and playwright, wore lemon Converse and pushed back strands of her short, bright blonde hair as she spoke. Despite the marriage referendum and the recent repeal of the constitutional abortion ban, it wouldn't be a 'new' Ireland, she warned, until the country faced up to its past: 'I get angry when people say, "But we never knew!" Everybody knew.'

Ann was one of the last to speak. 'I know she's here with me today,' she said of her daughter Evelyn.

Before everyone headed away, Carmel reminded the gathering of what was still urgently needed. 'No one has given an answer as to where the babies are,' she said.

After the commemoration was over, people returned to a side room off the main building for mugs of tea and coffee, chatting amongst themselves in little circles, brushing biscuit crumbs from their fronts, washing up their cups when they were done. Thomas Quigley was there and he introduced me to Sister Lorna Walsh, who was head of the Bessborough Centre's all-religious board. She was a solid-looking woman with white hair and a soft round nose, wearing boxy spectacles, a simple blue floral shirt, and a silver cross.

It had been announced in 2017 that the Bessborough estate was up for sale, and I asked Sister Lorna about it. She told me that the cemetery would be retained and that the Sisters would continue to take care of it. She and Quigley discussed how thousands of adoptees had good experiences. 'But you don't hear from them,' she said.

She spoke about Catholicism in Ireland before Vatican II and how strict it was. When she came to Ireland from her native England, she was surprised by the extent of the stigma faced by adopted people here. She did not, though, seem to make a connection between the stigma and the activities of her order.

After Evelyn's birth and death, Ann moved back in with the man she had been living with, and quickly became pregnant again. This time she was referred to St Patrick's on the Navan Road in Dublin, where she gave birth to twins, a boy and a girl. The twins were adopted. Again she returned to the same man, who was sometimes violent to her. Two years later, she became pregnant again, and returned to Bessborough.

At Bessborough the second time, she asked the nuns about her firstborn. They told her they had a record stating she had been there, but nothing about her baby. This frightened her, and after she gave birth to her son she decided she would escape with him. She sneaked into the nursery and grabbed her son. Then she just walked and walked, out through the gates and all the way to the train station with the baby in her arms, praying no one would stop her.

One day, her sister, peering down to the street from the top floor of a double-decker bus in Limerick, spotted Ann with a baby in her arms. The secret was finally out. Her mother took the news well, and visited Ann with money and new shoes for the baby, and with no questions asked. Ann still felt unable to tell her about the earlier babies, or about her time in the institutions.

Once, during a domestic fight, Ann ran out of the house to a priest's house on the corner. 'He said take off your top until I see where you're burned,' she said.

She endured it all. The next time she became pregnant, she didn't hide it or go to an institution. She had three more children: two sons and a daughter. Eventually, she started a new life for herself in her own house with her children.

★

Until 2018, Ann never had a document to show that Evelyn existed. A lawyer applied through the Freedom of Information Act for her records and she received a copy of her daughter's death certificate along with papers relating to her two stays in Bessborough. A social worker met her in Limerick to hand them over and talk her through any questions she might have. In the days before the meeting, her words came at a faster pace than usual over the phone. Finally, she thought, there would be answers. She expected that the records would show how Evelyn died. And, although it was highly unlikely, she hoped that maybe the records might even indicate where Evelyn's little body was buried.

We met in Cork so she could show me the documents. She was wearing a puffy parka, even indoors, looking shrunken inside of it. Her usual bottle of Lucozade sat on the table, untouched. She wouldn't eat a thing.

'Evelyn is a beautiful name,' I told her.

'It is, isn't it?' she smiled. Then her eyes fell back to the pages in her hands.

One document described her daughter as 'full time', but she was also said to have died from a complication of prematurity; Ann was troubled by the apparent contradiction. The records said she went to Bessborough the first time in April 1972, a couple of months before Evelyn was born; but she was convinced she went there earlier, since her bump was barely showing at the time. A maternity record gave her real name, but in the top right corner it also stated her house name and a code: 'Una YXD 95'.

In 1975, when she was in Bessborough for the second time, they gave her the house name Violet. The line on her chart regarding previous pregnancies was left blank, despite the fact this was her fourth child and she had given birth to her first child in the same institution.

The death certificate for Evelyn noted her birth at the Sacred Heart Hospital, the name for the maternity unit in Bessborough, on 24 June 1972. Her age was recorded as twenty minutes. She was marked as 'spinster' and as 'Daughter of Maid'. The cause of death was 'Atelectasis Prematurity'. Atelectasis is the collapse of a lung caused by the deflation of the alveoli, and it is common in premature infants. The informant on the death certificate was a Sister Redempta Pilkington.

Ann's labour was documented briefly. It began at 8 p.m. and her daughter was born at 1 a.m. 'Spontaneous delivery of a living female infant. Baby did not cry and did not respond to treatment. Died after 20 mins.' The record stated that Ann was given Seconal, a barbiturate that acts as a sedative, and an anaesthetic, two hours into labour. Under 'complication', it was recorded that on the day her baby was born Ann was given an injection of 'anti-D globulin', a treatment for women with rhesus-negative blood. Anti-D is usually given earlier in the pregnancy, to protect the baby against rhesus disease.

The baby weighed 5 lb. She was marked 'F.T.', full term. On a sheet headed 'BABY', columns that should have detailed Evelyn's weight and diet and progression were all empty. On the bottom were six lines of antenatal measurements of Ann's growing belly, by which an estimate of the gestation was made. By the second week of April, she was considered twenty-eight weeks pregnant and by the 19th of June, five days before Evelyn was born, thirty-seven weeks, making Evelyn just about full term, though abdominal measurements are not a very accurate way of estimating gestation. I tried to imagine a younger Ann during these checks, lying back to have the swell of her womb measured, maybe enjoying the chance to put her feet up for a moment.

Each of the various apparent inaccuracies or discrepancies in Ann's documents could have had an innocent explanation, but for Ann they were distressing. She had heard of records being falsified, and now her own documents seemed to be re-enacting the lack of control she felt in the institution.

At the top of the sheet, Evelyn's condition at birth was described as 'pale and limp'. The treatment listed was 'oxygen'.

Ann remembers screaming in pain during labour, and being told by a nun to shut up. In a vortex of her own noise, with her eyes screwed shut, she had no one to hold her hand or to help her breathe. Then the baby was out. The nun took the baby to a cot and told the pregnant woman assisting to rush and get the nurse. The afterbirth wasn't coming away. Ann told me she heard the baby cry, a high-pitched wail. The nun had her back turned but Ann could see an oxygen mask in her hand disappearing into the cot to meet her baby's mouth. The mask looked too big for a baby's small face. She felt a sharp prod into the flesh of her stomach and then the nurse's hand twisting something inside of her and a wrenching feeling. She passed out.

'I woke up in the ward, and they told me my angel went to heaven,' she remembered. 'I wasn't given any more information after that.'

She was told about her rhesus-negative blood, something she should bear in mind for her next pregnancy.

What did she want to call the baby?

Evelyn.

Did she want to see the body?

All on her own, feeling as though she had been turned inside out, the idea of going to see the dead body of her daughter was too much. She said no: a decision she would regret for the rest of her life.

That evening, she was standing by a window in the corridor near the ward when she saw two men walking in front of the house, one with a shovel and the other with a wooden crate on his shoulder, of the sort that oranges or onions come in. She wondered if her daughter was in that box. As they disappeared off into the grounds, she felt a wetness running between her legs, and realized she was bleeding.

Ann continued her normal work at Bessborough for a few weeks after her baby died, and then was sent home. She went back to working in the chipper and lodging with the married man.

No one in her family knew what had happened to her.

There was no sign giving the name of the cemetery on the Limerick Road, just south of the village of Sixmilebridge, in County

Clare. There was only a white metal cross, with flecks of paint missing, atop the rusted grey gate. In the distance there were a few cream- and white-walled bungalows. Across the road were fields, but nothing more. A few black crows hopped around in the boughs of a tall tree overlooking the graves, cawing to each other as they did.

This area used to be home to Ann's family, and many of her relatives were buried there. It was in this graveyard where she would be buried one day herself and where she had purchased a plot for her daughter Evelyn, a headstone above an empty grave.

Ann and I got a lift there with her friend Fiona, who also gave birth to a child who died at Bessborough. In the car on the way to Sixmilebridge, Ann explained that when she realized she was pregnant for the first time, it was just before her nana died. When her nana was being buried in the graveyard, her cousin, who was married and pregnant at the time, was forced to stay outside the gates of the cemetery. There was an old tradition that deemed it bad luck for a pregnant woman to enter a graveyard, bad luck for the health of her baby. But Ann couldn't tell anyone that she was pregnant, not even her own mother. So she stood there on the consecrated ground, praying silently to herself that the old belief was only superstition.

Now, in the same graveyard, Ann blinked in the sunshine. Her plot was one of the first that you came to when you passed through the gate, out at the very edge, so it was easy to find. We made our way over and stood on the overgrown grass at the edge of the low, sharp-edged border of the grave, the same pale and speckled granite as the headstone, polished to a smooth sheen. A string of oversized rosary beads was draped over the headstone, which bore a drawing of the Virgin Mary's face. 'In loving memory of' was written in black swirls. Between the two was 'Baby Evelyn Anne' and beneath that a large blank space where Ann knew her own name would be written some day. At the bottom it read 'erected by her loving mother, brothers and sisters'.

As we stood there, the heavens suddenly opened and a thick rain sheeted down. 'That's a good sign in a graveyard,' Fiona said. 'Means they're at peace.' Ann wanted Evelyn's body to be in that grave by the time her own body was put in the ground.

Outside Ann's home in Limerick, two boys were grooming a pony in the middle of the street, cleaning its coat with long slow sweeps of a brush. The trap they usually rode around in was laid out on the ground beside. Inside her home everything was pristine. A little dog yapped out in the garden, which was strewn with children's bikes and toys. Her daughter Leanne put the kettle on for us in the kitchen and sat up on a counter top by the window, having a smoke. Everyone said she was the spit of her mother when Ann was young, with long blonde hair and a heart-shaped face. We sat around the kitchen table and chatted about the trip to the grave.

'It affects her, I can see it,' Leanne said. 'You deserve to have your story told, Mam.'

It was years, maybe a decade or two, after she had her kids in the homes, sitting down watching a film on TV about the Magdalen laundries, that Ann turned to her mother and told her, 'I was in one of those places, Mam.' She'd been able, eventually, to talk about the babies who'd survived, but not until now was she able to talk about the institutions or about Evelyn. Tears began to flow and the words spilled out of her mouth, having been held back for so long.

In the end, it was Ann's mother who bought her the grave plot in the cemetery, where the headstone bearing Evelyn's name now stood.

'She told me if she had known, she'd have helped me keep them,' Ann said. The signals from the culture had been so powerful as to cause her to misjudge the likely reaction of her own mother. 'That's the hardest thing.'

9.

Sisters

On the day I went to meet Sister Mary Roche, in a modern extension of an old convent building on the site of Our Lady's Hospice in Harold's Cross, I was the only visitor to the permanent exhibition devoted to the history of her order, the Sisters of Charity. While Mary went to prepare a pot of tea and a plate of biscuits, I walked around the dark, quiet exhibition space in the Mary Aikenhead Heritage Centre, looking at the illuminated displays set into the wall, with little figurines representing the nuns and the people they interacted with, and an audio narration telling the story of the order.

One display told of how the foundress of the order, Mary Aikenhead, was born in Cork, in 1787, to a Protestant father and Catholic mother, and fostered out, for reasons unknown, to a poor Catholic family. Another told of how the Sisters of Charity was one of the first orders to work openly in society, breaking away from a tradition of enclosure in female congregations. Another dealt with the order's history of running Magdalen asylums. The one in Cork was in 'imminent collapse' when the Sisters were 'persuaded to rescue it'; in return, the Bishop released funds for them to build a new convent. This institution, unnamed in the exhibit, must have been Peacock Lane. 'Their aim was to save the souls of the thousands of street-walkers who eked out a living in Irish towns,' the narrator said.

The Sisters of Charity also ran a Magdalen laundry in Donnybrook, south Dublin, until 1992, when it was sold to a private company, which then operated it as an ordinary commercial laundry. They ran industrial schools, where children born in the homes were often sent if not adopted or fostered. They ran St Gerard's mother-and-baby home, St Patrick's Guild, and orphanages including the notorious Madonna House in Blackrock. St Vincent's Hospital in Dublin, the largest teaching hospital in the country, is the order's most enduring institution. In 2017, when the order's ownership of the hospital emerged as a potentially fatal obstacle to the relocation of the National Maternity Hospital to the St Vincent's campus, a new corporate structure was created to diminish the nuns' role.

After leaving me to finish the tour on my own, Sister Mary sat me down and poured steaming tea from a comically large teapot. I noticed the golden band on her pale ring finger, signifying that she is married to Christ. She did not wear a veil. Her eyes widened as she spoke about how headstrong and heroic the foundress was.

Sister Mary also told me that eight women who worked at the laundries were still under the care of the nuns in Donnybrook, and that a Sister who resided in the convent there might talk to me.

On an October day, Sister Eilis Coe, a woman in her late seventies, was waiting for me in the old-fashioned luxury of the Gresham Hotel in the centre of Dublin. I found her in one of the rooms towards the back, plainly dressed, like most religious Sisters. We sat side by side at a table and she asked me not to record, but allowed me to take notes. She seemed cautious about speaking to me and I thought it was unlikely she would tell me anything of interest, but I asked her about her work.

Sister Eilis told me she mainly worked on anti-trafficking initiatives in Ireland. The Sisters of Charity went to schools, she explained, to talk to students about the dangers of sex trafficking. They tried to use social media too. 'Like us on Facebook, follow us on Twitter, if that's the right way to say it,' she said. Sister Eilis described women she met selling sex on the streets of Dublin, whose abusive, drug-using partners pimped them out. 'Children need presents for Christmas,' she says. 'At Christmas there are more women on the street.'

Sister Eilis told me there were brothels a ten-minute walk from the Gresham. 'You have big long legs,' she said: maybe I could get there even quicker. The conversation seemed to be taking a strange turn. 'Sexual morality among Travellers was always very good,' she said. She mentioned that she'd recently had a 'notion' to write to the broadcaster George Hook, who had been fired for comments he'd made on consent. Then she said, 'If I left my money on the table and someone steals it, am I to blame?' She spoke about 'provocative clothes', about women attracting attention and drinking too much. 'Are they completely innocent?' she asked. 'You've contributed somehow.' She described some girls as foolish and 'half dressed'. 'First thing they do is taking off pants and put it in their handbag,' she said. I had an image of Sister Eilis lurking outside teenage discos. 'Girls in nightclubs are worse,' she said, with their high heels and 'not a stitch on'.

She talked then about the foundresses of the religious orders, women whose names often come up in Irish history. Mary Aikenhead, of course; Nano Nagle, who spearheaded a system of Catholic education for the poor and founded the Presentation Order; Catherine McAuley, who set up the Sisters of Mercy.

'All from aristocratic families,' Sister Eilis emphasized. 'Positions of leadership and authority.' Daughters of 'noblemen' and the 'upper class'. Her favourite was Mother Mary Arsenius of the Sisters of Charity, who set up a convent and a woollen mill in Foxford, Co. Mayo. She boasted that such women could rival Ryanair's founder for a business brain.

I asked her what she thought about the recent criticisms against the nuns. 'It's pathetic,' she said at first; but then she became suddenly reflective. 'It was terrible, looking back now,' she admitted. 'There were abuses, we did make mistakes.'

She herself spent a short stint working at the Peacock Lane laundry in Cork, when she was a teenager still in training. Baskets came in straight from the hospital wards, covered in blood and other bodily fluids.

'The nuns worked side by side with the women,' she said. Young Sisters took a vow of obedience and the hierarchy was absolute. 'You did what you were told,' she stressed. 'Don't speak out.' It sounded as though she was trying to make sense of the past, trying to justify it in her mind but realizing she might be unable to. There was pain in her face. I had, meanwhile, said almost nothing.

'You don't see it until afterwards,' she said.

Religious Sisters sometimes told me that the media didn't represent the whole story. I wanted to get their perspective, their side, and I told them so. I wanted to understand the experiences of the women who ran and worked within these institutions. It was easy – perhaps too easy – to vilify these women. Following the publication of the McAleese report, the historian Diarmaid Ferriter quoted Margaret MacCurtain – herself a nun and a pioneer of Irish women's history – observing that the nuns had been 'pawns in the struggle for control between Church and State, between bishops and departments of government' and that their voices needed to be heard.

Many of the religious Sisters I met led dynamic lives dedicated to work, sometimes even into their eighties. At the Haven, a centre for adult learning in Dublin, I met a petite, straight-talking and seemingly indefatigable woman, a member of the Sisters of Charity, who had advocated for access to education most of her life. I met another Sister of Charity at a convent in Dublin who had worked for years as a missionary in Nigeria. When she was a novice, she visited the Magdalen laundry in Donnybrook and was introduced to some of the inmates. She and other young nuns were encouraged to become pen pals with these women, she told me. I had never heard of this. I asked her what they wrote to each other about and she explained: nothing much, small talk. It was common in the institutions and within the convents for letters to be opened and read before being given to the intended recipient. What would these Magdalen women write to a nun?

Not long after that initial meeting, I received a phone call from this Sister to say that she had been told not to speak to me, that I should contact the congregation's office and they could give further information; she also said that the Sisters had been misquoted before and that they had been used. But then she kept talking. 'We did what we could,' she said. Of the Donnybrook inmates, she said,

'A lot of them were of low mentality. Used before they came to us and abused.' These women, she said, had nowhere else to stay. 'All our grandparents would have thrown them out, it was so embedded in the psyche of the time.'

I sensed that she wanted the motives of the order to be understood. I asked her about the letters she used to exchange with women in the Magdalen laundries, hoping that I could maybe see one. She told me they were 'trained always to tear up letters afterwards'. She observed, too, that some survivors start to feel abandoned as they get older, and some of the things they 'came out with' might not be accurate. When that happened, she said, 'The Sisters didn't protest. That's our policy.' The call lasted twenty minutes.

While individual religious Sisters were occasionally willing to speak with me, the orders as institutions – advised by lawyers and represented by communications consultants – generally refused to engage with my questions or requests for interviews. I went through a back and forth with the Sisters of the Sacred Hearts in the hope that I might be able to talk to members of the order who worked in their mother-and-baby homes. After meeting Sister Lorna at the Bessborough commemoration, I reached out to her about this.

'There has been such a negative version of what the Sisters did and words have been twisted to fit the negative agenda that Sisters are hesitant to talk freely about their work now,' Sister Lorna wrote in her email. She put me in touch with a Sister Eileen McLaughlin, based in the Sacred Hearts convent in Chigwell, and we arranged to speak over the phone to discuss 'the Sisters who would be happy to be interviewed, and where they presently are', as Sister Eileen put it. She told me that there were five Sisters who had worked in the mother-and-baby homes and whose testimonies had been given in an affidavit to the Commission. Three of them lived in the Sacred Hearts Convent in Cork, one in Scotland and another in Zambia. She listed each by name and role.

I was told in August 2018 that it would be possible to arrange for me to visit the Sisters that were part of the 'Cork community' by the next month. I then received an email around a week later to say Sister Eileen was speaking with the order's solicitor about matters related to the Commission and that he had 'valid concerns', given that they had been 'deliberate in dealing with the media' so far during the investigation and 'would not like the congregation to be questioned at a later date by other journalists as to why we were happy to deal with you Caelainn and not with them'. There were also concerns about 'the added stress any further interviews would put on elderly Sisters who are not too well'. I assured her my intention was not to cause them stress. A possible solution, she told me in a subsequent email, would be that she could send me 'copies of the particular Sisters' statements that were taken by one of our Sisters in preparation for their affidavits' and if I had further questions she would try to answer them.

She would be in Dublin soon and offered to meet to give me the statements. We agreed on a café but, at the last minute, she asked me to come to the hotel where she was staying. When I met her in the lobby, she was with the order's press relations representative, Wally Young, who worked for eleven years as a media adviser to Presidents McAleese and Higgins. He sat with us throughout the meeting, taking notes, having insisted I agree to everything being off the record before we started chatting. I was given no statements, no perspective from the Sisters, no useable insight whatsoever.

The first time I entered the Bon Secours Hospital in Cork, walking past an imposing life-size statue of the Virgin Mary, I asked where I could find Sister Marie Ryan, the head of the congregation in Ireland.

I was directed to the convent, at the back of one of the hospital buildings. I knocked on the red door of the old stone convent building, which looked out over a beautiful garden secluded by a border of hedges and trees. One of the Sisters answered and told me Sister Marie was out for the day. I called the number on their website later that day and left my contact details.

Just before Christmas, I returned to Cork, visiting Mary Gaffney again at Peacock Lane. On the Bon Secours Sisters' Facebook page, their profile photo was a close-up of a statue of the blushing Virgin, her eyes rolled up towards heaven, and her crowned child beaming at her, touching her face. A public event had been listed for that evening under the rubric 'GATHER Tuesdays'. The acronym spelled out Gather, Adoration, Time out, Hospitality, Explore, Reflect. 'Young adults are invited each Tuesday evening,' it read. 'An open invitation to meet with other young adults to explore aspects of faith and prayer.' I had just turned thirty. I wondered if I could still pass as a 'young adult'. I expected the event to be in the convent, but when I called the number listed, at the last minute, to confirm the event was on, a woman with a confident voice directed me to a house a short walk up a steep narrow road from the hospital. It was already dark, the moon three-quarters full and sirens sounding in the distance.

A short older woman with grey eyebrows and wispy hair, dressed in a fleece gilet, opened the door; I'll call her Sister X. Inside, it was warm and the sound of voices was bubbling away. I was a little late, and a group of maybe a dozen women – mostly laywomen, along with a few resident nuns – filled the living room, sitting on arm-chairs and dressed in Christmas jumpers, some wearing elf hats or novelty hairbands. An artificial Christmas tree with bright baubles twinkled in front of the fireplace and an angel in pink robes stood on the mantelpiece. The window curtains had a pattern of olive branches on them. I was handed a song sheet. Some of the women were from Cork and some from South America. Sister X joined us, adding whispery little quips here and there that made people laugh.

The laywomen all seemed to know each other – I gathered that they came together every week, sometimes to watch a film – but they made me feel instantly welcome. As the organizer, a lay-woman called Anne-Marie Whelan, strummed a guitar, I noticed the cartoon penguins on her jumper and smiled. She told me not to worry about introductions, as they were ready to start the songs.

The last song we sang was 'Silent Night'. When it came to the words about the mother and child, the holy infant sleeping in heavenly peace, I thought of Ann O'Gorman and her daughter, of the mothers who don't know where their children are buried, of the bones of babies still in a tank beside a playground in Tuam. I thought of how many times mothers have sung this song at Christmas, or heard others singing it, and felt the loss stick in their throat.

The kitchen table was laden with treats the women brought, Christmas-tree-shaped biscuits, mince pies and a home-made eggnog-type drink. Anne-Marie told me she was from Laois and that she worked for a bank before coming to work for the order. (Later I looked up her LinkedIn profile, which said that her current role with the Bon Secours is to develop 'creative evangelisation and vocations fostering programmes and initiatives for young adults (18–40)'. She started this work in November 2015, according to the LinkedIn page, the year after the news broke worldwide about the deaths and unaccounted burials in Tuam.) I told Anne-Marie that I was writing a book about the mother-and-baby homes and that I was hoping to speak to some of the Sisters to get their perspective. I asked if I could come to her office the next day to talk further, and she gave me her number.

I talked to the other women about my book, and mentioned the experiences of women who had had to keep the fact they had a baby secret for so long. There were students in their twenties from South America, for whom one of the Bon Secours Sisters, who came from Peru, seemed to be a real support so far from home. The others were middle-aged Irish women, clearly devoted to the order, who might in the past have become religious Sisters themselves but were reluctant to give up all their freedoms.

One of the Irish women told me that the mothers had been sent to the institutions for 'doing nothing wrong, let's call a spade a spade'. But she also believed only one side of the story was being told, excluding the perspectives of those within the religious orders and the Church. The Sisters talked about how Direct Provision for asylum seekers was going to be the institutional injustice that would be the subject of future reports. I exchanged numbers with one of the Sisters, who spoke particularly strongly on that subject.

Before everyone left, Sister X brought me into a prayer room. It was softly lit, with bespoke furniture and a little shrine and a statue of the Virgin Mary. There was a framed picture of a woman in a veil. 'She's our foundress,' she said, her voice soft and raspy. She told me that there were nearly thirty women, mostly retired Sisters, living in the convent on the hospital grounds.

I asked her about Tuam.

'The thing about it is, look what's happening nowadays,' she said. 'How many people living inside hotels, how many children homeless?' She wanted people to think about the injustices happening today. 'There will be a lot to answer for,' she said.

I asked her if she felt we were repeating the same patterns.

'I think they just want to cover up, they want to go back, look at another age as if it were today,' she said. 'They don't look at what's happening today.'

I tried to explain that, for many people, what happened in the institutions is not in the past: it still shapes their lives today. I explained that many mothers and adoptees I've spoken to still have religious faith but feel the Sisters haven't engaged with them.

'What do you say to someone when you don't know?' she replied. 'You'd love to be able to say something.'

I asked her what holds her back.

'I don't know anything, no one has asked me anything,' she said.

I told her I was trying to make sense of what happened in Tuam and elsewhere, how it's difficult to understand.

'It's impossible to understand,' she says. She seemed unconvinced that children were buried in the sewage tank: 'I find it very hard to think that anyone would do that,' she said quietly.

She joined the order in the 1960s, by which time the institution in Tuam was already closed. 'I should have asked,' she said, as if to herself. 'Hindsight is a marvellous thing. I didn't know there was a mother-and-baby home there.'

I asked her if she agreed there was a need for the Commission of Investigation to find answers.

'Of course I do,' she said. 'Of course I would love to be able to give people an explanation, to talk to them, to meet them.' Her eyes were wet.

Survivors wanted answers and not just meetings with nuns. But there had been an almost total lack of public engagement by the religious orders on the issue of the burials, and in this context I was moved by what Sister X said. It was a relief to see a nun show emotion about the burials.

She explained that she had a friend who was born in an institution and fostered out. I told her it was important to me to include perspectives like hers in the book and that I appreciated it. 'We think about it all the time,' she stressed.

One of the women who attended the event offered me a lift back into the city centre. My eyes followed the picture of a saint hanging from the rear-view mirror. One of the passengers, who had considered a vocation herself, had an aunt who was a nun in a convent so strict that she was not allowed to visit home, even when her father was dying. If the nuns simply acknowledged that people had been wronged, I suggested, if there was more openness and less silence, maybe there would be more understanding. The woman driving figured that the Bon Secours Sisters would have received legal advice not to speak on the matter, that everything had to be pre-approved, that it had all 'got very legal'.

Silence may protect against liability, but it only raises suspicion – particularly coming from a religious order whose institutions are publicly funded, and which continues to be a significant provider of healthcare.

We pulled up on the street where I'd asked the driver to leave me. A little stunned, I ducked into a chipper called Hillbilly's Family Restaurant for a late-night snack box. I checked my phone and saw a story via Facebook about Clint Eastwood on the red carpet of an awards ceremony with his secret daughter, who was adopted and then traced him. Maybe my algorithms are set to show me stories like this now, or maybe these stories are just everywhere.

I wiped my greasy fingers on a napkin and headed to the hostel dorm room where I was staying. 'Silent Night' was stuck in my head: the Virgin mother and the tender child. I thought of the small woman whispering to herself in the prayer room that she should have asked, she should have asked.

The next day was blustery and the Cork traffic was thick. I took the bus back towards the Bon Secours Hospital, planning to go to see Anne-Marie Whelan, the vocations officer. I stopped by the door of the house on the way, ringing the bell: I wanted to ask Sister X if she had known any of the Sisters who worked in the home in Tuam. Sister X answered the door. She said that my presence at the previous evening's event 'kind of took me off guard'. She believed I was there for the prayer meeting, not to research a book. 'It was a bit deceptive, wasn't it?' she said.

It went through my mind that maybe she had been advised afterwards that she shouldn't have spoken to me. I reminded her that when I spoke to her in the prayer room, I explained that I was writing a book and that I wanted to include the Sisters' perspectives. People always said their side wasn't included.

'We're here to help people, that's been my intention all my life,' she said. Relatives of hers had lost babies; she could imagine what a mother suffers losing her children. Her work was her life and she knew nothing about what happened in different convents. The way the children were buried in Tuam was impossible to understand. She said she didn't know any of the Sisters who worked in the Tuam home. 'I wouldn't say I slept last night, going over it and thinking about it,' she said. 'I hope that there will be some explanation when it does happen to come out, that it won't be as it is, and if it is, well, I wasn't involved with it.'

Another Sister joined her. They told me to go talk to Sister Marie Ryan, the head of the congregation.

Inside the hospital, I got a quick coffee in the canteen, passing the bain-maries filled with curry, sausages and chips. The big hall was decked out for Christmas; 'Grandma Got Run Over by a Reindeer' played over the PA. I sat in front of a table of people in scrubs and wondered what it was like to work in a hospital owned by a religious order that had been in the headlines in connection with the deaths of hundreds of children. There was a faded painting of Christ on one of the walls. The wards were all named after saints. On the wall beside the door of the canteen were framed collages of photos showing the Sisters.

Anne-Marie texted to say she was not available. I asked at reception for Sister Marie Ryan's office and was directed upstairs and through a ward to double doors with a security keypad and a sign that said something about a convent. A nurse buzzed me through to a corridor. The door of each room on the corridor had a name on it: Sisters of the order lived here. A nurse buzzed me through another door and across a walkway that connected the hospital building with the old convent. I followed her down a staircase and she handed me over to the first nun we met, who led me to a blue-carpeted room with a large table covered in blue cloth.

I waited for at least fifteen minutes, thinking of what I wanted to ask the head of the Bon Secours order in Ireland. I knew that in 2012, Sister Marie had sent a letter to Anna Corrigan, a woman searching for the burial place of her two brothers, who were recorded as having died in the Tuam home. Sister Marie wrote that there was a possibility that one of her brothers could be 'buried at the small cemetery at the home itself. This is located at the back of the home and was operated as a general grave.' Sister Marie had later claimed the Sisters had no information about the children's grave. I thought I would ask her about that. But the nun came back and told me Sister Marie Ryan wasn't available.

The religious Sisters I spoke to felt that a society once happy for nuns to care for the poor and destitute had now turned on them. They felt no one was telling their side of the story; but it also seemed clear that they had not figured out how to tell their own story. Some nuns were willing to speak openly with me, but the hierarchies and the secrecy of the orders made a deeper engagement impossible. There was an acknowledgement that mistakes had been made in the past, but there was no sign that any active search for answers was under way within the orders themselves. They understood that wrongs had been committed in the guise of doing good, but when they spoke of the good their orders did it was to distract from properly discussing the injustices. They were eager to have someone listen and yet scared to talk openly. They had become vulnerable to the one-dimensional social judgements all women have been subjected to, the inhumane absolutes of good and evil their religion taught us.

Back Gardens

I saw Teresa Killeen-Kelly again a year after our first meeting, this time in her office at the District Mental Health Association, directly across the road from Tuam's Catholic cathedral. I wanted to ask her about a one-time neighbour of hers, now dead, whom her mother had known very well.

Julia Devaney worked for years inside the mother-and-baby home in Tuam, after being transferred there from the Glenamaddy work-house, where she'd been institutionalized since she was a child. Her recollections had been recorded on audiotape by another neighbour, Rebecca Millane.

Teresa remembered Julia Devaney fondly. She had been a part of her life during her childhood, when her family lived on an estate near the Galway Road. She was an avid gardener and a dog lover, and she doted on children. 'We all knew she came from the home,' Teresa stressed. When Teresa got older and would be going out to dances, Julia would warn her that she 'couldn't go out dressed like that'. In the 1980s, a young woman on their street had a baby out of wedlock and was wheeling the buggy up and down the street. 'Imagine!' she remembered Julia exclaiming, scandalized by the sight. 'You wouldn't be able to do it in my time.'

I wasn't able to obtain the audio recording of Julia Devaney's recollections, but I did get transcripts. They give us the most detailed account we have of life inside the Tuam home, for the entire period of its operation.

Julia was a 'domestic' at the home. There were usually around ten of them at any given time. Some of them had come to the institution as children, like Julia. Some were mothers who gave birth to their children in the institution and then never left. 'It never dawned on us that the nuns were wronging us and we were entitled to our own lives,' Julia said. Some of them had well-defined roles. Peg was with the children all her life, Molly was in the sewing room and Eileen stayed with the school-going children.

To begin with, in 1925, there was no running water in the institution. Julia brought water in Delphi jugs to the nuns' rooms, along with carbolic soap, to wash. The dormitories that accommodated the children and the women were yellow-washed and painted by the domestics themselves. There was a big stone staircase which the children would clamber up, barefooted, to bed at night. Their boots would be left at the bottom, all tangled up in a mess of laces by the morning.

The County Council owned the property, and now and then it made inspections, conducted by a Miss Cross. She was apparently the sister of a well-known singer. While Julia was still a teenager, she and the other young women growing up in the home were told to hide by the nuns in case the inspector asked what they were doing there. Evidently, the domestics could not be presented as inmates, nor as employees, so their presence was simply hidden. But when the home closed, the County Council knew exactly how many domestics there were.

There seemed to be one grown man in the whole place, a caretaker called John Cunningham. There were also two male doctors, first a Dr Costelloe, followed by a Dr Waldron. They were hired by the County Council to tend to the medical needs of the inmates. Julia described them as driven by a sense of duty. The doctors' wives sent over old toys or books for the children. Julia described a doll's cot and a rocking horse belonging to Dr Costelloe's daughter, and a bespoke doll's house that looked exactly like the doctor's own house. The donations only seemed to leave Julia with a feeling of lack, a glimpse into the security and comparative luxury enjoyed by other children, the sting of being pitied by an outside world that saw her as inferior.

The gates were rarely locked, because there were bread vans and other services that needed to come and go throughout the day. They stayed open until the milk van came, which could be as late as 10 p.m. The domestic who was witness to many of the births, Bina Rabbitte, was in charge of the keys, and the inmates were wary of her. 'Bina was a devil, she was like a spy,' Julia said. Bina grew up in the home and was rumoured to have given birth to a child there herself.

Julia was conditioned to believe there was no other life for her than the one she knew within the walls of the institution. The domestics didn't go out the gate without permission, even if it was wide open. Their contact with the town was limited, never straying beyond simple errands or chaperoned trips. 'We would never, never, never be let out to a dance,' she said.

The first Mother Superior Julia spoke of was Mother Hortense. She was kind to Julia, and seemed somehow naive, having come to the workhouse very young and spent most of her life in an institution. Hortense's successor, Mother Martha, was more modern, and 'cute'. Martha the Bull, the girls nicknamed her. 'Big auld Queen Victoria of a one, a domineering big yoke,' Julia said. If someone wasn't where they were supposed to be, Martha would go on the warpath. There was a Sister Priscilla, who was childlike, and a Sister Anthony, who told the women not to cry, that it would be worse for them to be stuck in a bad marriage. Sister Gabriel, who was in charge of the babies, was always praying.

One domestic was remembered as being very pretty. When she was on a rare trip outside the home, to the Corpus Christi procession, a local clerk from Knock fell in love with her. She was around twenty-one years old at the time, and used to sneak down to the gate of the home to see him. But John Cunningham and Bina Rabbitte caught them.

The home was a maze of surreptitious transactions and unspoken histories, where eavesdropping was sometimes the only way to gain information. There was a room where Mother Hortense would work in the evening, and Bina would go there before bed. If Julia wanted any news, she would arrange her evening so that she found herself lingering longer than necessary outside that door. Even then, the ears of a bat were needed to decipher the frequencies in which they parsed their information. "'Twas a secret society,' said Julia. 'There was nothing open at all, it was all underhand.'

As a child from the institutions, Julia was always sent to the back of class at school, and her classmates would never play with her. When the teacher asked the children where they had gone for holidays during their summer break, she would always pass Julia out.

The nuns never taught the girls the facts of life. They were not told about periods or given sanitary towels or bras. When Julia had her first period, she hid it, using rags she found around the place. She learned what to do from the women who were there to give birth.

The nuns seemed to live frugally themselves, going to the sales in Dublin in order to save money, and making clothes for themselves and for the children. They wore shift dresses made from bed sheets, and these doubled as nightdresses. Julia didn't think they wore knickers. They seemed alien, almost sexless.

For the women who had entered the home in order to give birth, the day began at 6 a.m. Those with babies under ten days old slept with them in their beds and would bring them to the nursery towards the back of the building. Everyone was shunted out of the dormitories to Mass in the chapel by 8 a.m. 'A good eye was kept on those who were receiving Communion,' Julia said. After Mass, they gathered for a breakfast of porridge, milk, tea and bread, served on big trays. The mothers were sent to feed their babies, some by breast, others by bottle. Julia remembered that the Reverend Mother would nearly starve an infant in order to force a mother to breastfeed. A doctor would have to certify that the woman was unable to breastfeed before a bottle would be granted. (This policy changed in later years, according to a woman who told me she was not allowed to breastfeed her child.)

Then the mothers went to the laundry to begin work. In the earlier years there were only washboards and sinks, and a big contraption called a 'colander' for rolling sheets and drying them. A big cold bath outside was where the 'bowels' of the babies' nappies were rinsed out first. It was work that left backs aching and hands raw. In later years the council installed 'monstrous' washing machines and a wringer. They had hot water then too. The cloth nappies had numbers on them and each mother was responsible for her baby's own, as well as those of any other children she was looking after.

After the laundry, the women worked in the kitchens, scullery, dining room or dormitories. They polished and cleaned. They made the beds, removing the mattress protectors every morning, hanging them to dry on the iron rails of the stairs. At 5 p.m. they would put the covers back on again. No matter how many times the children were taken to the toilet, they still wet the beds. The stench of urine was everywhere, all the time, the whole place permeated with the smell of scared children. Julia remembers one young novice saying that she would rather mind pigs and that the whole institution was wrong.

Julia eavesdropped on the mothers as they worked. They often refused to talk to her, maybe worried she was a spy for the nuns. Some of the women would get into fights, mostly out of sheer frustration. Those that caused trouble were sent to the local mental hospital, or to the laundries. A doctor would need to certify that the women needed to be committed, Julia said, but that wasn't a problem, because the doctor would always do what the nuns told him to.

Rarely, a man would come to take one of the mothers out from the place and marry her. One time, a priest came with an inmate's parents and a man, who got down on one knee and asked for her hand. But he refused to take her child home, because he claimed it was not his.

There were swings and see-saws outside, but the children hardly ever played on them. Instead, they used to shout and screech, wheeling around playing ring-a-ring o' roses. Some would use their hands to lift porridge out of mugs instead of a spoon, with no one to show them properly. Julia described a 'terrible regime', the children rising at the crack of dawn in a 'cold barracks-like place', marched in twos like prisoners, their outside world confined to church or school. They went to bed at 6 p.m. The only food they ate was porridge and some starchy grub in the evenings. When Mother Martha took over, she started giving them bread and soup. They were pot-bellied, a sign of malnutrition. They called the caretaker 'daddy'.

An old man would sometimes bring them to see the chickens. They never learned the names of animals, never had bedtime stories to spark their imagination. They were destructive because they had nothing to do, and they were small for their age, almost stunted. They were fed mash but didn't really know what a potato was. 'In to wash your face and out to do the Rosary and out again and up to bed,' Julia recalled. 'I don't think there was any other institution as abnormal.'

Someone used to 'belt hell blazes' out of the children in the nursery. Julia could never work out who was doing it, because she didn't work there, but the beatings seemed to happen in the three little children's toilets, and the sound carried far. The neighbours could hear it, and sometimes when she was working in the garden, women strolling past would ask who was beating the children. Julia believed some of the mothers hated their situation and that they were the ones beating their children.

Every year, the children who were old enough would perform in a play, and the offspring of the local doctors would come to watch it. County Council members came to the home periodically for a meeting and were treated to a feast – 'beef and everything, a glorious feed'. The nuns were not in the service of God, but in the service of Galway County Council, Julia said. They kept big books for the council, with accounts of all the mothers and children, admissions, discharges, ages, origins and the names of the putative fathers. There would be advertisements for children available for fostering in the local papers, and babies were delivered to their new homes in the same ambulances that collected the ledgers for the council.

The moment when mothers and children were separated from each other was always painful to witness. 'The babies and toddlers whined and pined after the mother left,' she said. 'There was no effort to prepare them for the change, they weren't told they would be going.' The mothers, too, were distraught. 'No effort was ever made for mothers to keep their children,' she said. A few women were kept on as domestics, working without pay so that they could stay with their children.

The interviewer compared the nuns to a farmer raising chickens for slaughter, shocked that the nuns, educated women who were part of an international order, would treat children that way. 'Well, they weren't Christ-like, that's sure,' Julia said. She remembered the sight of children leaving the institution for foster homes: walking up the front path to a waiting ambulance, with a heavy pair of boots, socks, a new coat and change of clothes, and little knowledge of the world.

Sometimes girls were fostered out and then sent back on the grounds that they were 'slow'. These girls were sent to a Magdalen laundry, usually the one in Galway. Julia felt unable to intervene. 'You'd be lucky if next day you weren't in Ballinasloe yourself,' she said, referring to the mental asylum there.

At least three of the boarded-out girls came back pregnant. 'I don't think that they ever got out again,' she said. 'They were put into the Magdalen laundry.' The nuns pretended they were bringing the woman to a new job. Julia remembered that one woman was taken to a Magdalen laundry because her sister was also having a baby in Tuam. The nuns believed there was a weakness in the family.

Julia visited the Magdalen laundry in Galway herself once and noticed that none of the girls she knew there had their own names any more. She described them as praying like the nuns and speaking in a daft way. A child with the surname Corless was in the home while her mother was in the laundry. She was boarded out to a family, but they returned her and so she was sent to the laundry herself, alongside her mother. Julia heard that this girl then broke out of the laundry – a rare feat. Ordinarily, she said, 'When they went into the laundry that was for eternity.'

Julia said she was not religious herself. 'I suppose I got an overdose of it!' I could hear her laughing through the transcript. 'Nearer the Church, the farther from God!' She boasted about dodging Rosary, going out to weed the garden rather than picking her way through the beads. The garden was her escape. She felt proud when passers-by praised the flowers. She tended belts of wallflowers, polyanthus, asters, two glasshouses full of greenery and blossoms. The lawns were immaculately groomed. They grew cabbages, onions, lettuce, tomatoes, beetroot, parsnips and a big swathe of sweet pea. There were hens and pigs. The women would walk along a quarter mile of thick golden privet hedge on Saturday evenings, a reprieve after cleaning the whole place spotless for Sunday. 'How daft, the pride I had in the place,' she said. 'Had me heart and soul in it really.'

They were not completely cut off from the outside world. The children were sometimes invited to see a film by a lady in town, or the projector was brought to them. People would sometimes come looking to hire a servant girl. The bread van would often leave a cake for the domestics. The children's matching coats made them stand out. A crowd would sometimes gather at a particular corner, she remembered, nudging each other, gawking at 'the home ones'.

Julia repeatedly described the institution as unnatural, a place where children didn't even speak normally, with no one there to talk to them or to care what they said. 'It was a cold, sad, loveless place,' she said. 'Not like a home.' The most caring interaction some older children had with an adult in the home was when they were fine-combed for lice or checked for fleas.

In the 1950s, American couples started coming to take children to the United States. One couple came to collect a girl who was sick with measles, so they stayed in a hotel and visited every day while she convalesced. Later, when they'd gone back to the States with the girl, they sent back colour photos of her in a lovely bedroom with plenty of toys.

On one occasion, a woman gave Julia a ten-shilling note, and she decided to escape. Two of the domestics were working for a priest in Ballaghaderreen. She made it to the railway station, the money in her hand, but she just stood there frozen with fear. Eventually, two men were sent to bring her back.

The motto that helped her survive was that she couldn't miss what she never had. But in later years, when Julia watched children laughing and playing on the Dublin Road estate, running across the old grounds, she reflected on how different they were from the 'unhappy kideens' she had known inside the old walls. She never thought there would come a day when the home would be demolished and life would change. 'They had you brainwashed,' she said. 'Blinkers were put on us.'

Julia spoke, too, about the burial of children who died in the home. 'Sure they had a little graveyard of their own up there,' she said, simply. 'It's still there, it's walled in now.' Epidemics of whooping cough and measles were devastating: 'They used to die like flies.'

Mothers died in the home as well. One girl, after her baby was born, waited for her family to call, but they never did. She died when the baby was six days old. Julia believed it was of a broken heart. When the family came then to take her body, the nuns told them they should have kept in touch with her while she was alive.

The Galway County Council archives are housed on Nun's Island, across the main flow of the River Corrib from the city centre. In the centre of the island loomed the strangely organic stone mass of Galway Cathedral, with its rose-shaped windows and green dome, where the bodies of dead bishops were buried in crypts, including the disgraced Bishop Eamonn Casey. Across another stream of water was the convent of the Poor Clares, tucked away among green fields. Here I spent a day going through the county's financial records for various public-assistance institutions, including the mother-and-baby home in Tuam. I was hoping to learn something about the council's level of knowledge of the mortality rate and of burial practices there.

Expenses and income from the Tuam home were listed in each year's financial records, alongside figures from institutions for the blind, the insane, and the Magdalen asylum. They also documented the number of children and women in the home. In 1944, for example, there were 3 married women at the home, 110 'other females', 50 legitimate children and 224 illegitimate. The number of births in the institution each year was recorded, as was the number of deaths.

The accounts included valuations for the property and the furniture, and lots of detail regarding various costs of running the institution. But I could find no reference to burial expenses. This is, of course, consistent with a regime whereby burials handled by the Bon Secours involved the interring of remains in an unmarked mass grave on the grounds of the home.

In ledgers known as 'Manager's Orders', records were kept of the County Manager's decisions and the operation of the institution. The ledgers were not accessible to researchers, since they include identifying details of individuals; but the archivist sent me extracts. While there seemed to be no reference to burial expenses specific to the children's home in the records I was able to view, there *were* references to coffins. In 1946, the council accepted a Tuam man's tender for half a year's supply of coffins to the mother-and-baby home. Prices ranged from 16s for a small unlined coffin to £3 for a large mounted coffin. In 1947 another tender was accepted from the same vendor for 'small coffins at £1 each'. Whether the coffins were ever actually purchased was unclear. But the fact that the council was accepting tenders for 'small coffins' might suggest that some of the children who died in the home received traditional burials.

There were also references to children in the home being adopted to America, mostly related to payments for passport photographs, birth certificates or notary expenses. There was also an approval of the return of adoption expenses to a married couple. They had paid £99 9s od 'to defray expenses regarding proposed adoption by them of two children' from the home in December 1957. It was not specified why the fee had been returned, but presumably the adoptions did not go ahead. The sum of £99 in 1957 was worth the equivalent of more than €2,000 today.

On my way back to Galway city centre from the archive, I passed a wall that had a strange symbol on it, and inside the entrance to a private car park I could see a little graveyard and an ornate old building with stone carvings on the outside. I ventured in. The little gated graveyard with its crosses was for nuns.

An older woman in the car park came up to speak to me. She told me this was a convent for the Sisters of Mercy, with a modern building in the back that was a type of nursing home for the ageing nuns. She belonged to the order herself.

I asked her if she knew of the Magdalen laundry in the city, and she told me she had been stationed there herself for some time. She said the work there wasn't difficult at all, and dismissed the women complaining about it as money-hungry.

I asked if she would talk to me further about it, and she told me no.

Many of the women who gave birth in Tuam were no longer alive to speak about what happened there, and many went to their graves never telling a soul. While I worked in the archive on Nun's Island, leafing through dusty ledgers, I thought about Rosaline McKinney, an eighty-year-old woman still very much alive in the flesh and blood.

I first met Rose at a protest in Dublin, where she lived with her daughter. Over the next few months, I helped Rose apply for her records, which she wanted as evidence of what she remembered. One of eight siblings, Rose was seventeen years old, living on the family farm in Dunmore, a rural area of Galway, when crippling pain coursed through her body and her mother realized she was in labour. She had kept the pregnancy secret, not sure what was happening to her own body. At thirteen, she had left school to work the farm. Girls were taught about the Virgin Birth but not about sex or pregnancy. The local doctor was summoned and drove Rose not to a local hospital but to the mother-and-baby home in Tuam.

Rose spent a year there, and was allowed to hold her son only during feeding. The archivist on Nun's Island found Rose's name in the Manager's Orders for the Tuam home. I read that just over a year after Rose's son was born, her family began paying 30 shillings a month maintenance for the boy to remain there. Rose never knew about these payments to an institution where conditions were so poor. There was no record to say how long her son remained. Rose told me that he was fostered out after a few years.

Two years after she gave birth to her son, Rose became pregnant again. Her boyfriend came to the farm to ask for her hand in marriage, happy to be starting a family. But Rose's parents refused. 'They brought me back,' she told me, referring to Tuam. 'You had no choice in these things.' She gave birth to a daughter and remained in the institution, washing clothes and cleaning floors for the nuns. 'I wanted to keep her,' she said. 'I wanted to keep my son as well.' She was older this time, with a man who wanted to marry her, which gave her hope that they could take her daughter home. The nuns even allowed her boyfriend to visit, but they would not allow him to see his daughter. One day, her baby was gone. She doesn't remember signing any consent.

The nuns sent Rose to the Magdalen laundry in Galway, a place she described as 'the most vicious place you could ever live'. She washed clothes from first thing in the morning until 10 at night, sleeping in a dormitory with around forty other women. Many had also given birth to children in the institutions. A nun once hit her so hard across the face that she permanently lost hearing in one ear. She met a girl she went to school with in the laundry, a novice with the Mercy Sisters. 'Me and her were like that,' she laughed, winding her middle finger around her index, squeezing them tightly. Now they were segregated into different classes of women, a celibate bride of Christ and a 'repeat offender'.

After a few years in the laundry, Rose escaped one night, climbing over the roof with another girl and over the high outside wall.

She returned to the family farm on foot. 'The nuns came down to get me back,' she said. A local Garda sergeant was also with them. But her siblings were at home and refused to let Rose be taken back. 'I had my dog Prince beside me, growling,' she winked at me. 'They had to run.'

When we applied to the Sisters of Mercy for her records, they sent back a scan of a single entry in their register, the only record they had on her. There was nothing to show how long she stayed at the laundry or whether she had any medical care while there. There was no record of when she left. The entry in the admissions register, in spider-like cursive, noted her name, her age as twenty-two, her address simply 'Tuam'. It was dated 16 June 1959. 'By whom sent': Sister Patrick, and what looked like Horatius or Loratus, in Tuam. Under 'cause', the reason Rose was being sent to the laundry, two words were written: 'Penitent – twice'.

I spent a fair amount of time looking through the hundreds of death registrations of children who died in the Tuam institution. This place came into the national consciousness because of the way that dead children were buried there, and sometimes it seemed that not enough attention was paid to how those children had lived, and how they died. Even a tiny sampling from the bare details of the death registrations leaves plenty of space to imagine the dire conditions in the home and the suffering of babies and small children.

In 1946, forty-nine children were recorded to have died at the home in Tuam. In 1947, the number was fifty-two. I tried to imagine how the mothers, the women like Julia who worked there, and the nuns themselves coped with a child dying, on average, every week. A small corpse to lay in the ground, somewhere, every single week.

In 1946, Beatrice Keane was five years old when she died of 'congenital hydrocephalus', excess fluid on the brain, which if untreated can lead to pressure, intense pain, brain damage and death.

In 1950, Catherine Higgins from Headford died at four and a quarter years old, a little girl who might have already started school, marked as 'spinster', and the 'daughter of a farmer's daughter'. The first word in the box for her cause of death is 'imbecile', followed by 'meningitis 1 day'. Another child who died in the home around the same time, a boy, convulsed for twelve hours before he died.

Three-week-old John Joseph Mills, the son of a labourer's daughter from Tuam, died in October 1952 after three days of influenza and fifteen minutes of convulsions. He was labelled a 'congenital idiot' – apparently a catch-all term for children born with disabilities.

On the first day of December 1956, Rose Marie Murphy, two and a half years old, daughter of a domestic, died of bronchopneumonia. It was noted that she 'never developed normally' and was 'delicate'. At the end of that same month, two boys died, a four-and-a-half-month-old 'son of a small farmer', whose mother was in a sanatorium before and after the birth, and a four-month-old son of a domestic. Both died of bronchopneumonia, one day apart. A three-and-a-half-month-old girl, 'daughter of the farmer's daughter', died of bronchopneumonia a little more than a week after the boys.

In 1957, a six-month-old girl from Inishbofin died after a convulsive fit lasting fifteen minutes. A boy with no first name, son of a domestic servant, died after four days, of sudden cardiac failure.

Mary Maloney died in 1959. She was listed as a 'farmer's daughter'. Mary had suffered with chronic colitis for two months. Then over the space of two days, a bout of bronchopneumonia, an inflammation of the lungs, ended her short life.

Mary Carty, the daughter of a domestic, was the last child registered to have died in the home, at four and a half months old, in the middle of January 1960. She died after a convulsive fit. The record of her death noted that she was a 'restless baby'.

The mother-and-baby home at Tuam closed in 1961 – earlier than any of the other major institutions of the shame-industrial complex. Why did the institution close?

For a number of years leading up to the closure, there was official disquiet about conditions in the institution. In 1951, an architect submitted plans for renovations to the Department of Health. The following year, the County Fire Service Advisory Committee declared that the 'Children's Home in Tuam is a fire trap'. But the council wanted to determine the future of the institution before committing to urgent repairs – a sign, perhaps, that closure of the home was already being seriously considered.

In 1957, it was suggested that the children's home be transferred to Woodlands Hospital, which the Department of Health wanted a religious order to take over and run as an institution for 'mentally defective' children. The transfer would mean avoiding spending large sums on renovating the institution in Tuam, which was still identified as a fire hazard. But the County Manager warned that the institution was run 'by the Bon Secours Nuns under the jurisdiction of the Archbishop and they might not agree'.

In August 1959, a Dr O'Driscoll asked for a report on specific details relating to the home's operation over the past three years: a week's specimen diet, facilities for recreation, educational facilities, number of children born each year, number of admissions, number of adoptions and number of infants who died, as well as the daily cost of the institution.

On 10 October 1960, a Saturday, a group of medical officers, county managers and councillors discussed the 'allegations' made a year earlier by Dr O'Driscoll. (The records do not document any allegations by Dr O'Driscoll, merely requests for information.) The Visiting Committee was recorded as being 'quite satisfied' with how the home was being run. I thought of James Deeny's account of the wards in Bessborough that were immaculate and unimpeachable until Deeny peeled away the nappies of sick and potentially dying children.

In July 1960, a letter came from the Department of Health stating that the Minister for Health, Seán MacEntee, who fought in the GPO during the Easter Rising and whose brothers-in-law were influential members of the clergy, approved the transfer of mothers and children at St Mary's in Tuam to other institutions, and called for the home to be closed.

One of the main reasons for MacEntee's recommendation was

an estimate that it would cost £114,000 to improve conditions in the home and render it 'suitable'. It was cheaper to send the children to other institutions, which, as a result of a stated fall in the number of 'inmates', could provide accommodation for these children. The Minister's main concerns were 'unsatisfactory conditions in the Home, the high cost of bringing the Home up to modern standards and the fact that there is ample first class accommodation available for mothers and children in existing Institutions.'

At a County Council meeting in January 1961, the Minister's recommendation was met with resistance by some, most notably from the council's co-chair, Mark Killilea Sr, who was also a Fianna Fáil TD. As long as the home was located in Tuam, he said, 'the county has the benefit of the money spent there.'

The medical officer for the home, Dr Waldron, also opposed the closure. He argued that since the council had carried out 'desirable improvements' at the home and 'since the number of children accommodated there has fallen', it was in his opinion 'very comfortable' for the kids there. If the home was closed, there would be 'no such institution' for mothers and children in the West of Ireland. Waldron noted that the home 'also provides facilities for the Medical School of University College, Galway'. It is not clear exactly what Waldron meant by this, but the Commission of Investigation into the homes would later determine that the corpses of at least thirty-five infants – some or all of whom might have been stillborn – had been sent to the university for use as anatomical subjects.

Dr Waldron also noted that there were 'ten or twelve girls who have been there for many years whose only Home it is' – the domestics, like Julia – and who would have to leave if it closed.

The opposition of the TD and the doctor did not change the Minister's decision. The County Manager envisaged an ongoing decrease in numbers, and that 'the continued operation of the Home will become more uneconomic'. The Assistant County Manager stated that 'the Home still constitutes a serious fire hazard'. The engineers confirmed that the works carried out so far had not reduced that risk and 'in other circumstances' the Fire Officer 'would probably have condemned the Home as unfit for use for its purposes'. The Assistant County Manager added that 'the standard of comfort in the Home is not all that it should be'. The lack of central heating was a 'serious defect'.

As closure approached, there was difficulty finding adequate institutions for some of the Tuam children, particularly those described as 'mentally handicapped'. There was a report of a three-year-old who was 'removed from Tuam Home' to the mental asylum in Ballinasloe, and died shortly thereafter.

On the final night, Julia remembered walking out the gate with John Cunningham and Nurse Burke, the last to leave. All the children were gone already, sent away in batches, on minibuses or in ambulances, mostly to the Sacred Hearts at Sean Ross Abbey and Castlepollard. It took two days to send them all off. The mothers who had yet to complete their year of penitence were required to finish their terms elsewhere. There were cows and a farm at Sean Ross, she heard. The mothers worked the land. 'The nuns owned the place, not the council, as in Tuam.'

A year later, while working at the Grove, a hospital run by the Bon Secours in Tuam, Julia met an older man and was married. The nuns at the Grove were 'as natural as ourselves', unlike the nuns who ran the home. A beautiful-looking nun called Sister John Baptist, who worked in the home, left the congregation entirely because of what she saw there. 'They knew well that the home was a queer place, 'twas a rotten place,' she said. 'I feel a sense of shame that I did not create a war,' she said. 'But then again, what could I have done?'

In October 2018, more than a year after the test excavations found evidence of significant human remains on the site of the home, I attended a press conference at Government Buildings in which the Minister for Children, Katherine Zappone, announced the decision that the mass grave would be exhumed. The government had opted for the most extensive form of excavation, though the gardens of the surrounding homes would not be entered. Full DNA analysis would be carried out where possible.

A report released by Geoffrey Shannon, the State's Special Rapporteur for Child Protection, who sat on the panel alongside Zappone, had determined that the government was bound by international human rights law and the constitution to investigate whether the right to suitable burial had been observed. It was also bound to determine whether the children's right to life had been respected, and this would involve investigating and confirming the causes of death. There was no clear indication of how long the process would take. The estimated cost was between €6 and €13 million. The Bon Secours Sisters had already pledged €2.5 million towards the cost of the exhumation, at the government's request.

I asked Zappone if this would set a precedent for the other institutions. I expected her to dodge the question, to say they were focused on Tuam for now. But she indicated that it could set a precedent.

I walked out of the building feeling a strange sense of comfort – a feeling that the country could trust itself and that, finally, the right thing would be done.

The day after, I took the bus to Tuam. The trees were already stripped and hungry-looking in the disappearing sun, the long lines of low stone walls blotched with lichen. I noticed new housing developments on the edge of the town and thought of families moving here. An Eastern European man had told me that before he moved to Tuam for work he googled the place, and the first thing that came up were news stories about hundreds of children buried in an unmarked grave.

In the empty field beside the Tuam Coop Livestock Market, a lone donkey lay on its side. The car park of the cathedral was packed with schoolboys in navy blazers, some sucking at cigarettes against a wall. Girls in long school skirts and jumpers milled around on the other side. Beside the Presentation Sisters convent I started up a conversation with an 86-year-old nun who was wrapped up in a deep pink scarf and rainjacket, a walking stick in hand, though she stood very straight and steady. In all honesty, I was eager to talk to anyone who looked old.

I asked her if she was from Tuam.

'Not for long, I'll be dead soon,' she told me.

I asked her if she had heard the news about the exhumation of the burial site, and whether she remembered the home.

'We were enclosed, we wouldn't have known,' she said. 'Terrible, them buried on top of each other like that. We hear a lot about it nowadays.'

I wanted to speak to people living on the estate about how they felt now that the decision had been made. I had a rough map that Teresa Killeen-Kelly had drawn for me on a scrap of paper in her office, directing me to a woman's house backing on to the burial site. Teresa didn't even tell me the woman's name, just told me to go to the house.

I was wearing a bright yellow rainjacket and felt very much like the outsider I was, back in this place to take advantage of their news. Tight-knit communities must be wonderful in many ways, I thought, until you fall out of the fold. A man on his couch seemed to lock eyes on me as I passed his window. I walked until I reached the house indicated on the map.

A woman answered the door in her dressing gown; she was not expecting visitors, but she invited me into her living room and sat me on her couch. Her name was Jacqueline. She pointed out the window, between her shimmery pink drapes, to the surviving segment of the institution's old stone wall. Any time she sat in here watching TV it was lurking out there, a remnant of the dark past. On the other side of the house, the wall ran between her garden and the burial site itself. There was a crack in it and she believed that as soon as the digging started it was likely to collapse.

Jacqueline grew up on the estate and went to school with children from the home. The Mercy Sisters used to punish her for talking to them, but it didn't stop her. 'We used to get beaten for talking to the home children,' she told me. There were two girls she remembered. They were always made to sit at the back of the class and didn't have uniforms. They all wore the same brown coats. 'They did treat them different,' she said. 'As if they were dirt.' The children were told not to speak to them. In the summer, the nuns would put some of the cots outside and they could see the 'kideens' from the street. She was madly curious to see inside the place, beyond the walls, but when they were caught looking in she said a caretaker would close the gate or scare them away. 'It was sinful to look at the small ones,' she said. They were so wasted away it made her feel uneasy.

A few people apparently found bones while digging in their gardens at various times over the past decades. 'Not chicken bones either,' she said. Most of them just reburied what they found without thinking too much of it.

As we sat and talked, a friend of hers arrived. He explained how during the 1990s, when he was building a new shed in his garden, he found 'various bones' in the topsoil. He was used to butchering pigs and didn't think much about it. 'The whole place is a graveyard,' he said. 'That's what the name means.' He meant the name of the town: the Irish word for tomb is *tuama*.

Unlike some residents of the estate, Jacqueline believed the ground should be dug up and the bodies of the children accounted for if possible. 'They should have been buried properly,' she stressed. Her face had become strained and there was anger in her voice.

Out through her kitchen, we walked to the garden, the sky filled with crows. At the end of the garden there was a big gate like the type you see on farms, with long fat rungs you can climb over, bolted shut on one end. Beyond that was the entrance to the memorial garden.

On a nice day, Jacqueline didn't feel she could sit out with a cup of tea any more, or have people around to enjoy the garden. She would be worried what people would say.

Along the side of the old wall, she brought me to a spot that didn't seem marked in any way, but which she clearly knew from memory. 'My dog is buried there,' she said. 'They won't be digging there.' That was her only demand, her red line. When they buried the dog they made sure not to go down too far, worried about what might be brought up.

After I left Jacqueline's house I walked along the lane that passes beside her garden, opened the little gate and entered the odd-shaped patch of land that was to be excavated. On my previous visits it had been boarded up, and this was the first time I could step inside. The smell of turf smoke was in the air and the light was fading. I counted out steps along the edges of the area. Twenty steps along the wall perpendicular to the boundary along Jacqueline's house. Seventeen steps along the wall that separated the memorial garden from the children's playground. There were flowers laid at the foot of the Virgin Mary in the far corner, along with rosary beads, snow globes and angel figurines.

Later, walking away from the burial ground, I met a young man with a neck tattoo, sitting in his car. He told me that the children should be left there. His friend remembered when Famine bodies had been dug up on a nearby corner. He claimed to have photos on an old phone.

As I left the estate, another lanky young man in a grey tracksuit, holding a can of beer in one hand, stopped me.

I asked him about the children's remains, and he said he thought what the nuns did was wrong.

Then he asked, 'Are you single? Are you on Snapchat?'

The Assumption

The Feast of the Assumption is celebrated on the 15th of August. The assumption was the transportation of Mary to heaven. Not only did the Mother of God never commit original sin, she defied death. At the end of her earthly life, it was not just her soul, but her physical body, that was assumed into heavenly glory.

In the final hours of the Feast of the Assumption in 2018, towards the end of a blazing summer, I arrived in Knock, a pilgrimage site in County Mayo. The tiny village was put on the map on a Thursday evening in August 1879 when the Virgin Mary and other saints appeared to a young girl and a housekeeper, who ran to gather others to see. The witnesses then spent two hours in the pouring rain reciting the Rosary before the vision.

I went to Knock during the week of the Novena, one of the shrine's holiest and busiest times. The Archbishop of Tuam, Michael Neary, was giving Mass that evening. I had come from Tuam, where I'd stood in a steady downpour of rain waiting for the last bus. People sitting in a car parked across the road assured me it would come, and after half an hour it appeared, like a miracle. After an hour or so of driving through small towns and wide-open farmland, we arrived in Knock village.

A young man in a camouflage hoodie emblazoned with the words 'LIFE IS SACRED' was waiting to get on as I disembarked. The bells were already sounding for the evening's Mass. Crows were wheeling and squawking over the roof of the old St Mary's convent building, once home to the Daughters of Charity, where I had booked a room, the last one available in the whole nunnery-turned-hotel. I was taken to the tiny room in an extension of the original house; a miniature plastic well of holy water was stuck to the wall beside each door. The bed was narrow and the room plain, with the feel of a retirement home; I guessed that ageing nuns had lived here.

On the main road, shops sold all kinds of religious figurines and holy souvenirs. The Lady of Guadeloupe shop was run by Human Life International and gave out free pro-life information packs, its window displays showing off plastic foetuses for sale, and books on how to find the perfect husband or wife. When I was a teenager I had come to Knock once on a school trip and almost missed the bus home because I was busy rummaging in the shops, buying religious snow globes and shot glasses decorated with the figures of saints, eyeing up neon-glowing light-up icons of the Virgin Mary that I couldn't afford.

Archbishop Neary entered the basilica in an elaborate procession, followed by men in navy blazers and women dressed all in white, with veils and what looked like labcoats. These were the 'stewards' and the 'handmaids', voluntary workers at the shrine. One of the first announcements made during Mass was that their committee had voted that day to rebrand, and both men and women would now simply be known as volunteers. I wondered to myself if it had something to do with a certain TV show, adapted from a certain novel, about a misogynist dystopia.

The Tuam Cathedral choir was singing and Archbishop Neary was dressed in white robes, with his bishop's magenta skullcap perched atop his head. He spoke of the Assumption and of the Blessed Virgin Mary, the Immaculate Mother of God. There were thanks given for the power of God to gather his children together from all over the world through the Church and for the way faith gave people a sense of belonging and a sense of who they are. He waxed lyrical about the innate gifts of mothers and how they knew instinctively what was best for their child. These were simple ideas that, coming from an Irish Catholic bishop, carried a particular sting for me, after hearing so many testimonies of women who had been told they were not fit to mother, that they couldn't give a child the life they deserved, and of adoptees denied the basic knowledge of who gave birth to them.

After the Mass, the busy church emptied and hundreds of people filtered out into the night, lighting candles nestled in cardboard holders as they went. The sun had finally relented and it was dark outside. They carried the flickering lights as they joined a procession, chanting the Rosary aloud and walking along the Stations of the Cross, along a grassy slope. When the Stations of the Cross were finished and a final address given outside the Chapel of the Apparition, Archbishop Neary stood in the darkness as people came up to greet and thank him. I shook his hand and told him I had just come from Tuam and was writing about the homes.

He nodded his head and said, 'Okay.'

I told him I would be interested to talk to him about it. I mentioned that there were many adoptees and mothers I had spoken to who still had strong faith.

'Okay, okay, okay,' he answered each time. The lines on his face seemed exaggerated in the shadows. He looked exhausted, and guarded. He advised me to email his secretary, and turned away.

The day after, in St John's Rest and Care Centre, next to the basilica, there was a talk about using children's liturgies as a way to revive the Church. The idea, it seemed, was that the children would bring their parents back to the pews. I sat for an hour listening to the enthusiastic presentation, thinking about the Church's dismal record in child protection and its treatment of families that didn't fit its mould. Afterwards, I took a seat at the tables beside a hole in the wall from which ladies in aprons and paper hats served tea and sandwiches. I sat sipping coffee that tasted like water that had been used to soak a burned pan.

Soon the others cleared out, hurrying to Mass, save for one man sitting on one of the long benches amongst the rows of tables, where pilgrims came to slurp their tea and refuel on sandwiches and biscuits. The hall was empty now and this man was taking a break between shifts. His sandwiches were home-made, hidden in a crinkled nest of tin foil, next to a mug filled with milk. The shiny rectangular badge on the right lapel of his navy blazer had his name printed on it. He was a Knock steward, volunteering at the shrine, helping during Mass and shepherding pilgrims into the church. His navy tie was branded with the shrine's emblem in the Virgin Mary's signature powder blue. He wore grey trousers with a faint pin-stripe, the same colour as his moustache, and sturdy shoes.

I had walked over to his table to ask him if he knew where the Bon Secours burial plot might be, showing him a graveyard listing on my phone that detailed the number of the plot in the new cemetery.

He shook his head, unsure where exactly it might be. He seemed like a kind man and was happy to talk.

I told him I was writing about the mother-and-baby homes and had just come from Tuam.

'I was born there,' he told me. 'In the home.'

I asked if I could join him at the table and if I could take notes as we spoke.

He asked me to use the name Jim, rather than his real one, because many of the people he volunteered with at the shrine did not know his story. He hadn't even told his own children. I was conscious that we were the only people chatting in the canteen, but he seemed at ease.

He had always known that the people he called mammy and daddy were foster parents, but they raised him as their son. Jim used to shave his foster father, pulling the wrinkled skin taut so the blade could run smoothly. The ritual brought them close. Jim shaved the only father he ever knew half an hour before he died. He inherited the small farm and had lived there ever since.

Before he was married, he told his fiancée the story of his adoption, fearing that she might take the news badly. 'I was sort of ashamed of myself,' he said. But she understood and told him she loved him.

Jim lived in the Tuam institution until he was around six years old. His memories of his time there were few and fragmented. At dinner, there would be a gang of lads around his age and they would all be sitting down at a big table to eat. When it was time for bed, the plates would be snatched away from underneath their noses. The nuns demanded obedience and gave out punishments. 'If it wasn't words it was a slap across the jaw.' He remembered other boys being struck and beaten by the nuns. He remembered being afraid of the nuns. There was a yard where he would some-times play. He didn't remember ever going to school while living in the home.

Sometimes people came in to take kids away. One couple stuck in his mind, because they pointed, saying, 'We'll take this lad.'

He was between six and seven years old, he figures, when some-one came and picked him out. He was boarded out to a farming family. The family had a dog, a little collie, which terrified him at first. He had never seen a dog before. He was given his own room and his own bed, a privacy and comfort he had never known before. 'I had a great life with them,' he told me. He went to dances when he got older and sometimes would walk a girl home. His friends had money when he had none. 'I was never referred to as a home baby,' he said; but then he thought back to his school days and remembered there was the odd bully who would tell people he was from the home.

When he was in his early thirties, Jim went to a priest to ask for help searching for records that might help him find his mother. He was told to leave that subject alone. 'I said, Father, you were never in my position,' he remembered; but the priest refused to help.

For more than a decade, Jim worked as a labourer for Galway County Council. When the priest couldn't give him any answers, the council was the next authority that he turned to. He told them he wanted to know where his mother was. A woman who worked there, since retired, helped him obtain some basic and non-identifying information. He found out that his mother was only sixteen when she gave birth to him. After doing her time in the home, their records showed, she went to England.

In 2014, when Jim first heard about the burial site in Tuam, the news made him think of his daughter. His words came slow then, catching in his throat, and I noticed his eyes had filled with tears. His daughter was stillborn. He lifted his large, fleshy hands to make a cradle. He was showing me the way he held his dead child, his eyes cast down towards the shadow of where she once lay. His thick hands, the kind that were always freckled from being outdoors, seemed like they could lift the weight of the world.

'I held her in my arms,' he whispered. 'When we put that little baby into the ground . . .' His words failed him. The silence of the canteen enveloped him. There was no chatter audible, even from the women on their break in the kitchen, in their hairnets and aprons. I was conscious of the fact that people he knew could walk in and wonder why his eyes were full of tears as he spoke to a stranger. He told me where they buried his stillborn daughter, in a tiny coffin. He explained how it comforted him to be able to visit her grave.

The Pope was due to visit Knock the following week. In the local chipper, warm with the smell of hot oil, I had listened to a woman behind the counter whispering with a customer about the cost of the visit and the fact His Holiness was only coming for an hour. She seemed to think it was a waste. Security had been stalking around the town for months in preparation, and attendance had been low for the Novena week because people figured the whole place would be on lockdown. Jim would be working as a steward at the shrine that day, in the presence of the Pope when he said the Angelus and delivered Mass. At the same time, there was a vigil planned at the site of the home in Tuam.

As a devoted Catholic and a man who had dedicated much of his life to the Church, he felt conflicted. 'I believe in the priests and the Church,' he said. He didn't want to rock the boat. He wasn't even keen on lay people giving Communion. But if he wasn't signed up for a shift at Knock that day, he would have chosen – despite the presence of the Pope – to go to the vigil in Tuam. If he got the chance to shake the Pope's hand, he would tell him: 'Look for my mother.'

After he drained his mug of milk and finished his sandwiches, not a crumb escaping from the nest of tin foil that he scrunched up into a shiny ball, Jim led me out to the car park beside the canteen. A compartment in the driver's-side door of his van was stuffed with folded-up documents, a blue plastic hair brush and a small can of Jungle mosquito spray. He fished out a piece of paper from the mix and gently unfolded it.

It was a photocopy of his birth certificate, registered in the district of Tuam. His birth date was in June 1945 and his place of birth was recorded as 'children's home'. In the boxes for the name and dwelling place of father and the father's profession, there was only the wide slash of a pen. Between the two boxes was his mother's full name. 'Bina Rabbitte present at birth, children's home, Tuam,' another box read. Jim kept it with him everywhere he drove, hoping that at some point he would have the courage to approach Catherine Corless and ask her to help him find his mother. Everyone else had failed him. Some day, he hoped to go to her and ask for her help in finding out where his mother was, whether she was still alive, or buried somewhere herself. 'I'd die a happy man if I knew,' he said.

After speaking to Jim, I headed to the cemetery near the shrine in Knock, hoping to find the plot where the Bon Secours Sisters were buried. Up on top of a hill overlooking the basilica, there were several fields of graves. In the first graveyard, a sign notified passers-by that witnesses to the apparition were buried there. The only person around was a large man standing awkwardly by the gate, rocking slightly. As I came nearer his eyes were fixed on me and his hand moved to the crotch of his trousers, groping at himself. I passed him as I made my way into the graveyard, and then hesitated. I worried he might follow me in, and even though it was broad daylight I wondered if it was safe. Then I saw another man coming down a path towards me. He was old, sporting a blue jumper and yellow-tinted glasses, and he was smiling. I asked him where the Bon Secours plot might be, but he didn't know.

I ventured further up the hill and eventually found the Bon Secours plot. A stout statue of Our Lady in flowing veils, her hands clasped in prayer, stood barefoot on a rock, the grey concrete plinth below reading 'Bon Secours' in large, deeply engraved capital letters, in a crude font. The plot was on two levels and took up the space of around eight regular graves. There were two headstones either side of the statue, thin slabs of plain concrete. The details were squeezed tightly together, just names and death dates. It looked like an engraved spreadsheet. On one of the slabs, the names of seven nuns, who died between 2005 and 2017, took up only half the space. On the other there were twelve names, from 1948 to 2001. These were likely the twelve nuns re-interred from where they had been originally buried on the grounds of the Grove Hospital, in Tuam. There were several bunches of synthetic flowers on the gravel surface.

I thought about Jim and his quest for answers. Jim's mother was only sixteen when she had him and he wondered whether he had brothers or sisters out there. When he thought about that, a fear gripped him, that he might have a sibling who died, who might be buried in the unmarked grave at Tuam. 'Thanks be to God I was one of the lucky ones,' he had told me in the van. 'But she might have had another baby landed in there.' His eyes filled with tears again, brushing them away clumsily with his big hand. 'I'd dearly love to know, had I a brother or sister?' If he won a million euro, he would give it up to know if he had a sibling, even if they were long dead.

He had visited the graveyard near Maam Cross, but never found a headstone that matched his mother's name. He often drove through Tuam, on his way to other places or on his own quiet pilgrimage. Next to the birth certificate that always travelled with him he also kept a stone that he had taken from the little lane in front of the gravesite, beside the playground, on the old grounds of the home.

On the train back to Dublin that evening, I looked out at the fields aglow in soft evening light, cows lying down in huddles.

Across the aisle from me, a grandmother was holding a moon-faced baby boy by the pants as he clambered across the table, trying to reach the phone his mother was typing on.

'He's a handful,' I said to her, laughing.

'Like a bag of eels,' she nodded.

The baby turned his attention on me then, wide-eyed and gurgling. His four-year-old sister was sitting beside them in a pink top, directing a constant stream of chirpy questions at her granny.

The granny pointed out a field in the distance and told her, 'My daddy grew up there.'

The girl's brow furrowed. 'Where's your daddy now?' she asked.

'He's in heaven,' her granny replied.

'He died?' she asked.

The woman with the refreshments trolley gave the baby some plastic cup lids to play with, and gooed at him.

I tried to imagine the rows of cots in the dormitories of the home, the babies raised in an institution, without a loved one there tending to them every moment. Children were sponges, soaking up every subtle change, learning and adapting with a fierce speed, consumed by a rabid hunger to take everything in, grab it with chubby little fists, mouth it and taste it and throw it away in order to pick up the next new thing. Every experience was momentous.

I thought of the children, like Jim, who stayed in the home until he was school-aged, with no real memories other than being smacked and running around in a yard. Children who never knew what a dog was. Children who were grown now and didn't know who their mothers were, who stayed awake at night wondering if they had a sister or brother buried in a septic tank.

12.

'You're here because nobody wants you'

In the black-and-white snapshot, the frame packed with figures, a column of women file through a Dublin street. They are flanked on both sides by straight-backed gardaí, and a priest is visible at the front of the procession. The women, who are inmates of the Magdalen laundry in Seán MacDermott Street, wear white veils. Two of them, near the front, are carrying a flower-covered plinth, on which stands a statue of the Virgin Mary.

The photograph, whose date and provenance are unknown, was discussed in the McAleese report on the Magdalen laundries, in a section dealing with the question of whether the Garda Síochána prevented women from escaping from the institutions. The report quoted a peculiar account of the photo provided to the committee by the Garda.

> The photograph was subsequently investigated by Gardaí and it was discovered that this is not exclusively a Magdalene procession but a community procession attended by lay people and members of the Children of Mary, a lay Catholic group. Some of the women in the photograph are residents of the Sean McDermott St Asylum, however it is a May procession. The women are carrying the bedecked statue of Our Lady as they have the honour of doing so. The Gardaí are in attendance in veneration of Our Lady and for no other reason.

Similar assurances were provided by the priest who is visible at the head of the procession, and who was interviewed by the Garda for their submission to the McAleese committee. This priest, unnamed in the report, was chaplain to the Seán MacDermott Street laundry in the 1960s. Apparently keen to dispel any idea that the women were treated as prisoners, he described an outing he brought some of them on.

> So I went down to 30 of them and I said 'I'll take you to the pictures provided you don't let me down. That we'll go, enjoy the picture and com[e] back'. I said 'it's on your honour'. And the Sisters agreed on my honour! God if it happened today! I walked up Sean McDermot Street, collar and coat the works. At that time . . . with 30 women!

★

In June 2018, in the courtyard of Áras an Uachtaráin, a soldier stood poker-straight in an immaculate green army uniform, ready to meet a fleet of buses as they pulled up at the President's stately home in the Phoenix Park. When more than 200 women emerged from the buses in a stream of colour, the gaggle of press photographers snapped furiously, capturing images that vividly depicted how much had changed in the relationship between the Magdalen women and the State.

The first Magdalen survivor to get off the bus – silver-haired, in a turquoise dress suit – led the way carefully across the cobblestones, leaning on a cane. Others pumped the air with fists and cheered, even while grasping sticks and strollers. They moved in flashes of silver pumps and lilac heels, salmon-pink linen, little black dresses, floral skirts. Each of the women was allowed to bring a guest, and most came with a family member or a friend by their side. A man in a kilt and bow tie stood looking impossibly proud.

'Penitents' was what the Sisters called these women, but Gabrielle O'Gorman always refused to be a penitent. In the courtyard of the Áras, she wore a sleeveless coral jumpsuit with a dramatic frill in the front, a diamanté choker around her neck, and electric-blue shades perched on her head.

Gabrielle was born in St Patrick's mother-and-baby home in 1945, to a woman who grew up in an industrial school after Gabrielle's grandmother died in childbirth. Not long after returning home from the institution, her mother was thrown out for being pregnant. Gabrielle stayed in St Patrick's with her mother until she was four years old, though they weren't allowed to bond. Gabrielle described a distinct memory of lying with other nappyless toddlers on a sheet soaked in their own urine under the big window panes of the conservatory, where children were put to get some daylight. She remembered children with 'dropped rectums' because they'd been left to sit on little enamel potties for so long.

At four, Gabrielle was sent to St Philomena's orphanage and residential institution in Stillorgan, south Dublin, also run by the Daughters of Charity; it was a holding centre for children bound for industrial schools. Her mother left for England, coming back to visit her daughter once a year. Gabrielle believes her mother wanted to try to keep her somehow, but wishes she had been adopted, to save her from a childhood in institutions. She was raised by the nuns, never going to a proper school, spending most of her time cleaning. At twelve, she was sent to Lakelands in Sandymount, the same industrial school her mother was raised in, run by the Sisters of Charity. They were taught nothing about sex other than that they should keep their purity. The first time she saw a girl menstruating, she thought she was dying.

One of the many cruel ironies of the shame-industrial complex was that girls who had learned nothing of sex in the institutions were more likely to end up pregnant out of wedlock, and thus to be re-institutionalized.

When the girls in Lakelands reached the age of sixteen, the State no longer provided capitation payments for them, and the Sisters of Charity sent them away. Gabrielle went to London. 'The best thing was to get out of Ireland,' she told me. 'We had no choice here, people didn't believe you, you were nothing.' But a sixteen-year-old girl with little exposure to the real world could hardly live independently in London, and so Gabrielle found herself living in a convent. When she started dating a boy, becoming more free and sure of herself, her mother brought her back to Dublin to meet her grandfather, who was a lodge keeper at the Goldenbridge industrial school. She was told to get down on her knees and pray. She returned to working for the Daughters of Charity at St Philomena's. One night, she stayed out with a boy. The relationship was not sexual, but when she came back to the convent in the morning, two nuns and a fat-bellied garda were waiting with her case already packed. They told her she was being taken away for her own safety.

Two nuns took her to the Magdalen asylum on Seán MacDermott Street, operated by the Sisters of Our Lady of Charity of Refuge, which had capacity for 150 inmates. They tried to put her to work, but every day she stood her ground and refused. She had nothing to be penitent for. The older women who worked in the steam-choked laundry prayed constantly and seemed brainwashed, and she did not want to become one of them.

Gabrielle refused to wear the rough fabric uniform, and would approach any handyman who came into the place, hoping to convince him to help her leave. After six weeks she managed to escape, pulling another girl along with her, knocking over the older women trying to stop them, bursting out through the laundry door. The other girl brought them to an aunt's house for shelter, but the aunt called the guards and they were dragged back to the laundry.

The same two Sisters who had brought her to Seán MacDermott Street now came for her again, driving her all the way to the Good Shepherd laundry in Limerick. She was forced to wear a uniform and her name was stripped from her: inside the walls she was now called Stella. The Sisters repeatedly tried to demean and shame her. One day, a nun made her kneel down and told her, 'You're here because nobody wants you.'

After two and a half years she was sent to Dublin, where nuns met her at the station and set her up with a job in a hospital, but she didn't last long. She fled to England and remained there. The nuns would always have control of her in this country, she felt; and if anyone knew she was once in a Magdalen laundry, she would suffer from the stigma of that.

Gabrielle returned to Ireland in 1993 for a vigil for 155 Magdalen women exhumed from the grounds of the High Park laundry, operated by the Sisters of Our Lady of Charity of Refuge. Mary Raftery told the story of the exhumation in a 2011 article in *The Guardian*. 'The nuns had been dabbling on the stock exchange,' she wrote. When their investments turned sour they had to sell a portion of their lands to a developer. 'The snag was that the land contained a mass grave.' The nuns and the developer agreed to split the cost of exhuming, cremating and re-burying the remains of the inmates buried there. When the grave was opened, it was discovered that it contained not the 133 bodies for which the nuns had records, but 155. The Sisters had no names for 45 of the women, except for their institutional names: Magdalen of the Good Shepherd, or Magdalen of Lourdes. Justice for Magdalenes Research subsequently found the names of 106 more High Park women, buried in unmarked graves in Glasnevin.

Inside the Áras, Gabrielle danced down a corridor lined with portraits of former Presidents. A bronze bust of de Valera looked at us cross-eyed. Walking out to the gardens, through the lavish reception rooms, I bumped into Mary Merritt, a short and determined woman with a glossy dark bob. At eighty-seven years old, she was thrilled that her experience was being officially recognized, but also painfully aware that there were countless other women who never got to see it. 'It's a shame it took so long to happen,' she said, running her hand over a book on one of the tables. She wanted to write her own memoir, but so much was still unanswerable. 'I don't even know who my mother is, it just says I was born in the workhouse,' she told me.

Mary was raised by Mercy nuns in an industrial school and made the legal ward of the nun in charge. She laboured for them on their farmland. When she was seventeen, she was caught stealing apples because she was hungry and sent to the Magdalen laundry at High Park. She remained there for fourteen years. The one time she escaped, she turned to a priest for help. The priest raped her. With no understanding of sex, all she could tell the nuns was that he had undressed and hurt her. When she discovered that the priest had made her pregnant, the nuns sent her to St Patrick's on the Navan Road. 'We know what happened to you,' a nun told her. 'You keep your mouth shut.' Her daughter was taken for adoption, and Mary spent a year in the institution before being sent back to the laundry again. Then one day they put her out. She found a job in a laundrette, eventually moving to England and meeting the man she would marry. Inside the warmly lit room of the Áras, a harp lilting away nearby, she was defiant. 'I gave them hell,' she said, her smile tight with fury.

In a big marquee out in the garden, I spotted a woman I'd met before. Jane Conlon was born to an unmarried mother and sent to St Patrick's before being fostered out. She spent time in Seán Mac-Dermott Street laundry in 1984 when she was barely nineteen years old, after being abused for years by a priest, the serial abuser Bill Carney, who followed her from institution to institution, all of them run by the Sisters of Our Lady of Charity of Refuge. Jane took me by the hand and led me to meet a few other women. One of them – only forty-something, with streaks of purple in her hair – told me that her father had sexually abused her and that she was put in a Magdalen laundry because of it. Magdalen women often say therapists are shocked when they hear their stories. Shock can sometimes share the same face as disbelief. In this room, there was no shock between the women, only recognition.

At a table towards the very back I spotted Mary Gaffney, who had travelled up from Cork for the day. Then a hush fell over the room and eyes turned to the stage.

'Share your experiences with each other,' President Michael D. Higgins urged the women. 'Quite frankly, it will help us all in Ireland.' He spoke about Magdalen survivors reclaiming their rightful place in history. Their stories had been buried, denied, distorted, deliberately forgotten, and 'even erroneously justified' by those who preferred 'an accommodating amnesia'. The President said they had been failed by the religious orders, by the State and by a society that actively colluded in their incarceration. 'The treatment of vulnerable citizens in our industrial and reformatory schools, in the Magdalen laundries and in mother-and-baby homes represents a deep stain on Ireland's past,' he said. 'A stain we can only regard today with great shame, profound regret and horror.' Around the room, some of the women had tears running down their faces. 'I apologize to you, survivors of the Magdalen regime.'

After the reception with the President, the Magdalen survivors travelled to the city centre for a dinner at the Mansion House, as part of a two-day event called Dublin Honours Magdalenes. The fleet of buses received a Garda escort; some of the women told me that it made them feel nervous. When they alighted from the buses, they were met by a welcoming party holding home-made signs that read 'The women of Ireland salute you'. They walked through the crowd – beaming, gobsmacked and vindicated, their cheeks wet with tears. Grey-haired men stood openly crying, clapping them on. Women pressed their faces against the railings to serenade them with 'Molly Malone' as they made their way inside. Even for those who had never left Ireland, this was a kind of homecoming, to a country that accepted them and embraced them. A country that believed them.

The banquet hall of the Mansion House was set up for an evening of entertainment. The Lord Mayor of Dublin, Mícheál Mac Donncha, spoke of the closure of the laundry on Seán MacDermott Street, shut down because it was no longer commercially viable: the domestic washing machine did more to abolish these institutions than the State ever did. He mentioned that it was the birthday of James Connolly, a hero of the Rising who did not die for a State founded on abuse and the robbery of children. 'No more, no more,' he urged, to loud applause.

Watching the Lord Mayor speak, I thought about a journal article I'd read by Peter Murray. It tells the story of Mary E. Murphy, a sixteen-year-old worker at the Jacobs biscuit factory who was charged with boxing another girl in the face and calling her a 'scab' during the 1913 Lockout. Murphy was sentenced to one month at the High Park reformatory, on the same grounds as the Magdalen laundry, a place of detention for minors since the Children's Act of 1908. Connolly was reported as saying that 'if there was any shame left among the custodians of our public morality, the clergy', they would denounce Mary Murphy's detention at High Park from every pulpit. The Sisters of Our Lady of Charity of Refuge asked the *Irish Times* to clarify that the reformatory was as distinct from the Magdalen institution as a hospital is from a prison. Reformatory windows that overlooked the Magdalen grounds were deliberately glazed to obscure the fallen women.

James Larkin, too, launched into a defence of Miss Murphy – at the expense of her fellow High Park inmates. In London's Albert Hall, he was reported to have urged his audience:

> Think of the statesmen that would send a pure, clean-minded, clean-souled girl of sixteen to spend a week's holiday with those who had forgotten their race, their sex and their soul. Think of a Christian Government [hisses] who had put her there that she might be soiled, and that in years to come people might say she had been in a home for fallen women – the Magdalene Asylum.

Mary Murphy's father visited his daughter at High Park, and she told him that inmates of the reformatory attended chapel at the same time as the Magdalen women. 'I would rather see my daughter in Siberia than in such a place,' he said.

On the second day of the Dublin Honours Magdalenes event, I joined a group of survivors packed into another coach, for a trip to High Park. After a lurching sharp turn up the road to the old convent grounds, a building site loomed into view. Someone said there were still sixteen women in the nursing home on the grounds, women who had 'never seen the outside'.

Respond, a housing organization connected with the Franciscan Brothers, have their offices in High Park. They also took over another convent building, owned by the Sisters of Charity, in Waterford, and operated housing for Cura, the pro-life crisis pregnancy agency. In the midst of a worsening housing crisis, as the State used hotel rooms and B&Bs for emergency accommodation, High Park became the first 'family hub', operated in partnership with Dublin City Council.

We walked into the old chapel; the women who once worked in the laundry at High Park still knew their way. We dovetailed with mothers and children living in the emergency accommodation. A young boy in a school sports uniform sat next to his mum, a blonde young woman in a summer dress with a tattoo on her thigh. Light filtered through elaborate stained-glass windows behind us.

A spokesperson for Respond stumbled a little through his speech. The organization was planning 101 apartments on the site. 'High Park has a bright future,' he said. 'We will never forget you or its past.'

One of the women living in the homeless accommodation then addressed the Magdalen survivors. 'We walk in your footsteps daily,' she said. 'No matter what we've been through, it's nothing near what you suffered. Being strong is the only option you've got.'

The lane that runs behind the old Magdalen laundry on Seán Mac-Dermott Street was empty, the tiled white cross on its outside wall still intact. The old fan vents loomed on top of the wall of what was once the laundry room. The sound of a choir singing was hanging in the air.

It was late August 2018, and the Pope was arriving. I was arriving too, by the back lanes, avoiding security blockades to reach Seán MacDermott Street. The newspapers over the previous weeks had suggested that Pope Francis might stop by the former laundry during his tour of Dublin, en route to the Pro-Cathedral nearby.

There were crowds in Seán MacDermott Street, but they were not gathered outside the old convent door, with the carved faces of the Virgin and child above the arch. They were clustered a short distance down the street, opposite the church where the bones of Matt Talbot lie, a Dublin man sainted for beating his addiction to the drink. A big sign advertised the Shrine of the Venerable Matt

Talbot. Across the road, there was nothing to acknowledge what women endured behind the walls of the laundry. The building, owned by Dublin City Council, was unmarked and vacant. The back of the property was being used to store building materials; I'd been in there, wearing a hard hat and steel-capped boots, with a woman from the County Council, which was planning to sell it to a Japanese hotel chain. (Shortly after the Pope's visit, in the face of opposition, the council voted not to sell the property; and in June 2019 the council voted to create a 'site of conscience' there.)

The street was expectant and tense. People who grew up in the area told me that, back in 1979, Pope John Paul II was meant to visit this area but never did. People still nursed the slight.

Mary Kelly, a sixty-year-old woman in a white T-shirt that said 'I ♥ Pope Francis', remembered going to the laundry when she was a kid, seeing the women inside. Local historian Terry Fagan was there, a man who often shared stories about the heroes in the community who helped children escape the industrial schools. His friend Christy told me about a friend's uncle or grand-uncle who put two children in the convent when he couldn't support them. When he went back, a few years later, to bring them home, only one was there.

Someone else said, 'No one listened to the working-class people. The working-class people knew what was done behind the walls of these institutions.'

Then the papal motorcade arrived. It sped past the door of the Magdalen laundry. Outside the church, the Pope shook hands with the mostly elderly people waiting. Among them was the mother of the new Lord Mayor of Dublin. She told me she also used to bring her laundry to the Magdalens and that she still lay awake some nights thinking about that.

In white robes and skullcap, the Pope then mounted the Popemobile, waving through the bulletproof glass as he sped off down the street.

13.

Churchmen

In the summer of 2018, as the visit of Pope Francis grew closer, I wondered if the Holy Father knew about the two men of God – one a priest, the other a bishop – who had been tasked with entertaining a vast crowd of young people at Ballybrit racecourse in Galway in 1979, as the helicopter carrying Pope John Paul II approached. Both men were later exposed for having secret children with unmarried women. Both had preached the Church's teaching on sexual morality while living as hypocrites.

Father Michael Cleary, the celebrity singing priest, was a tall and charismatic man who went on TV and radio condemning contraception and abortion. He talked about how 'there's a cross to be carried in Christian life' which meant he had to 'restrain' his 'sexual appetite'. In reality, he had been in a sexual relationship with his housekeeper for a decade.

In 1967, after a performance, Father Cleary met a seventeen-year-old girl called Phyllis Hamilton, survivor of sexual abuse within her family home, who had been put through a religious-run orphanage and a psychiatric institution. In the book she wrote about her relationship with Father Cleary, Hamilton described the first night he kissed her, and the time he masturbated in front of her on a couch and then exchanged vows with her, claiming they would not be married in the eyes of God until their relationship was consummated. She didn't know what 'consummated' meant, and so he explained that they had to have 'full penetrative sex'. She described sex as 'a small price to pay for the feeling of being loved for the first time in my life'.

The first time Hamilton became pregnant, Cleary sent her to a doctor in Waterford for a pregnancy test, then to a gynaecologist in

Dublin, and then to a friend of his in London. While in London she found work, but she soon returned to Ireland, and for the rest of her pregnancy she lived, along with two other expectant mothers, in Cleary's parochial house on Griffith Avenue, in Dublin, where the priest had set up a kind of informal mother-and-baby home. At least some of the women who stayed there, Hamilton later wrote, were referred to Father Cleary by Ally, a Catholic agency that helped to place women who were pregnant out of wedlock in accommodation before they gave birth. Not long after having her first child, Hamilton found Father Cleary having sex with another woman who had stayed in the house when pregnant.

After Hamilton gave birth, Cleary performed the christening. Hamilton was then driven in a car by a friend of Cleary's to Temple Hill, where she handed her son over to a nun. She later recalled that everyone around her at the time was saying she was unfit to be a mother, and she felt she had no control. She immediately wanted her baby back and rang to ask if she could visit, but was told she was a 'selfish little bitch' and that her son was already with a family. This was before she had signed away her rights to the baby, and initially she refused to sign, but Cleary threatened to take the baby and disappear. He brought her to sign the papers.

Hamilton kept the second baby she had with Father Cleary. She was officially his live-in housekeeper, and was considered to be just another unmarried mother with her son. Cleary even brought her to collect the unmarried mother's allowance. She became pregnant a third time, after being raped by a trainee priest. This time she went to the US to give birth, and her daughter was adopted.

The other famous churchman who was on stage with Father Cleary at Ballybrit in 1979 was the Bishop of Galway, Eamonn Casey. Casey was an unusually prominent and influential member of the hierarchy, and co-founder of the Catholic charity Trócaire, whose Easter flat-pack cardboard boxes I remember assembling and filling with coins as a kid.

At the beginning of the 1970s, while Bishop of Kerry, Casey had had a relationship with a distant cousin of his, an American woman called Annie Murphy. She became pregnant, and after the pregnancy started showing, Casey introduced her to people as 'an American in a spot of trouble', as if he was doing a charitable thing by allowing her to stay with him. A social worker at the Rotunda Hospital placed Murphy with a family in the city. After she gave birth in the Rotunda, she came under pressure from Casey to choose adoption. The social worker advised her to go to St Patrick's on the Navan Road, describing it as 'a home for unmarried mothers' where she could make up her mind about adoption. She clung to a desperate hope that Casey would change his mind, that he could somehow be with her and help her raise their son.

Reading Annie Murphy's memoir of these events, I thought back to my conversation with Sister Éabha in Henrietta Street. Sister Éabha told me that on at least three occasions that she could recall while working at St Patrick's, she had been quietly told that the father of the baby to be born was a priest. She also recalled another Sister telling her that Bishop Casey had been in one evening, and that he had walked down the corridor to sit in a chair in her office. 'He was so natural,' the Sister told her. It did not occur to Sister Éabha at the time that the Bishop was there to visit – and, perhaps, to apply pressure to – the mother of his own child. When the scandal broke eighteen years later, she was very upset to learn that Casey's child had been born in the institution where she worked. I asked her what she felt when she heard that women were coming into St Patrick's carrying babies who had been fathered by priests, and what did she say about it, if anything. She told me that she put it to the back of her mind. 'What were they about?' she thought. But she accepted it and went on with her work.

What was Bishop Casey doing in St Patrick's mother-and-baby home? In her book, Annie Murphy wrote that it was on her fourth day at St Patrick's that Bishop Casey visited, the Sisters 'practically gobbling him up as they knelt to kiss his ring and "My Lord" him'. She was in the dowdy dress she had been given to wear, while Casey was in episcopal splendour, 'talking charmingly to the

Sisters as if they were mental defectives'. She figured the Sisters thought he was a marvellous man to come all that way to visit a fallen woman. 'How were they to know he had come from Kerry to force his mistress to give up his son?'

She described St Patrick's as a black-steepled building behind stone walls, accessed through a wrought-iron gate. 'It was a prison,' she wrote. 'I had slept with Eamonn month after month without any sense of guilt, but now I was, yes, ashamed.' Pregnant women seemed to be endlessly on their knees polishing the floors under the watch of smirking pictures of the Virgin Mary, 'who had got a child without you-know-what'. In the yellow-painted nursery, the babies lay in iron cots painted white, dressed in white gowns. When a bell rang, the mothers knew they were allowed to go see their babies.

Murphy remembered one elderly nun, Sister Ignatius, who came up to one of the pregnant women polishing the floors and told her to take a rest. The Sister then got down on her hands and knees to start polishing the floor herself. Another nun hissed at her to get up, that she was setting a bad example. But Ignatius carried on. 'I had done an unforgivable thing: lumped all the nuns together,' Murphy wrote. 'That nun must have been under a Gestapo-like discipline for fifty years and she had kept her freedom.'

Murphy was hospitalized twice during her stay at St Patrick's, the first time for an infection and the second time for deep-vein thrombosis in her leg. She received no medical attention at the institution; on both occasions, friends brought her to hospital. On the second occasion, a doctor who was also a family friend told her that it was the Irish view that children without fathers were better off adopted. He also told her that it was not medically advisable for her to have another child. She had still not made up her mind about adoption, and now she had reason to believe that this could be her last chance to be a mother. After she recovered, she had Casey drive her to the US embassy so that their son could be added to her passport. Then she flew home with the boy to her family in the States.

In 1993, on the *Late Late Show*, Annie Murphy sat wearing a neutral jacket and a light pink scarf as audience members picked apart the book she had written, claiming she was a liar, that another man was the father of her son, that she had smuggled condoms into Ireland. She was unflappable, standing over her story. 'If your son is half as good a man as his father, he won't be doing too badly,' Gay Byrne said as the interview came to an end. 'I'm not so bad either, Mr Byrne,' she said, to scattered applause.

In 1975, the year after Annie Murphy gave birth to Bishop Casey's child, Casey spoke at the national conference of Cherish, an organization set up and run by unmarried mothers to support women in their situation, of which he was an early patron. At the time, the chairperson of Cherish, Maura O'Dea, estimated that more than half of Irish women who became pregnant outside of wedlock were rejected by their families. 'If the parents could only be got to act in a sympathetic and responsible manner, the hurt to many an unmarried mother and her child could be greatly lessened,' Casey said at the event. 'The bitterness resulting from rejection has caused permanent damage to many a girl.' He asked people to consider the effect of the father's absence.

In 2019 it emerged that Casey, who died in 2017, had faced multiple allegations of child sexual abuse, including an allegation brought in 2005 by his own niece, who said he raped her and abused her for a decade from the age of five. At least two other women accused Casey of abusing them when they were children; one of them received compensation from the State's redress board and the other a settlement through a High Court case, which was in process when Casey died. It has also recently been confirmed that two dioceses were aware of additional allegations of sexual abuse against Casey, dating back to the 1950s.

Long before these latest revelations emerged, we knew about how the Church in Ireland (and elsewhere) generally treated clerical abusers: it moved them from parish to parish, allowed them continued access to vulnerable people and children, and didn't inform the civil authorities of what it knew or suspected. As with the Church's treatment of women pregnant out of wedlock and their children, the priority was secrecy. But whereas women and children suffered for secrecy, male abusers benefited from it.

My visit to the diocesan house in Ennis, as described in Chapter 3, was shadowed by something disturbing I had heard from a reliable source: that the diocesan archivist there had been convicted of sexual abuse.

I was uncertain about whether I should confront the archivist with what I'd heard about his past. This man had spoken frankly about institutional abuse in the Church. He had introduced himself simply as Joe. When I asked him his full name, he told me it was Joe Summerville.

When I finished in the archives, Summerville drove me to the train station. The hospitality of Summerville and Father Nash, their willingness to speak so openly and to allow access to the archives, felt meaningful, a break from the silence. But I couldn't stop wondering about what I'd been told. I googled the name Joseph Summerville, and found reports about a man of that name who had been convicted in 1996 for sexually abusing a teenaged boy while working as a school chaplain in Tuam in the late 1980s. He had been defrocked by the Church, and served four years in prison.

During the same online search, I also came across an article by a Joseph Summerville in the Catholic magazine *The Furrow* in 1983. Summerville criticized the possessive way priests spoke about believers, and he embraced the concept of 'Pobal Dé' – the people of God – in preference to the 'clericalist mould'. He also wrote about the role of women in the Church. The question of women had become synonymous with the question of celibacy, he said, arguing for recognizing women on women's terms. 'Otherwise we are only abusers of women.' The abuse for which he was convicted began five years later.

I later got confirmation from a senior Church figure that the Joe Summerville working in the archive in Ennis is the Joseph Summerville who was convicted of sexually abusing a minor in Tuam.

I thought seriously about the fact that this man seemed to want to shed truthful light on the Church's past. I had no reason to believe that Summerville's work as an archivist gave him access to minors, or that he wasn't complying with the terms of his conviction. And unlike many abusers, Summerville had been punished. For these reasons, I considered not including his voice at all. But in the end I concluded that there was no way to include his views on the Church or on the history of institutions without being transparent about his own past. Knowing I was a journalist, he spoke – as a Church-employed archivist – about past institutional abuses, the rights of women and the patriarchy of society, without any acknowledgement of his own part in the Church's history of abuse. I didn't see how I could let that silence stand.

On the first day of the World Meeting of Families, in August 2018, I took the number 4 bus to the RDS. Some of my fellow passengers were discussing the news that hundreds of tickets for the Pope's visit had been applied for by people who were planning to boycott the event. An older woman talked about how at the beginning of the century every mother wanted her son to be a priest. 'They ruled in anger instead of love,' she said.

Two young women in the back of the bus, across the aisle from a priest and an elderly couple, were having a good joke amongst themselves.

'You don't realize how many people are religious till you see something like this, all them priests and nuns,' one said, hugging a Lucozade bottle.

'Praying for forgiveness!' Her friend laughed, slapping her thigh.

As the Archbishop of the city hosting the World Meeting, Diarmuid Martin seemed to be juggling a number of conflicting agendas. At a press conference following the announcement that Dublin would host the event, he had stressed that Ireland, 'despite what many think, has a strong family culture'. He noted that the country 'has a much higher marriage rate than Italy and a much lower incidence of divorce' and boasted that 'the fertility index in

Ireland is 2 whereas in Italy it is 1.4.' But he warned that 'Ireland is a very open country and is open to all the pressures of Western secular culture regarding marriage and the family.'

In a radio interview with Marian Finucane in the run-up to the event, Archbishop Martin struck a somewhat different note. He suggested that Pope Francis had decided to come to Ireland because the country had changed. He described Pope John Paul II's 1979 visit as a historic 'high point' in the life of the Catholic Church in the country, which was followed by 'a decline and a change'. But he admitted that 'All in Ireland feel that Ireland has changed for the better.' In the Pro-Cathedral, where the Pope would pray, there was a candle to remember victims of abuse; the candle had been there for a number of years. 'He obviously will have to address the question of that part of our history,' Martin said. 'It's important, I believe, that he doesn't address it as part of our history but as part of our present, because the wounds are there and new wounds are emerging.'

Then, as I watched at the RDS, Archbishop Martin again spoke of the Church's legacy of abuse with more directness than churchmen were generally able to muster. 'Particularly in Ireland – because of the industrial schools, the day schools, the Magdalen laundries, the mother-and-baby homes, the children abused by priests in parishes – the numbers of those abused is immense, and the numbers that have come forward is only proportionate of that,' he said. He was, in part, responding to the publication of a vast grand jury report on clerical sexual abuse in Pennsylvania.

Following publication of the Pennsylvania report, former President Mary McAleese stated on national radio that despite Pope Francis's seeming commitment to change, he continued to put 'defence of the institution first'. She spoke, too, of a meeting she had while President, in 2003, with the Vatican's Cardinal Secretary of State, Angelo Soldano, during which he proposed that the Irish State indemnify the Church against the compensation claims of abuse survivors. It was a huge revelation, from a former President now pursuing a doctorate in canon law. 'It strikes me as impossible to believe that all bishops acted equally negligently by coincidence,' she said. 'We heard it through the media, we heard it through the courage of victims, we heard it through lawyers, we heard it through government. We never really heard it openly, spontaneously from our Church.'

In a stadium usually used for rugby matches, concerts and the annual Dublin Horse Show, rows of chairs were lined up in front of a stage with an altar and two big screens either side. Mass was held there every day of the World Meeting, and speeches were given by members of the Catholic hierarchy. The keynote address on the first day was given by Archbishop Eamon Martin, the Primate of all Ireland. He was standing in for the original speaker, Cardinal Donald Wuerl, who had withdrawn after being implicated in the Pennsylvania report. Wuerl was Bishop of Pittsburgh between 1988 and 2006, and was heavily criticized after the grand jury found that there was 'wholesale institutional failure that endangered the welfare of children' in the diocese. Wuerl's speech was to be titled 'The Welfare of the Family is Decisive for the Future of the World'.

On the stage, with a large silver cross hanging on his chest, a magenta sash around his waist and matching headpiece, the most senior figure in the Catholic Church in Ireland talked of marriage between a man and woman 'open to life', of the benefit of chastity for young people living 'surrounded by a contraceptive, anti-birth mentality', and of the commodification of childbearing.

I spoke with the Archbishop at the side of the stage after he had descended. When I asked him about the mother-and-baby homes, he described them as 'a shameful chapter, really, in the life of the Church and indeed in the life of the society'. His voice was high and soft. 'We can't put this story into the past and think it never happened, neither can we easily explain it away.'

The family was the vital cell of the Church and society. 'If society and if the Church abandons any families, we are storing up trauma,' he said. 'I hear stories of families even in the sixties who felt abandoned by their Church, who felt abandoned by society. I look back and I wonder what was it about our teaching, what was it about our attitudes as a Church which percolated into society and which influenced, which dominated in many ways, society? What was it that allowed us to abandon and exclude people who were faithful members of our parishes, our neighbourhoods?'

The Archbishop talked as well about the Church's responsibility to be on the lookout 'for where we may be repeating this kind of behaviour today'. I told him about Jim, the steward in Knock, who had got no help from his local priest when seeking answers about his birth mother. The Archbishop seemed moved by the story and said the Church a few years back had petitioned the government, saying, 'We need to do something about the law in this country, the tracing rights for families.' In Northern Ireland, where he was based, adopted people had the right to their original birth certificates (whereas in the Republic, they may access the original birth certificate only with the permission of the birth mother). He said the Archdiocese of Armagh was collecting its records to hand over to the State, and he hoped 'effective and swift tracing rights' could be established. What happened in the past, he suggested, was an 'aberration of Church teaching'.

At a stand for the Diocese of Elphin in the World Meeting's main conference hall, Bishop Kevin Doran – a tall, thin man with a distinctive grey-and-white beard – was finishing up for the day when I asked if he'd speak with me.

Doran, a native of Dublin, was seventeen when he entered the seminary in 1970. Days after he was ordained as a priest, he 'came across that whole experience of crisis pregnancy' when a pregnant young woman came to him. He accompanied her to what he described as 'our own Catholic pregnancy care service', a new agency called Cura. 'Actually, I was mistaken by the counsellor for the father,' he laughed. 'The young woman didn't want to go in to the counsellor without me.' I wondered if that counsellor was accustomed to priests coming in with women they had made pregnant.

That experience caused the young Father Kevin Doran to feel that it wasn't enough to just say he was against abortion; the Church had to offer alternatives. His early years as a priest coincided with declining demand for the secrecy provided by mother-and-baby homes, and an increase in the number of women who were willing and able to travel to Britain for an abortion. Energy within the Church that had gone into building the punitive institutions was now increasingly channelled towards preventing abortion. 'I was involved back in the early 1980s in setting up a pregnancy care agency called Life Pregnancy Care,' Bishop Doran told me. 'It still exists, although the name of it has changed to Anew.'

A few weeks before the World Meeting of Families, Bishop Doran spoke at an event in Dublin marking the fiftieth anniversary of the Papal encyclical 'Humanae Vitae', which hardened the Church's stance on artificial contraception. Doran warned that the encyclical was being ignored and needed to be freshened up for the current generation. Doran advocated for Catholic teaching on sexuality in schools and argued that the 'contraceptive mentality' was directly connected with the 'surprisingly high' number of people ready to accept same-sex marriage: when love was 'separated from its pro-creative purpose', it was difficult to explain why marriage needed to be between only a man and a woman. He also argued that contraception prevented women from saying no to men who wanted to have sex with them. 'It may seem to some that contraception has liberated women insofar as it allows them to take control of their own fertility,' he stated. 'But the fact that they are less likely to become pregnant also takes away from women one of the principal motives or freedoms for saying no to unwanted sex.'

'Please just make it stop!' the Minister for Health, Simon Harris, begged on Twitter following Doran's comments, saying, '[Religion] will not determine health and social policy in our country any more.'

I mentioned to Doran that, in the aftermath of the referendum that overwhelmingly overturned the constitutional ban on abortion, a priest in Cork had suggested bringing back the mother-and-baby homes. 'Oh yeah?' he said. 'I suppose if they did come back they'd want to be, do you know, a lot more supportive.'

When I asked him about the mass grave at the Bon Secours home, he said, 'I think the jury is out as to what exactly happened in Tuam. From what I understand, the babies buried there were buried in a very ordered kind of way.' He must have missed the coroner's report, quoted widely, that described the bodies as buried in a haphazard way. He talked about high infant mortality in the rural West of Ireland. I wondered what it would take for him simply to say it was terrible that hundreds of children had died in an institution and were buried without any name to mark them.

Eventually, Doran's secretary realized an interview was going on and tried to interrupt it. 'I have to put up with all the abuse that he gets in the media,' she told me.

One evening, following an exchange of emails, I had a long phone conversation with Willie Walsh, who was Bishop of Killaloe from 1994 to 2010.

Walsh was born in 1935 in Roscrea, the town where Sean Ross Abbey had opened a few years earlier, and as a child he knew about the mother-and-baby home. As a teenager, he was aware of a young man from the area who emigrated to Australia, supposedly because he had made a girl pregnant. It left a strong impression on him: pregnancy outside of wedlock was a disgrace, and people felt unable to remain in the community. 'We didn't have a sense that it was wrong that these girls should go into a home,' he said.

Walsh grew up on a farm. He was familiar with the ways that animals reproduced, the bulls and cows, the boars and sows, the whole messy and physical cycle of life. But it was a while before he understood that the 'same cycle applied to humans'. Those matters weren't spoken of. He believed at one stage that babies were found under cabbages.

He was aware that children were being sent from Sean Ross Abbey to adoptive parents in America and he was almost jealous, feeling that those children were lucky. At twelve he was sent to boarding school, then the seminary in Maynooth. As a young priest, when he returned home from Rome where he had been sent, he had vague recollections of celebrating Mass at the chapel attached to the mother-and-baby home.

He never questioned any of it until years later. 'It wasn't touching my life,' he said. 'Looking back now, these girls obviously suffered a great deal.' It was clearer to him that in many instances the women had 'little or no say' in their child being adopted, and 'that was very unjust'. There was 'very little respect for a girl who became pregnant outside marriage'. Even as a former member of the Church hierarchy, he recognized the hypocrisy. 'While as Christians we preached the importance of dignity of every person, we didn't apply that in practice,' he said.

At the seminary in Maynooth, they were taught that 'any sexual pleasure outside of marriage was wrong and was sinful'. For celibate priests, sex itself in any form was a threat: to their reputation, their job, their life's ambition. 'Sexual sin was one of the worst possible sins,' he said. The Church's teaching on justice distinguished between different levels of wrongdoing – stealing a euro wasn't as bad as stealing a thousand euros – but the Church 'allowed no such distinction in relation to sexuality', he explained, with 'any offence against sexuality regarded as grievous'. Women represented a temptation and hence a threat. Walsh was taught little about how to support people who failed to uphold the Church's strict moral code on sexuality, and he felt that nuns, too, 'were victims themselves of a system in which they were trained'. The clergy enjoyed a huge degree of public reverence – 'They could do no wrong' – but he personally knew two priests who fathered children and remained in their positions.

Before the publication of Pope Paul VI's 'Humanae Vitae' encyclical of 1968, Walsh had been expecting the Church to soften its stance on contraception; instead, it was hardened. That led Walsh to question the Church's teaching on sexuality, including its attitude towards unmarried mothers, but he never raised his doubts in a public way. 'You were kind of conditioned to think the Church was always right,' he said. 'Questioning wasn't that welcomed.' Indeed, it was seen as disloyalty to the hierarchy and to the Pope.

He remembered the vans with 'Magdalen laundry' written on the side. 'I began to think this is a kind of cheap labour,' he said. 'I began to realize, somehow, this wasn't right.' But he still didn't speak out about it; and, speaking to me, he couldn't 'recall any serious discussion when I was bishop on mother-and-baby homes'.

He asked me if I'd ever heard someone say they were going to beat the Devil out of me. He had experienced it himself as a child: 'It was all right to beat the Divil out of us,' he said. 'That justified some cruelty.'

I asked him about the claims by the Sisters of the Sacred Hearts that they had no burial records for hundreds of children who died at their institutions, including Sean Ross Abbey.

He said it didn't surprise him that the burials weren't recorded, but he wondered why the nuns would not speak openly about it. 'If a child died and they had been baptized, they were gone straight to heaven,' he said. 'I hate to say it but I think there was a certain attitude that their remains didn't matter, they were gone to heaven and their remains were of no great importance.'

I had never heard this idea expressed so directly before, by any person, religious or otherwise. I had read about *cillíní*, informal graves in unconsecrated ground where unbaptized babies were traditionally buried, because the Church refused them a Catholic burial. But the idea that a *baptized* baby's remains would be considered 'of no great importance' seemed completely at odds with Catholic practice in non-institutional settings. Walsh did not endorse the idea that a baptized child's remains 'didn't matter', but he did attribute it to the religious orders that ran the homes.

He was clear that the unmarked and unrecorded burials at Tuam, and also in Sean Ross Abbey in his hometown, where a thousand children died, could not be justified. 'I feel sad about it, shame about it, we didn't see how wrong these things were,' he told me. 'It is a past that we should have some shame about.'

One day at the World Meeting of Families, I bumped into my local parish priest, Father Gaughan. I remembered him striding through the park in his dark clothes, and I knew that my father had had to ask him for permission to get married outside the parish, but I had never spoken to the man. I introduced myself and we had a brief conversation, during which he mentioned that he had been a chaplain at a Magdalen laundry. He lived a few doors up the busy road I grew up on, in a semi-detached house opposite the church, a priest who had a reputation for being more conservative than most.

I went to visit him not long after the World Meeting. He brought me into his living room, and we sat facing each other in armchairs, his a large beige affair with white lace over the back. He sat back in it with his legs stretched out in front of him, his feet on a pouffe, dressed in a dark suit, his hands clasped over his stomach. In notable contrast to the various times I'd visited religious Sisters, there was no rush to make me tea. His hair was still as black as I remembered, but thinner. Tortoiseshell-framed glasses perched on a long thick nose. I had never been in a priest's house.

I had looked him up online before going to visit and learned his full name was John Anthony Gaughan. He'd been born in Listowel, Co. Kerry, in 1932. He had a doctorate in philosophy and had published a number of historical books and papers. He even had his own website, which listed his publications and awards. It was noted on another website that he used to say Mass for Kerry GAA footballers prior to All-Ireland Football finals in Croke Park.

I wanted to talk to him specifically about the few years in the mid-sixties when he was chaplain to St Mary's convent and the Magdalen laundry in Donnybrook, run by the Sisters of Charity. He had no qualms about the subject and launched right in. 'As I recall, there were over a hundred girls, old and young,' he said. Every morning at 7 a.m. he performed Mass for the 'nuns and the ladies, the females who were there'. He was impressed at how well the place was run, like a girls' boarding school. He recalled the big concert put on by the inmates at Christmastime, attended by local people who contributed to the running of the laundry through donations, and by the Lord Mayor of Dublin. 'The girls of course were very good-looking,' he remarked, unprompted, 'like Marilyn

Monroe, and it was a very enjoyable night.' His voice was academically nasal but softened by the Kerry undertone.

The story of one young woman was at the front of his mind. He had been contacted by someone – either a curate in Finglas who was once a classmate of his, or a local Garda sergeant – about a young woman living in a flat in the parish who had been working in a chemist shop as an assistant and had committed infanticide.

'She was a very nice little country girl and she had this baby and apparently she panicked,' he said. 'She had the baby in the bathroom and she wrapped it up in the local newspaper.' He commented on the fact that she was good-looking, and on how quiet and polite she was. The young woman gave birth in the bathroom of the flat she shared. Her flatmates did not know about her pregnancy. She was afraid the baby would scream and make a noise, so she suffocated it in her panic, and left the baby's body in the entrance of a local church. When the local Garda sergeant tracked her down, he called Father Gaughan because he felt it would be 'appalling' if she went to jail.

Father Gaughan contacted the Sisters of Charity to secure an agreement from them to take her into the laundry for a while, if possible. The young woman still had to go to court. Father Gaughan wanted to appear as a representative for her, but was warned by an assistant bishop not to. 'They'll think you're the father of the girl,' he was told. He secured the help of a woman from the Legion of Mary, and then went along to the court anyway. Having been assured by the advocate that the woman would go to the Magdalen laundry, the judge, Gaughan recalled, 'sentenced' her to go there. (It seems to me likelier that this was not a sentence following a verdict, but rather a condition that satisfied the prosecutor that it was not necessary to try the woman on the charge of infanticide, a verdict juries were sometimes reluctant to reach.) In his mind it was the best possible outcome for her: avoiding jail, her reputation and secret maintained. 'It was done quietly for her sake.' The relatively short 'sentence', I gathered, was linked to the fact that her family was considered 'respectable'.

He told me the gardaí sometimes referred women for placement in the laundry. The Lord Mayor would come to their Christmas party, watching the women perform on a stage. The laundry had contracts from 'big places' and van men who transported the finished product. 'The Sisters were unpaid servants, if you like,' he said. 'They donated their lives and their skills.' He claimed the nuns worked alongside the women. The inmates were 'vulnerable people' with nowhere else to go, unwanted by their families. 'A sheltered existence, that's what they needed,' he said.

The laundry in the mid-sixties, in his account, was a place from which the inmates were free to leave: 'All these very beautiful young girls popping in and out.' One family contacted Father Gaughan because their daughter, 'a lovely little girl', was using drugs and selling sex on the streets. 'They asked me to do something about her,' he said. 'She was happy with what she was doing.' He saw her and other 'little girls and their little skirts' on a freezing Christmas Eve, 'like schoolgirls on corners'. He thought it was awful but left her be because she said she was okay.

Father Gaughan was also familiar with Madonna House, the orphanage near Blackrock. He spoke of the Sisters of Charity bringing up 'little foundlings' who had been brought in by the gardaí. He baptized some of these children – on one occasion, to much disapproval, at the same time as the child of a government minister. Although he had lived for three decades in Blackrock, he had almost nothing to say about Temple Hill. He described it as a 'small little operation'. I told him about the evidence, recently in the news, of illegal adoptions: birth certificates falsely listed the adoptive parents as the birth parents. 'Oh, I see,' he said. 'That was illegal?'

I asked if he ever knew anyone who had been an inmate in the mother-and-baby homes.

He said no. 'Certainly not one of my girlfriends!' He convulsed into a wheezy roar of laughter.

The room was unlit, and the daylight filtering through the window was fading, until we were almost in darkness. I asked him how much of the stigma against women who had sex out of wedlock came from the Church.

'It was part of it,' he said. Then he accused the media of 'pooh-poohing morality' but blackguarding people if they fall. The attitude of the Church was different, he assured me. 'It sets out the moral principle, preaches it, exalts everybody to follow it, then when people fall? Mercy. No attack on them, no judgement on them, the opposite to the media.'

I found it hard to believe that he was convinced by his own rhetoric. 'Do you believe the Church was that forgiving?' I asked.

'They weren't actually, on that issue,' he admitted. 'I agree, I agree.' He thought about it some more. 'I suppose I didn't want to see it,' he said. 'I only wanted to know from people what they wanted to tell me themselves.'

Before he moved to Blackrock, he worked in poorer areas of the city. He remembered seeing women trying to cope with poverty, drunken husbands and children with addiction. In Cabra West, not far from the St Patrick's mother-and-baby home, he was in charge of a sodality of teenaged girls, hundreds of them, who often left school when they were around fourteen to work in glove or stocking factories in the city, getting up at dawn to go to work. 'A lot of them got pregnant with their boyfriends,' he said. 'Mothers came in to me and said, "He'll do the decent thing and he'll marry her."' He thought this was very just, that it acknowledged the responsibility of all involved.

He had also worked in a mostly affluent farming area, where 'it was the opposite attitude' if a girl got pregnant. 'They left the little girl in the lurch,' he said. 'It was the girl's fault, she shouldn't have allowed it to happen. He'd walk away from it and she would be an unmarried mother, which was appalling.' He didn't agree with it, he said, but he acknowledged that he never spoke up about it at the time. 'I wouldn't interfere,' he said. 'I felt that it was inevitable, and talking about it wouldn't improve the situation.'

Even as a priest?

'Yeah.'

I had made the mistake of misinterpreting him. He reminded me that he was 'basically conservative' and that he believed the Church stood for sexual morality and the 'secular world' didn't. 'Women and men can do what they like about sex,' he said, in the secular world. 'Women can use their bodies any way they like.'

14.

'You don't know what you're going to find'

A woman I know told me something over coffee one day that she'd never previously mentioned: her mother was born in one of the mother-and-baby homes, and the father was a priest. She described attending the priest's funeral, with an archbishop present. She told anyone who asked that she was his grandchild.

We were both around thirty. Neither of us had children yet, but the idea of being pressured into giving a baby up for adoption was difficult even to contemplate. 'I'm not getting broody or anything, but I can't imagine what it would be like to have my baby taken away,' she told me. She joked about how, if it had been us, we would have fought off the nuns to keep our kids. But I knew that it was a pointless thought experiment. The women who entered the institutions were told they were shameful, that they couldn't provide the future a child deserved. They were promised that giving up their child was a great and redemptive act, allowing a good and respectable couple to experience the wonders of parenthood. A married couple could give their child everything.

The conversation was an example – one of many, for me, while working on this book – of a strange paradox. It was hard for me and my contemporaries to imagine ourselves into the not-so-distant past of the mother-and-baby homes and Magdalen laundries and the profoundly alien ideas that underpinned them. And yet, many people of our generation were still living with the legacy of the institutions.

The day after I first went for tea with Sister Goretti, I met with a 33-year-old adoptee who asked me not to use her real name; I'll call her Niamh. Dressed in a highlighter-pink hoodie, she sat low in a soft chair at a Starbucks, describing the day she first found out details about her birth mother. She was around twenty years of age at the time. In a dowdy room on Merrion Road, where the Sisters of Charity had a house, she was served tea and biscuits by an older nun, who then handed her a photocopy of a letter written by her birth mother and left with the nuns when Niamh was two years old. Her mother's name was Tippex-ed out on the photocopy. The nun left her alone in the room to read it.

The letter was bluntly honest on certain subjects, Niamh said. 'How difficult the pregnancy was, how she resented me growing inside of her, but how she came to love me. And there I was with a nice cup of tea and a saucer.' She realized their handwriting was similar.

Niamh wanted to make contact with her birth mother and, at her request, the Sisters wrote to the address they had on file. Her birth mother reacted angrily, telling the nuns they'd brought stress upon her elderly parents by getting in touch.

'I had no control over that, you don't really have any control,' Niamh told me. 'That's life as an adopted person, lack of control over your own life.' There was a time when she feared she was 'the result of something bad that happened' to her mother, 'some damage'. When she was young, she was terrified of ending up in a relationship with an unknown sibling. (This fear was felt by many adoptees, and was not unfounded. I spoke to a woman from Dublin who gave birth in St Patrick's and whose son traced her. When they reunited, her son realized he had briefly had a sexual relationship with her daughter, his half-sister.)

A few years later, she again asked the Sisters to help her make contact with her birth mother, due to a genetic health issue. This second attempt, again, was unsuccessful. It was emphasized to Niamh how cold and angry her mother had been on the phone. The Sister asked Niamh if she wanted to leave a letter in case her birth mother made contact in future, and she did so, agonizing over it, saying nothing that might create any sense of guilt, expressing gratitude to her birth mother for giving her life. Then, contrary to the original understanding and without asking Niamh, the Sisters sent this letter directly to her birth mother.

At the time I spoke with Niamh, she was hoping to start a family with her husband, and all the old feelings – of guilt and rejection and a need to connect with her mother – surged up again. 'You can never escape it,' she told me.

While scrolling through Twitter one day I noticed that the @Ireland account, which is curated by a different person each week, was tweeting about being adopted from Bessborough. It was Kieran McGuinness, the singer from Dublin band the Delorentos, who had written a song inspired by his birth mother and his experience of adoption.

In a corner of a café near St Patrick's Cathedral in Dublin, Kieran told me about his happy childhood with his adoptive parents. He always knew he was adopted. When he was thirty years old, before getting married, he went into the offices of Cúnamh, the organization formerly known as the Catholic Protection and Rescue Society. At their office on South Anne Street, in Dublin, Kieran met a social worker who began the process of tracing his birth parents. When they read him out the non-identifying details from his file, he felt as though he was listening to a podcast, completely detached. His girlfriend was in a pool of tears beside him.

According to the file, his mother had entered Bessborough around a month before he was due, and stayed with him there for four weeks after his birth. 'Apparently the nuns came up on the train with me in a basket,' he told me.

Within three months of his first meeting at Cúnamh, he established contact with his birth mother, and they wrote letters back and forth. Kieran learned that, subsequent to his birth, she had got married and had children with her husband. When he and she were reunited, all the family were present. She told him that getting his letter had freed her from that secret. She kept apologizing; he told her, again and again, that she had nothing to be sorry for.

The song 'Petardu' was a way for him to work out his feelings around his adoption and to try to see things from his birth parents' perspective. When the song came out, in 2012, Today FM started playing it nearly every day and he found himself doing interviews about his adoption. When he pledged to give profits from the song to Cúnamh, the gesture prompted some people to comment about the history of the agency, particularly its role in bringing pregnant Irish women from the UK to Irish institutions, sometimes without their consent. To him, Cúnamh was just an agency that had helped him reunite with his mother.

That such a donation would be controversial is indicative of the minefield faced by Irish adoptees. Even for the rare person who has a straightforwardly positive experience tracing a relative, the history of the institutions and the agencies casts a dark shadow.

In 1987 – the year the law on illegitimacy changed, and shortly after the closure of Temple Hill and St Patrick's – the Adoption Board made fewer adoption orders than in any of the previous twenty-four years. Most adoption agencies were now providing their own 'counselling service' for people wanting to trace their origins. Adoptions were becoming rarer, but the reckoning with Ireland's troubled history of adoptions was intensifying. It became ever clearer, over time, that many adoptees were affected by two separate but related scandals: the use of false registrations to sever any documentary link between an adopted child and their birth mother, and the tendency of adoption societies and religious orders to supply false or misleading information to people seeking to trace a parent or a child. As far back as 1997, in an interview with the *Irish Times*, Sister Francis Ignatius Fahy of St Patrick's Guild admitted that the agency had sometimes supplied false information to adoptees and that some of their 13,000 files on adoptions included misleading or false information. Because of such practices, adopted people and mothers often feel they can't trust the information they are given.

Ann Valentine, who worked for the St Louise Adoption Society connected to St Patrick's mother-and-baby home, told me that she used to go through records of other agencies when helping people with traces, often seeing irregularities. Doctors who organized illegal adoptions often destroyed their records, or they were left in the attics and cupboards of their family homes. It was said that nuns had special files in relation to famous people or those in positions of authority. There was also talk of the creation of fake passports in order to send children abroad. The Franciscan Sisters of St Clare at Stamullen once refused to give her even non-identifying information from their records when she was assisting an adoptee. Ann felt that the culture of some of the religious adoption societies was corrupted by the power they had. 'It was like playing God,' she told me. 'You were giving someone a baby.'

The mother-and-baby homes were built on the premise that conception out of wedlock was a scandal that had to be hidden. The State's policy of closed adoptions, whereby adoptees had no fundamental right to know the identity of their birth parents, was entirely consistent with that premise. What becomes clear, when you talk to adoptees, is that the need for information about or a connection to the person who gave you life is profoundly at odds with the secrecy of the system. Not every adoptee wishes to trace his or her origins, but many do; and in Ireland, because of the fraught history of adoption, the still largely unchanged rules regarding information, and years-long waiting times for searches via Tusla, the tracing process is often deeply frustrating.

As I worked on the book, it seemed to me that the legacy of the homes was everywhere, just under the surface. I began to meet people born in the institutions around the same year as me, in some cases by pure chance. At a house viewing, the woman whose room was up for rent – I'll call her Catherine – told me that she was born in Bessborough in 1988, the same year I was born. At a café off Grafton Street, we sat over flat whites like a bad stereotype of millennials, chatting about her intention to try to trace her birth mother.

Catherine's childhood was a happy one and she always knew she was adopted. She was never told much about Bessborough, but she was told that when she was brought home to her adoptive parents' house, her granny had insisted on washing her. Catherine suspected this was a 'moral thing', rather than a result of her infant body being actually dirty after her stay in the institution. She was baptized twice, first at Bessborough, and then a second time in her parents' local parish – another form of cleansing.

When Catherine was a young child, her adoptive parents brought her on a trip down to Cork to visit the mother-and-baby home. When they reached the doors of Bessborough, her adoptive parents were not allowed to accompany her inside, and she was shown around by the Sisters. She told her mother afterwards that she had seen 'lots of fat women' inside.

In a box her adoptive parents kept for her, there were documents compiled by the nuns. Her birth mother's address and name were redacted at the top of the letter, but her signature was visible, the name barely legible, at the bottom. In the letter, Catherine's birth mother provided some background on her pregnancy, her age at the time, her occupation, her likes and dislikes. She said she had received some photos of Catherine as a baby and asked if it was possible to get any more.

Searching online for the name she had learned from the signature, she quickly identified a woman who she believed to be her birth mother. She was wary of going any further without guidance. She considered adding her name to the Contact Preference Register, operated by the Adoption Authority of Ireland, which can help blood relations find one another without the assistance of agencies. She wasn't sure if she wanted to meet her birth mother, or wished only to receive information about genetic medical conditions. She spoke to someone from the Adoption Authority about making that decision. The man on the phone described the experiences of adoptees and mothers tracing each other, and the system that enabled and controlled this process, as a 'fractured landscape'. She could only speak with a social worker if she actively committed to making contact with her birth mother.

'You don't know what you're going to find,' she told me, by way of explaining why she felt uncertain about the possibility of making direct contact with her birth mother. She didn't have any idea what the chances were of making contact; she didn't know how the process might affect her, or her birth mother. Maybe her mother had had a traumatic experience in the mother-and-baby home; maybe she had problems with mental health or addiction; maybe the conception was the result of an assault; maybe, by initiating a trace, she would do harm.

When she told people about being born in a mother-and-baby home in 1988, they were surprised. She could see them wondering why a woman would give a baby up at a point in history when, it was felt, there were more options. It seemed that while the stigma of illegitimacy had largely fallen away, there was a different sort of stigma attached to the belief that her story was an anachronism. From the letters in her possession, Catherine was aware that her biological grandmother and aunt knew about her mother's pregnancy and that they were supportive, but it was kept a secret from everyone else.

The last time we met for coffee, Catherine had recently spoken with a social worker from Tusla and was now committed to tracing her birth mother. She visited the General Registration Office during her lunch break one day and printed out her original birth certificate, with her mother's name.

A Buddhist nun in France recently told Jess Kavanagh to take a look at her ancestors. Jess knew her mother had been born in 1956 to an Irish woman and a Nigerian man, and adopted from a mother-and-baby home, but she didn't know which one. Her mother had died of cancer when Jess was in her early twenties. Now, in her early thirties, Jess was acting on the Buddhist nun's advice.

As a young Irish woman of mixed race who often 'passed' for white, and sometimes found herself expected to agree with people's complaints about 'them Nigerians coming over here', Jess had developed what she described to me as a 'linguistic arsenal' for talking about these things. When she pointed out her own heritage to people, there was often an uncomfortable silence. It felt like it was her responsibility to explain her own identity. Nowadays Jess often finds herself performing alongside younger black Irish artists who are completely at home in their identity and proud to express it. 'Mam never got to see that,' she told me.

Jess always knew her mother, Liz, was adopted. 'It was obvious. My grandparents were white and my mam was black.' Jess used to joke around with Liz, asking if she was definitely her mam. Labels in her family were flexible; her sister, twelve years older than her, called their grandparents Mam and Dad.

When Jess first asked her grandmother, Nana Betty, about Liz being adopted, Betty got annoyed and told Jess that her mother shouldn't have told her that. 'She was adopted from birth, it doesn't even count,' Betty said.

'Adopted from birth' was only part of the story, as it turned out: Liz's birth mother was Betty's own sister, Kay. After Kay was sent 'to the country', to an institution run by nuns – presumably a mother-and-baby home – and handed over her daughter for adoption, Betty adopted the baby herself. Kay moved to London to find work, and Betty raised Liz as her own daughter, sending her over every now and then on visits to 'Aunty Kay' in London. Liz didn't find out until she was fifteen that Kay was her biological mother.

When Liz was still a child, Betty took her and her sister (who was also adopted) to the orphanage in Blackrock, hoping to adopt another child. While the nun was showing Betty the babies in their cots, the kids wandered off to another room, where they followed the sound of crying to a closed closet. Inside they found a baby. 'A black baby crying on its own in the dark,' Jess remembered Liz telling her. The nun told Betty that the baby was sick and probably wouldn't make it. Betty decided that if the baby was going to die, she was going to die with a family. The baby girl lived and grew up to be her youngest aunt, Ana. When the news of the human remains at Tuam broke, all Jess could think of was that it could have been her mother, her aunt, her uncle. 'Their alternative fates are hard for me to consider,' she said.

Jess also wondered if the way baby Ana was being treated had something to do with the colour of her skin. Racial discrimination in the institutions is part of the Commission's terms of reference, thanks at least in part to lobbying by the Association of Mixed-Race Irish and the advocacy of one of its founders, Rosemary Adaser. Like many mixed-race children who went through the mother-and-baby homes, Rosemary was never adopted; instead, she spent ten years in an industrial school. She has spoken publicly for years about how racism was endemic in the institutions. She was made to unblock toilets with her hands because of their colour, and was told by the nuns that no man would ever want her because she was black. When she was old enough, she moved to the UK. When I met her in London, we spoke about how the mother-and-baby homes did much to conceal the reality of mixed-race relationships. The shame-industrial complex was effective at finding homes in Ireland and America for illegitimate white children. But mixed-race children were a more obvious rebuttal of the myth of Irish moral and racial purity, and they paid a price for it.

Liz was eighteen years old and unmarried when she gave birth to her first child, Jess's older sister. Nana Betty wanted to adopt the girl and help raise her. In the 1970s it was still difficult for a single mother to get a lease, never mind a job. But Liz was determined to raise her daughter herself, and did so. Although Liz was outspoken about most things, she never confided much to Jess about this history. 'It's a very Irish thing, we just get on with things,' Jess told me. She saw it as her mother's way of protecting them.

Jess and I went one day to the General Registration Office to try to find her mother's birth certificate: Jess wanted to know where her mother was born. The ledger for the year in which Liz was born didn't list birth dates, as most other ledgers did, and it listed multiple Elizabeth O'Neills. Jess remembered someone saying her mother's middle name might be Bernadette. Sure enough, we found an Elizabeth Bernadette O'Neill. We applied for a photocopy of the birth certificate. The piece of paper shook lightly in Jess's hand as she checked the details written in the boxes.

The location of the birth was Castlepollard. The 'informant' was a nun. I scrolled through an album on my phone to find photos of a commemoration I'd attended at Castlepollard some months before, and Jess looked through pictures of the chapel where her mother would have been baptized.

On a scorching July afternoon, the sky unexpectedly blue, my friend Ruth sat on a garden deck with a black sarong wrapped over her head, the table behind strewn with empty bottles from the night before. I was telling her about the stories people had been sharing with me when she cut me off. 'Did you not know my mum was adopted?'

I did not know, and so she told me. Her mother, Clare, was born to an unmarried woman and adopted by a married couple who lived in Blackrock, not far from where I grew up.

As a child, Ruth remembered going to visit her mother's adoptive parents, strictly religious people, in a lavish house. Clare's parents had another adoptive daughter, Gina. Clare always knew she was adopted and it was made out to be something special. But that came with expectations, questions about identity that couldn't be voiced, and shame.

Ruth told me that her Aunt Gina became pregnant out of wedlock, and gave birth in a mother-and-baby home – in 1988, the same year I was born.

With Ruth's permission I contacted Gina, acutely conscious that if my own mother's circumstances had been slightly different, she could have ended up in the same position.

Gina told me that she was born in Castlepollard in 1966, to an unmarried woman from Offaly. She was twenty-two years old when she became pregnant herself, and in 'denial with a capital D' when her sister Clare, Ruth's mother, came home from being away in the US. 'She took one look at me and said you're pregnant. Your tits are huge! Get yourself to the doctor.' Clare told their parents about Gina's pregnancy over tea. Later, their mother confronted Gina. 'I believe you're thinking of starting a family,' she said.

Her adoptive mother, whose brother was a priest, arranged for her to stay at Denny House in Donnybrook. She didn't know anything about mother-and-baby homes. 'I didn't know these places existed, I felt I was being punished.' She had to hand in her notice at the office in Blackrock where she worked.

Denny House was 'a posh one', she told me. 'Nice compared to what other girls went through.' The matron in charge dressed all in grey and was very strict. The other women were mainly from the inner city. Gina – a middle-class girl who had attended Sion Hill, a school run by Dominican nuns – was viewed in a different light, and the matron took her under her wing. Counselling was provided by the Catholic crisis pregnancy agency Cura. Gina was at Denny House for two months before giving birth and two months after. She had to do chores, cleaning out the fireplace and hoovering the floors, but it 'wasn't the worst place'.

When her labour started, an ambulance was called. A cousin of hers came to the hospital but her mother stayed away. The matron at the hospital said, 'Here's a girl who sleeps with every Tom, Dick or Harry.' Other women's husbands were there with them on the ward. 'I was the only one who didn't have anyone,' she told me.

When her mother came to visit, she brought a big salmon to thank Gina's cousin for being with her. I remembered my mum telling a story of how my dad insisted she cook a whole salmon for my christening party, worried about impressing the family. In middle-class south Dublin in the late 1980s, it seems, a big fish was an antidote to illegitimacy.

Gina's mother and her uncle, the priest, advised her to get the baby adopted. But her sister Clare urged her to keep the baby and said that she would help. Gina was determined to keep her son. Afterwards, her father would tell her he was glad. But her mother didn't offer her any support, and she was no longer welcome in their home.

A friend from school helped her find a 'sort of flat'. It was a garage off a house, with a hole in the floor. At one stage she used a cinder block as a chair. It was 'an awful place to bring a baby', she told me, but it was all she could afford. A five-minute drive away, her parents lived in a house with an extra kitchen, bedroom and sitting room upstairs, renovated for Gina's grandparents.

She worked various jobs, and her father would slip her a few quid when he could, saying not to tell her mother. Social welfare and rent allowance made it just about possible to get by. Her son was a live wire in a tiny space. When the boy was three years old, Gina's parents suggested that it 'wasn't too late': she could still put him up for adoption.

15.

Two Mothers

The first time Gráinne had sex, she was eighteen years old, a country girl studying in Dublin. She and her boyfriend had been going out for a few months, intimacy limited to 'a bit of a snog' before they slept together. It was the summer of 1981, and contraception still required a prescription from a family doctor. Gráinne had been taught that sex outside of wedlock was a sin, but for her this gave it the appeal of a rebellious act. Personally, she had no hang-ups about sex: it was, to her mind, a beautiful thing.

When she started losing weight and throwing up, she thought she was seriously ill. She didn't know whether to feel relieved or not when a doctor told her she was pregnant. 'I never thought for one minute something would happen other than I would have the child,' she told me.

When she told her parents, their reaction made her feel that it would have been better if she had cancer. Gráinne felt herself become a different person in their eyes. 'Whore, prostitute, sinner': she listed off the names her mother called her. 'I had always been loved,' she told me. 'I didn't know this woman.'

Gráinne and her boyfriend had broken up by that point, and her parents made her swear she would not tell him that she was pregnant. And if she'd told anyone else, she should now tell them it was a 'false alarm'. There was a relation who was a nun with the Sisters of Charity, involved in adoption. Gráinne remembered the phone call made that same day to the nuns. 'Yes, it's a moral issue,' she heard her mother say.

She went to Bessborough when she was around six months pregnant. Her name was changed. She felt she was treated better than most because it was known she had a nun in the family. She had a room of her own. Anyone who asked where she had gone was told she was staying with friends of the family. 'We staffed the nursery,' Gráinne said. 'We cared for babies of the girls who had gone.'

Her labour was induced early so she could be sent home sooner. At some point they gave her Pethidine, a synthetic opioid. She remembered being told she'd had a boy, then passing out. She wasn't allowed out of bed for three days. She was allowed to visit her son in the nursery and to hold him. Then her parents drove her home. Six weeks later, she went back down to sign the adoption papers. Gráinne agreed to the adoption because she was told it was the best thing for the baby; that she would be selfish to keep her son; that she would have no future and neither would her child.

She soon started a new relationship. She confided in her new boyfriend about the baby she had given away and the deep sense of loss she felt. He was understanding, and this deepened the relationship. She wanted to get pregnant again, and within a few months she had. 'We had a dream we'd run away together,' she told me: they were going to leave Ireland to raise their child together.

But the dream did not last long. She had not even told her parents about her boyfriend, feeling that they were scrutinizing her and would not approve. She was still in her teens. Soon, rather than planning a new life for her young family, she was paralysed by the thought of the shame her parents would feel. Instead of running away from Ireland with her boyfriend, she cut the relationship dead and ran in a different direction. 'The only thing I could think to do was to take myself off,' she told me. The Rotunda Girls' Aid Society referred her to Ard Mhuire, the Good Shepherd Sisters' mother-and-baby home in Dunboyne. A minibus brought the women to Holles Street for check-ups. They were put to work folding and packaging greeting cards in a prefab near the convent, and Gráinne cleaned the chapel sometimes. A priest came for Mass, and during confession gave her what she felt was his attempt at a practical solution. 'The priest asked me if I enjoyed sex,' she told me. His advice was, 'If you're one of those women, find a boy and get married.'

Ard Mhuire had a coin-operated phone box. At one point during a phone call to her mother, she ran out of money. Her mother rang the operator to call her back and was told that the call had come from the Good Shepherd convent. Gráinne felt immediate relief. The only reason she was giving the baby up was to keep it secret from her mother. 'Now I can keep him,' she thought.

After giving birth in Holles Street, her baby in the crib beside her bed, she spoke to her mother from a phone in the hall. When she said she wanted to keep her baby, her mother raised a fresh objection: 'How could you do that? What if your first son traces you and finds out you kept this child?' The doubt her mother planted 'kept eating into my brain', she told me. She hated the thought that her firstborn would conclude he was the lesser child.

The taxi hired to bring her from Holles Street to Ard Mhuire stopped at St Patrick's on the Navan Road, where she handed her son to a nun at a side door. He would stay there while the adoption was arranged. She moved back home to the countryside, but every week she took a bus to the city to visit him, usually on a Thursday, along with other passengers going for a day's shopping. If there was someone she knew on the bus, she had to act jolly and make up a story. She visited for six weeks and then finally gave her consent to the adoption.

When I started speaking to people about the mother-and-baby homes, I sometimes wondered about a woman I used to know, the mother of an ex-boyfriend. Blánaid had had a child when she was young and unmarried. The child had been adopted, I knew that, and she was trying to locate him. I didn't know if she'd been in one of the institutions.

One day, I searched her name online, and found her artist's website. I felt nervous about contacting her, unsure if she would want to talk. But I found a link to a 1997 policy document, written by the Adoption Review Group and stamped by the Department of Health, which listed her name as a representative of the Barnardos Birth Mothers' Support Group. I sent the email.

When we spoke on the phone, she was surprised to hear what I was writing about. 'I wouldn't think young people would be inter-ested,' she said.

The first time I met Blánaid, I was a college student, nineteen years old, creeping across her front garden with my boots in my hand, trying to sneak away from their family house after secretly staying the night with my boyfriend. She spotted me from a win-dow and I think she might have waved.

Just before Christmas of 2018, I sat in her kitchen for the first time in ten years. She was taller than I remembered, nearly as tall as me, slender and well dressed, her hair a long soft blonde-ish bob. She apologized for having a cold. We laughed about the time, years ago, when she put out uncooked rice in the garden for the birds, with the kind intention of fattening them up before winter, and we had to tell her it might make them explode.

Blánaid was twenty-four years old and living in London when her mother had an accident. She moved back home to Ireland on St Patrick's Day, in 1975. One night, she ended up back at the house of a man she knew, living in the city. 'We had sex,' she told me matter-of-factly. 'I flew out of the place knowing I was pregnant.'

In London, she had been on the pill, which was almost impos-sible to get in Ireland at the time. 'You wouldn't even dream of it.' It was still illegal in Ireland to sell condoms to unmarried people.

Her pregnancy made her sick very early on and her mother copped on very quickly, bringing her to a doctor she hadn't seen before. The appointment still sticks in her mind. The doctor told her if she was stupid enough to get pregnant, she was too stupid to have a baby. She remembered his moralizing and judgement – more intensely than from any nun. The feeling Blánaid was left with from the doctor was, 'You'd done wrong and you had to make up for it. It was the worst shame.'

She grew up in a middle-class Dublin suburb. She wasn't aware of anyone who had become pregnant out of wedlock, or any single mother raising children alone. 'I felt like I was the only person,' she told me. 'It was like I had landed from outer space, there was no one else like me.'

Her father was heartbroken by the news that she was pregnant. 'He was crippled by his respectability,' she told me. She herself was a devout Catholic at the time. Her brother took her to a church outside their parish so she could anonymously attend Mass, but she was too ashamed to confess to a priest that she was pregnant, and she was afraid there would be no forgiveness. After her son was adopted, she did speak to a priest but found little understanding. The experience broke her trust in her own Church.

She knew she would never be able to take her son home and raise him there. 'I wouldn't have put them through it, because I loved them,' she said of her parents. It was never an option – 'never for one second'. She understood that she was expected to give her baby up for adoption. 'Everybody thought it was best for the baby,' she said. 'At times I thought it was best for the baby. I couldn't offer him anything.' The decision was hers, but everything pointed in the same direction. 'I can't say I was forced,' she told me. 'I was conditioned.'

Blánaid had just started working in the computer department of a semi-state sugar company. Her boss knew about her pregnancy, but it was kept secret from others in the office. She was on probation and worried she would lose her job if she chose to keep her son. There was no other single mother working there, as far as she was aware. The ban on married women working in state jobs had been lifted only a few years before. The unmarried mothers' allowance, introduced in 1973, wasn't much to live on, and there was still social stigma against renting to single women with children.

Blánaid was advised by her doctor to go to St Patrick's Guild, and so she met with two nuns in the Haddington Road office. 'From then it was like a machine,' she told me. She remained in work for six months of the pregnancy. Being tall meant it was easier to hide her bump and the added weight.

St Patrick's Guild referred her to the Dominican Priory on Dominick Street in Dublin, a short walk from the Rotunda maternity hospital. There she spoke with one of the priests involved in the Catholic agency Ally about a placement with a family. Her parents knew about her pregnancy, but it had to be kept secret from the neighbours. It was surreal to think of a pregnant woman going to a sanctuary of white-habited men, dressed in their scapulars and capuces, rosary beads hanging from their leather belts.

In the seventies, even as institutions like St Patrick's and Bess-borough continued to operate, there was a new effort on the part of Catholic agencies to hide unmarried mothers within the private homes of respectable families. And the system was being profes-sionalized: social workers were now increasingly involved in the institutions and agencies. Since the early seventies, Ally had gath-ered lists of volunteers with whom they could place women. They would often work as unpaid au pairs in these houses in return for room and board. Countless families around the country provided rooms to unmarried mothers who then went on to give birth in the institutions and had their children adopted. Few are speaking up now.

Women who experienced the institutions tried to offer help to other women. The documentary film director Paul Duane, who was adopted from Sean Ross Abbey in 1966, told me about how when he reunited with his birth mother, she told him that she always kept a room free in her house for any pregnant woman in crisis who might need shelter and the time to make a decision for themselves. She became pregnant as a teenager and her own father drove her to Roscrea and collected her. The family was consid-ered well off, and so she was given preferential treatment, but this resulted in a deep and lasting guilt at having seen other women indentured, unable to leave until their babies were adopted but also unable to take them home.

Through the seventies and eighties, his birth mother became a successful businesswoman and married. Her husband knew about her child. Keeping a room free for a woman needing refuge 'was a way of coping', Paul told me. She spoke to him about how abortion could be the better choice for some women, how being separated from a baby was often a lifelong trauma. She trusted him to under-stand, and he did.

★

In November, when she was beginning to show, Blánaid was sent by Ally to live with a family in south Dublin. Blánaid described the family as 'jet setters of the time'. She looked after their two young children, did work around the house, sewing for the wife. Blánaid had worked as an au pair before, so she had the skills, but she was made to feel like the family was doing her a great favour. When she went out for a walk, she sensed her absence was resented. The family had photos of all the other women they'd 'had in', clearly proud of doing their Christian duty.

One night, only a week or so after Blánaid had moved in, they were 'having a bash' and there were people drinking downstairs. Blánaid, in bed, heard snippets of the conversation. 'I was the topic,' she told me. 'They were laughing about it.'

Her parents let her come home, where she was hidden away for the remaining months. People who asked were told she was in London. In January, when she went into labour, she was brought to St Columcille's Hospital in Loughlinstown, rather than one of Dublin's maternity hospitals. A cousin who had adopted children from Temple Hill gave Blánaid the loan of her own wedding ring so that she could pretend to be married, but the matron and the nurses on the ward knew the truth. She was put in a room on her own, not on a normal bed but a cushioned 'bench thing', under shelves where they kept spare nappies. She had taken no maternity classes and no one stayed with her through her labour. After she gave birth, a nurse placed the baby on her tummy. 'That love,' she said, exhaling. It was instant for her and immeasurable.

She was kept in the hospital for ten days, because of high blood pressure. The same cousin who lent her the wedding ring then drove her to Temple Hill. She carried her son to the side door and handed him over. Many times over the next three and a half months, she took two buses to spend the permitted half-hour with her baby. Her mother came with her. She showed me a photo album, with shots of her in a blue turtleneck and flared jeans, her hair auburn, holding her son swaddled in a yellow blanket and wearing a yellow Babygro, just as Cathy Garton described. Her mother is in a tweed coat with a crimson hat on. The wall behind her is pale blue and the carpet an ugly brown paisley.

One time she went into the wrong room by mistake and saw the rows of cots, trying to make out if her son was there among them. She always worried how the babies were treated, what her son's life was like when she wasn't there. 'Even getting the photos developed, I had a feeling of shame,' she told me. There was no ring on her finger, no husband beside her.

She still thought about ways she might be able to keep her son. If she got married, she thought, her son could be legitimized in the eyes of the Church and the State. Before signing the final adoption papers, she met the father again in a pub and gave him a photo of their son. She tried to raise the possibility of getting married, but 'he didn't absorb it', she told me. They were not in love, and it would never have worked.

St Patrick's Guild informed Blánaid when her son was going to be adopted, but after months of visits she couldn't face a final goodbye. She had a small gold medallion, with a cross in relief on the front, especially made for her son. The words 'Love and God Bless' and the year were engraved on the back. She crocheted a blanket for him also and bought a teddy. It was meant to go with him when he was adopted, but he didn't receive it from the Guild until he turned twenty-one.

When she went back to the Guild's offices on Haddington Road over the years, making appointments to see Sister Gabriel and Sister Francis Ignatius Fahy, she would always bring a small envelope with a donation. She had been made to understand, when she came to ask could she have photos of her son or information on how he was doing, that these things cost money. She handed over her money, not large sums, but huge for her at the time. 'You were begging for information,' she says. 'You were at their mercy.' The nuns decided what was written about her in the file and the details her son might one day be given. The nuns held the information on where her son was, and with whom. She had signed the adoption order, giving up her rights as a mother. After the adoption, she was expected to keep her son's existence a complete secret.

When Pope Francis visited Ireland and publicly told mothers it wasn't a sin to search for their child, she was watching on TV, holding her grandson, in floods of tears. 'It was the first time someone said, you didn't do wrong.'

In 1991, when Blánaid's father died, her mother told her that her aunt had had a baby out of wedlock. She no longer felt like the black sheep of the family, the anomaly bringing shame upon a respectable household. In the same year she joined the Barnardos Birth Mothers' Support Group. Most of the women in the group had been through the institutions. She began lobbying for a voluntary contact preference register to which people could add their details, hoping for a match with a blood relation. She met with government ministers and tried to explain why it was important. Adopted people weren't entitled to their own birth information. There was resistance from the Adoption Board and the government. In the end, a voluntary group had to set up a register themselves, launching in 1999. Six years later, the State's Adoption Board established a National Adoption Contact Preference Register.

For her own part, Blánaid was hoping to reunite with her son. Sister Francis Ignatius Fahy at St Patrick's Guild reached out to Blánaid's son about a reunion; he was in his early twenties.

Blánaid never got a response from her son. She looked up his name once in *Iris Oifigiúil*, a government gazette of legal notices published twice a week until the late eighties, that used to list adopted children by their new adoptive names and dates of birth. Apart from searching the births ledgers, it was one way for mothers and adopted people to trace each other independently. Later, with the advent of social media, Blánaid found him online. It gave her peace just to know he was alive and seemed happy in life. She wanted to respect his decision.

'I love him the same,' she told me. In the living room, she showed me pictures of her holding him, in a frame alongside photos of her other two children.

16.

The Castle

In October of 2018, I was in Donegal with a friend, visiting her aunt. On the way back to Dublin, I asked if we could make a detour to Newtowncunningham, a small town between Letterkenny and Derry city. I had seen images of an abandoned building that was once a mother-and-baby home called the Castle. There was hardly any information about the Castle in the public domain.

When we got to Newtowncunningham, the old boarded-up house was visible from the road, set back from its gates in an overgrown field. It was raining, so we ducked into Coyle's pub across the road to have a drink, charge a phone and see if anyone remembered anything about the place. A few regulars were perched on stools at the bar. We sat at a corner table, looking at old photos on the walls of local movers and shakers. I asked a young woman working the tables if she knew anything about the Castle. She told me I should talk to the woman who ran the place. I waited up at the bar for a few minutes until a woman came out from the back. Her name was Patricia. She had light grey hair and wore a pink shirt. 'The girls would come in here at night just for a mineral,' she told me. 'Most were professional girls.' I tried to imagine the pregnant teachers she described, sipping on phosphorescent TK red lemonade.

One woman from the Castle who came into the bar told Patricia she had a friend in Belfast who would send postcards home for her, so that her family would believe she was working there, and not pregnant in a small town in Donegal.

We left the pub and crossed the road to the gate of the Castle, which was set into a stone wall. We waited until there were no cars passing and then hopped over the gate. The grounds were completely overgrown. The two-storey house was derelict, and covered in sad attempts at graffiti. The HSE wanted to demolish it, and planning permission had been granted for a new primary care centre, but the project had stalled due to planning board concerns about demolishing the eighteenth-century building.

After we climbed back over the gate, I made my way across the road and a few doors down to a house whose address Patricia had given me. It always feels an unnatural thing to do, to turn up on people's doorsteps. It tests the nerves. One of my first jobs was selling bins door to door in Dublin. I remember one person who had an entire conversation with me through a letter box, and another who invited me in to a 'living wake', making me do my pitch in front of a very weak but smiling old man on a couch and two middle-aged women, sitting around a table laden with ashtrays, glasses and a whiskey bottle and cans.

When I raised the subject of the institutions with people, the conversation usually went one of two ways. They either became suddenly tight-lipped, talking about the good the Church did or how 'those were the times', or else they started very suddenly to tell you intensely personal stories about loved ones or experiences they'd had themselves. Sometimes they did both.

Norah Doherty was open and relaxed: 'What do you want to know, like?'

We sat in her neutral-toned living room with daytime TV droning along in the background. She told me that the Castle opened as a mother-and-baby home in the early 1980s. This was news to me, and a bit of a shock. It was one thing for the homes to stay open into the nineties, as some of them had, but it was hard to believe that a new institution had been established so recently.

Norah explained that the institution was founded as a cross-border initiative by the Bishop of Raphoe and the Bishop of Derry. She was the 'house parent', employed by the health board. The women were sent to hospital in Letterkenny or in Derry to give birth.

The job was advertised in a newspaper, though she didn't think, casting her mind back, that the ad mentioned many specifics. Doherty had experience as a nurse, but this position did not require nursing skills. The house parent was the person in charge. During the interview process, Norah met with a social worker from the health board, a social worker from the Derry Diocese and a priest from Derry. The institution could accommodate around fourteen women. They were referred through the pro-life crisis pregnancy agencies Cura and Life, or by social workers attached to the local health board.

'It was people generally who wanted to get away from home, not because of their parents but because of their neighbours,' she told me. 'Ireland being what it was.' The women came from all over the country, including from across the border. We all knew of women crossing to England for abortions, but I had never heard of women travelling from the North to the Republic to give birth. 'We had Protestant women as well . . . three or four,' Norah said. 'We also had a Pakistani girl. She fell out with the father, she just needed to get away. It was a safe home.'

The women usually came when they were around six months pregnant and could stay for six to eight weeks after they gave birth, though that wasn't strictly imposed. They generally used that time to make up their minds about adoption. 'They wanted to keep their babies, but those circumstances . . . It just couldn't happen, like. They wanted to continue their education, finish whatever they were doing.' Some were studying, some were in the middle of their college exams. They cooked their own meals. On Sundays, most went to Mass. The women paid £16 per week at the start, and in later years the fee rose to £35.

Norah didn't advise when it came to the decision about their child. But she tried to listen and to support them. 'They'd just come and cry,' she said. Social workers, usually from the counties the women were from, would come at least once a week. The women would have their babies with them in their bedrooms and they were completely responsible for them. Some mothers brought older kids with them to the Castle, and they would attend the local school while in Newtowncunningham. I asked why women would go to such lengths to hide a pregnancy if they were already raising children as single mothers? 'They didn't want to be seen pregnant,' she said. 'I made a mistake once, I can't be seen to make a second mistake.'

Some decided to keep their babies, and at least a couple, according to Patricia in the pub, didn't actually return home but remained in Newtowncunningham and got married there. Some children being placed for adoption went to what Norah described as a 'crèche' in Fahan, an orphanage called Nazareth House.

We spoke about where the shame came from. 'None of the girls who were there felt ashamed that they were pregnant,' Norah said. The shame came from other people, it got into their heads from outside. There was one woman who took her baby son home to Sligo, but the local priest refused to baptize him because she was unmarried. 'That wasn't right,' Norah said. 'Who are they to say I'm not going to baptize the baby? An innocent baby.' The woman came all the way back to Newtowncunningham and the local priest did the baptism. 'Then you wonder why people have stopped going to church?'

The news about Tuam was horrifying to her. 'I just can't find the words to describe the Tuam situation,' she said. 'It's like the Nazis. A mass grave. To be a Christian country and to do that. It's hard to get your head around it.' At the same time, she wasn't surprised. 'Nuns and that,' she said. 'People who were supposed to be next to saints, because that's what nuns were. They were revered.'

The Castle was the only institution under investigation by the Commission that had operated after 1998, making it subject to the Freedom of Information Act. I applied to Tusla for records from the Castle relating to admissions, discharges, adoptions and funding. I was told that I would have to narrow my query – there were limits on the resources that could be devoted to a request – and so I applied for a sample of different records, hoping it would be in some way representative. I got the impression from the FOI officer that, four years after a state investigation was launched into institutions including the Castle, there were still boxes of unsorted files sitting around offices. I was told I was the first person to make a freedom of information request regarding these records.

Amongst the records I received were shop receipts from Centra – for milk, scones, chips, peas, curry, bananas. Then there was a diary. Most of the names in its pages were redacted, but the diary gave glimpses into everyday life within the Castle. An entry from 1999 mentioned a call with a social worker in Sligo and, in relation to an inmate, 'better form today – she walked to town'. A mum came to visit. There were plumbers, engineers, and a washing machine making a banging sound. A woman was to be brought to 'the clinic' – 'she's for admission tomorrow to be induced'. It noted she was 'very quiet'. One girl was 'looking forward to tomorrow' – her due date, I guessed – but was warned 'it might not happen that quickly'.

The diary noted phone calls from people asking to place women in the institution. A man was told they 'couldn't take the girl' until there were more staff. A women's refuge was mentioned. Someone phoned to say 'that the girl has refused to come and they were going to court to get an order'. What looked to be 'LIFE' – the name of one of the Catholic crisis pregnancy agencies – was written in brackets next to a note about a request to place a woman in four to five weeks, after someone else left. Women walking to town were asked to pick up baby food or post a letter.

From admissions records running from 1998, when the Freedom of Information Act went into effect, all the way through to 2006, I was able to see the number of women who came to the Castle each year. In 1998, there were 12 admissions. In 1999, there were 13 admissions, and one baby died.

In 2000, a total of 15 women were admitted to the Castle, and in 2001 there were 10 admissions, including '3 not pregnant'. Were these women who panicked after a sexual encounter? Or had they come with a child or children needing some other kind of help?

The last years of the Castle saw a growing number of admissions of children – in some cases the older kids of pregnant women, but in other cases apparently child-protection cases. From other North Western Health Board documents it was clear that from the late nineties, the Castle was also intended to serve as a residential service for twelve-to-eighteen-year-olds. There were records of expenses for birthday presents, video rentals, emergency clothing and school uniforms.

The records referred to structural problems with the building, damp and fire-safety concerns. In 2003, a report noted a 'major roof problem', requiring up to €10,000 to repair. The service had diminished, and there were plans to relocate it, 'funded hopefully by the Crisis Pregnancy Agency with a voluntary organization like St Mura's Adoption Society and Cura adopting the project with the board as partner'.

Two years later, in 2005, an inspection found the roof still unfixed, with a hole now allowing water into a bedroom at the back. One of the stairways was in a dangerous condition. The building needed to be assessed 'to confirm it is fit for human habitation'. As was the case with Tuam in 1961, the eventual closure came on the heels of the local authority debating whether to invest to make the institution safe. Despite these problems, there were '4 girls' admitted in 2005. In 2006, the Castle's final year in operation, there was a single admission.

When I called the Derry Diocese to ask for information on their involvement with the Castle, the woman on the phone was incredulous at the idea that there had been any involvement. When I phoned the Diocese of Raphoe's office in Letterkenny seeking information about their involvement with the Castle, the archivist told me she was shocked to hear it had been in operation as late as 2006. She had seen nothing about it in the records.

She went away and found a directory for the Diocese in 2003, reading out a reference to a Ballaghderg mother-and-baby home. I searched for Ballaghderg – a village north of Letterkenny – but found nothing about a home there, and the Commission's terms of reference do not include an institution in Ballaghderg. On a whim, I rang a local business in the village. A friendly woman in her sixties, whom I will call Mary, answered the phone. She had never heard of a mother-and-baby home in the area, where she had lived for more than twenty years. But she did know about the Castle. She told me a lot of girls were referred there through Cura. 'I've been in it,' she said then. 'When it was a mother-and-baby home.'

I asked in what capacity, thinking she might be telling me that she had gone there to hide a pregnancy. It turned out she'd worked as a volunteer for Cura during the nineties, offering women what she described as companionship.

In Mary's experience, women were terrified to tell their families when they got pregnant out of wedlock. Following the X Case ruling in 1992, constitutional amendments established the right of women to travel to access legal abortion, as well as the legality of providing information about abortion and referrals to abortion services elsewhere. Women who contacted Cura in the 1990s and early 2000s might have found the number in the telephone directory. It wasn't unusual for women to contact such agencies in hope of getting information about ending a pregnancy, not realizing they were anti-abortion. Was concern about women going abroad for abortions a motivating factor for Cura's referrals to the Castle?

'Absolutely,' Mary said. 'We were protecting the child.'

Mary told me that Cura wanted women to make an informed decision with all the options – which included travelling from all across Ireland to conceal their pregnancies in the Castle. She described one mother who sent all her letters to a friend in Belfast to repost, and I wondered if this was the woman that the barwoman in Newtowncunningham had described, or if there was a woman in Belfast who provided a kind of service.

If a woman was referred by Cura to the Castle, someone in the Letterkenny office would organize a volunteer to go visit them. Mary explained they also acted as 'birthing partners' for the women. She told me that she tried to be careful never to say anything that would influence their decision, but that some people definitely gave their opinions on the 'best option'. She felt there were women, especially from the country, who if given the right support might have been able to keep their babies. She remembered three women she was involved with who made that decision. She would role-play with them, pretend to be their parents and practise how they might break the news. This was a distinct departure from the long-established Catholic view that adoption was the best option for a woman pregnant out of wedlock. The Church's new emphasis on encouraging a woman to give birth instead of choosing an abortion actually predated the X Case. As Bishop Casey put it when speaking at the opening of a Cherish branch in 1975, 'It took the frightening growth of abortion among us to bring most people to recognize and acknowledge the basic goodness of the unmarried mother.'

In the late nineties, Mary told me, a woman came to Cura determined that her baby was for adoption: 'no way in God's holy earth' she was able to take the baby home. She went to the Castle, and a social worker organized an adoption. A Cura volunteer had taken photos of the woman with her child at the Castle. She printed them out and gave them to the woman in a little album. When it came time for the foster parents to take the baby, the mother decided she couldn't do it. The woman went to her parents and showed them the book, told them this was her son. The mother asked her why she felt she had to go away. The father stayed silent and then stood up and put on his coat. He said he was going to meet his grandson.

'There was such a stigma, such shame,' Mary told me. 'Women were terrified to bring their baby home.'

Mary had told me that she didn't try to influence women's decisions; but her stories left a different impression. One of the first girls she met through Cura 'came looking for an abortion'. She was with her boyfriend. 'Have any of you had brothers or sisters that have children?' Mary asked them. They said no. 'This would be the first grandchild,' Mary said then. She told me that after she spoke those words, a light came into their eyes. Years later, she saw them with a child around the right age and knew they hadn't travelled for an abortion.

Mary advised me to look up the Bishop of Killala, John Fleming, who was at one stage President of Cura. I did so, and read about how, in 2005, four Cura volunteers from Donegal protested against the organization distributing the government's official Positive Options leaflets to clients, because it offered information on obtaining an abortion abroad. The four were suspended by Cura for speaking publicly about it. 'Cura would not be involved in any activity or practice which would make abortion a more likely option in a crisis pregnancy situation,' Bishop Fleming assured people that year. The agency was receiving hundreds of thousands of euros in government funding each year.

The controversy went on for a few years, with the government suspending Cura's contract over its refusal to give clients full information on services available. Cura's state funding eventually resumed, and continued until it announced its closure in 2018, following the abortion referendum.

Mary told me that the former Bishop of Raphoe, Séamus Hegarty, had been involved in setting up the Cura office in Letterkenny, along with four or five 'society people' in the town. These were doctors' wives, dentists' wives. 'A pedigree,' she said. When Hegarty moved to the Diocese of Derry, his successor Bishop Philip Boyce kept up the involvement. A priest would always say Mass for the volunteers and offer spiritual guidance.

Later, I called the number listed on the Diocese of Raphoe website for Bishop Boyce and spoke to a woman called Marie, who asked me why I wanted to talk to him. She told me he was away on a pilgrimage and that the Castle 'wouldn't have had anything to do with the Church' anyway.

Mary told me that women from Donegal who came to Cura wouldn't be sent to the Castle. They'd be referred to other Cura offices further afield, where no one would know them. She knew there had been some sort of house similar to the Castle in Galway, and possibly one in Athlone.

I asked her about what would happen now that Cura was closed. She figured women would turn to 'Mr Google'.

Mary was right about Mr Google. In the first months of 2019, when women began to access legal abortion in Ireland for the first time, many searched online for where to go.

A website offering counselling and scans to women with unplanned pregnancies appeared in search results with the same name as the government's official information service, MyOptions. It was eventually traced to Eamonn Murphy, an anti-choice campaigner who had been involved in running unregulated crisis-pregnancy agencies in Ireland, dating back to the nineties.

17.

The Dead and the Living

In April 2019, nearly five years after Catherine Corless's findings about the mother-and-baby home in Tuam made worldwide news, the Commission of Investigation released an interim report on burial practices in the institutions, where thousands of children died.

At a press conference in Government Buildings, Katherine Zappone, the Minister for Children and Youth Affairs, emphasized one of the interim report's key assertions: that there were people who knew more about how and where children had been buried than they had yet disclosed. She looked to the TV cameras at the back of the room and said, 'Let us know where they are buried.'

After the press conference, I sat down with the report and went through it page by page.

Section 4.41, on page 36, caught my eye.

In 1994, a former Bessborough resident contacted the Congregation of the Sacred Hearts of Jesus and Mary requesting documentation about her time in the institution and making a formal inquiry about the burial place of her child. The child was resident in Bessborough with his mother in 1960 and subsequently died in St Finbarr's Hospital later that year.

The report went on to say that, on foot of the former resident's request, the Sacred Hearts contacted St Finbarr's Hospital. The hospital chaplaincy passed the request to the hospital administrator, who determined that the child had been buried in the Cork District Cemetery, Carr's Hill. However, the report stated, this information was not shared with the child's mother. Instead, 'a member of the

[Sacred Hearts] congregation' told her that the baby 'was buried in the congregation burial ground at Bessborough'.

These dates and details were very familiar to me: they matched the story I'd been told of baby William, the brother of Carmel Cantwell, whose mother, Bridget, had searched for information about his burial for years. I took a photo of the page and sent it to Carmel in a private Facebook message.

'Jesus Christ,' she wrote back. 'Why has no one told my mother?'

The burials report was released on a Wednesday, just before the Easter weekend. On Good Friday, I stood at the gate of Carr's Hill cemetery with Carmel and her three-and-a-half-year-old foster son. The last time I'd seen Carmel was at the commemoration in Bessborough the previous summer, at the headstone she and her mother placed for William near the spot where, close to a quarter of a century earlier, Sister Sarto had said he was buried.

Carr's Hill is located off the Carrigaline Road, south-east of Cork city centre. There was no car park for the old cemetery, and so Carmel had to leave her car in a lay-by with the words 'no parking' painted on the ground, at the side of the road where trucks and cars barrelled along at blinding speed. The gate was painted black with a little cross on top, and a yellow sign was affixed to it warning that we were being watched by CCTV.

A significant number of Bessborough children died in the district hospital, later called St Finbarr's. A former administrator of the hospital, who had access to mortuary records, confirmed to the Commission that the South Cork Board of Assistance assumed responsibility for the burial of Bessborough children who died at the hospital and that 'many of these children' were likely buried at Carr's Hill. But the burial book where these details might be listed had not been located.

Carr's Hill was established as a municipal burial ground during the Great Famine, when other cemeteries in the city ran out of space for the dead. The night before I travelled to Cork, I spoke on the phone with Pat Gunn, a local historian who told me he had long petitioned for the local authorities to take care of the cemetery, to cut the grass and make it more accessible. It was hard for the Cork City and County Famine Group, of which Pat Gunn was a member, to hold a memorial for the Famine victims, since the road was so dangerous, there was no safe place to park and the way to the cemetery was not easily accessible. He told me it was a 'forgotten place'.

Carmel, her little boy and I made our way up the track. We climbed through a dilapidated farm gate, continuing up through the thick grass of a barely marked path. On the other side of a low fence was a field of cattle.

On our way up the lane, we noticed two people behind us, a middle-aged man and an older woman. The cows in the next field were spooked and giddy, jostling and bounding with an unusual energy. At the top of the field, the wall and gate of the cemetery came into view, but wire closed off the path.

Around twenty cows lined up side by side to watch us attempt to get past the last obstacle. We suspected that the wire that ran up the field, separating the cows from the rough path, which now barred crossing from the path to the cemetery gate, might be electric. Carmel ducked under it to be safe but her back brushed against it, the sting of the electric current flinging her forward on to the ground. She got up quickly and brushed herself off.

Carmel was a member of the Mother-and-Baby Home Collaborative Forum, established by Minister Zappone to represent the interests of survivors. She had also accompanied her mother, Bridget, when she testified before the Commission, and had written to Zappone about her story. After reading section 4.41 of the interim report, she emailed the Commission asking it to confirm that it referred to William.

Now, having heard nothing from the Commission about its findings regarding the child who was clearly her brother William, here she was with her face in the dirt, trying to visit the place where he was buried. The State's health service owned this cemetery, and a state commission had published a report suggesting that over a hundred Bessborough children could be buried here – and yet, people trying to visit were made to navigate rusty gates and electric wire. It was surreal. I found a big stick to hold down the wire so that Carmel's foster son, and the man and woman we'd encountered, could pass easily.

The cemetery was a big, sloping field lined by a wall and trees. In the middle of the field was a giant cross, made of steel bars and wire mesh and supported by wires fixed to the ground. A plaque explained that it dated back to the 1950s and was the work of a taxi driver from Cork named Jack Sorensen, who thought there should be a monument to the dead and made it with his own hands. A big stone plaque nearby, marking the 150th anniversary of the Great Famine and the thousands of Cork people who were buried there, had been unveiled by the US Ambassador in 1997. This was thought to be the biggest mass grave in Cork, with tens of thousands of bodies from the workhouse, plus an unknown number of people who ended up here because they had been institutionalized or simply because they were too poor. It is not clear when the last burial took place. On the radio the day before, I had heard a local man saying that he remembered seeing a cart going to Carr's Hill with the feet of dead bodies, including the bodies of children, poking out from under a tarpaulin. There was not a single headstone in the entire field.

The five of us stood looking up at the cross. Carmel told the two strangers about her brother. The old woman said that a relative of theirs, a woman in her fifties, had only recently found out she was adopted. She was contacted by the State and told she was one of the people named in the records of St Patrick's Guild, illegally registered as the natural child of the people who'd adopted her. Her birthday, too, had been falsified. Her whole identity was a fabrication.

In the absence of a gravestone to visit, Carmel looked around the cemetery, assessing it. 'It's not depressing,' she said. 'I'm going to tell my mum it's not depressing.' It was far away from the walls of any institution, in an open space, the sky arching from one horizon to the other, uninterrupted by buildings, only the taxi man's strange cross, erected in tribute.

There was the flash of a rabbit's white tail bounding away as I walked through the swarm of brambles and nettles that covered most of the burial field. There were two wooden structures that looked like beehives – but who comes to an overgrown paupers' graveyard to tend to bees? Someone had hung a fake Christmas wreath on a gorse bush, and there was a plastic figurine of a deer in the undergrowth. Carmel's foster son, with a head of dark curls, rambled around in the flatter patches, nattering away to himself, wearing a top emblazoned with the word 'happy'.

I went up to the top of the gentle slope then back down to the very end, looking for any sign of a headstone in the field and finding none. At the top there was an arched opening in the wall, looking out on to another field. At the edges of the field, there were little clusters of bones among the undergrowth – the remains of animals, or so I hoped.

Back at Carmel's house, she showed me letters and emails sent and received over the years regarding requests for information about what happened to William.

In the mid-nineties, when Sister Sarto showed Bridget the spot in the Bessborough graveyard where William was buried, Bridget assumed that she'd been told the truth. Carmel began to have her doubts, though, particularly after talking to other people who'd received misinformation from religious orders.

In 1999, Carmel and Bridget went to St Finbarr's Hospital looking for William's records, but the department they spoke to couldn't assist them. Not long after that, they managed to obtain his birth and death certificates. Bridget then became seriously ill, and for a long time they dropped the search. They sent the first freedom of information request in 2013. The next year, they were given a tour of Bessborough and asked the director to request information about the burial from the nuns on their behalf. In 2015, through a solicitor, they wrote to the nuns, the statistics office, St Finbarr's Hospital and the registrar's office seeking William's records. They received confirmation from the local diocese that William was baptized in St Michael's Church the day after he was born. The HSE said it held no records on William's burial or relating to his stay at St Finbarr's Hospital. Carmel also inquired with Cork City Council about burial records in the graveyards.

After Carmel read the details of William's burial in the interim report, she called a solicitor working with the Commission, with whom she'd previously been in contact. 'I was sobbing my heart out,' she told me. She was told that, for legal reasons, the Commission couldn't say anything or give information about individual burials. The Commission would later issue a statement to the *Irish Examiner* claiming that it would be 'an offence . . . to disclose or publish any evidence given or the contents of any document produced', and thus 'we cannot inform the families'.

Now, Carmel knew, documentation had existed all along to show that the Sacred Hearts at Bessborough had written to St Finbarr's Hospital on foot of Bridget's request for information in 1994, and that the hospital had been able to determine that William was buried at Carr's Hill. How had this not come to light before? Why had Bridget been told the false story that her son was buried near the nuns' plot at Bessborough?

Between 1922 and 1998, the Commission found, over 900 Bessborough children died. The Commission had been able to determine the burial places of only 64 of these children.

Fourteen adult inmates died at Bessborough, according to the interim report. Nine of these deaths were recorded as being related to pregnancy or childbirth; no cause was given for the other deaths. No burial place for any of these women has been found. There were also women who never left the institution, and who were considered 'domestic servants' by the time of their deaths. Between 1927 and 1985, twelve such women were buried in a private plot owned by the Sacred Hearts. The headstone was broken and unreadable, and the Commission notes that, 'It is unlikely that the headstone bears the names of women buried in this plot.' One of these women entered Bessborough in 1922 at the age of twenty and died in 1984, aged eighty-two. Each of the nuns buried in that plot had a carefully placed cross inscribed with her name.

The Commission judged it 'highly likely' that children had been buried in the grounds of Bessborough. But having engaged forensic archaeologists and studied aerial photography and old maps, the Commission was unable to locate any physical evidence of a children's burial ground, and 'did not consider it feasible' to excavate the 60 acres of the current Bessborough estate, let alone the 140 acres of the original estate that had subsequently been sold.

The Commission could only speculate about the number of Bessborough children buried in Carr's Hill because the HSE – which owns the cemetery – had not yet been able to produce records on who was buried there. Mortuary records with details of burials existed at St Finbarr's until 2001, and the Commission was trying to track down a burials book that had apparently been transferred to Cork University Maternity Hospital. There had reportedly been a caretaker who had a burial register and who lived near the cemetery. The Commission made 'house-to-house inquiries' in the area, trying to find the caretaker, but without success.

The Sacred Hearts, according to the Commission, 'were able to provide remarkably little evidence about burial arrangements'.

The hospital administrator who found the record of William's burial in 1994 wrote that a book called *A Tale of Two Hospitals* had reminded him about the records. The book, by Sister M. Emmanuel Browne, details the history of the workhouse and St Finbarr's Hospital, where the Sisters of Mercy continued as matrons until 1978. 'Cork Workhouse was among the worst in Ireland,' Browne writes. 'One dreadful example of its callousness was the existence of the paupers' grave known as "Carr's Hole".' A decent burial was important. People feared the shame of dying in the workhouse and being buried in an unmarked shallow grave. 'The poor dreaded it beyond all else, but they had no other choice of burial ground.'

★

In records I obtained through a freedom of information request, there were minutes of an August 2014 meeting between two employees of Tusla and a Sacred Hearts Sister. The nun's name was redacted, but the document described her as the 'director' of Bessborough between 1981 and 2007: this was clearly Sister Sarto Harney. She had requested the meeting to inquire about files that might relate to her, concerned about being at a disadvantage if there was a future inquiry into the running of Bessborough and she could not 'account for her time'. The meeting took place a few months after the Tuam news broke. The two Tusla officials told Sister Sarto that they couldn't give her the sort of files she had expressed interest in, and that she would have to send in a request for specific records like anyone else.

The two Tusla officials had a few questions for Sister Sarto. One of them, Lesley Honan-Loucks, had been involved in research for the McAleese report, looking specifically at pathways between Bessborough and the Magdalen laundries. The officials would almost certainly have been aware of a HSE draft report from 2012 that had flagged grave concerns about the high death rates at Bessborough, the legality of adoptions, and payments made by mothers, families and potential adopters, and called for an investigation into the mother-and-baby homes. This was two years before the news broke about the mass grave at Tuam.

Sister Sarto was asked about the burial place of stillborn babies. She said she would check with the caretaker, but didn't know his or her name. When asked where babies might have been buried, she suggested 'family graves'. Sister Sarto claimed that only three babies died at Bessborough during her time, from 1981 to 2007. She said all three were buried in the Sisters' cemetery. Sister Sarto also claimed that the institution trained women for jobs as cleaners and that the girls 'loved' it there. She mentioned a box of pictures of babies and birth mothers she had kept, along with thank-you notes from women who they had 'helped'.

In contrast to Bessborough, the other two Sacred Hearts mother-and-baby homes – Sean Ross Abbey and Castlepollard – had areas clearly designated for the burial of children. But as at Bessborough, no burial records survived: either they were never kept, or they were lost or destroyed. The Commission's interim report cast serious doubt on all of the claims made by the order with regard to the burial of children. An affidavit provided to the Commission in relation to the burials 'was, in many respects, speculative, inaccurate and misleading'. The Commission found it 'difficult to comprehend' that the Sisters knew nothing about burials in Bessborough. The Sisters' affidavit stressed that the infants buried at Sean Ross and Castlepollard 'were laid to rest without any cost accruing to the coffers of the local or central government'. I read this as a dig at the State, suggesting authorities were unconcerned about where babies were being buried so long as it saved them money. But the claim was refuted by the Commission, which noted that it had seen a bill for coffins 'sent by Sean Ross to a local health authority'.

According to records, more than 1,000 Sean Ross Abbey children died in the institution or in the hospital in Roscrea. Twenty-nine mothers also died, the majority for reasons arising from pregnancy or childbirth. There was a designated children's graveyard on the grounds of the institution, but no headstones or burial records. At the time of the report, a test excavation of the graveyard had recently been completed, with forensic screens set up on a part of the grounds and gardaí present around the clock.

In Castlepollard, the third mother-and-baby home established by the Sacred Hearts in Ireland, 220 children died (either in the institution or in connected hospitals), as did eight mothers who succumbed to complications of pregnancy or childbirth. Babies were buried in a narrow corridor of land accessed by a lane leading from the old stately house. The graveyard was bounded by a low wall on one side and a high wall on the other. It was said that there used to be another low wall bisecting the plot, with a locked gate, separating the nuns' burial plot from the area where the babies were put in the unmarked ground. A stone cross was erected in memory of the Sisters, but no mention was made of the children. At a Castlepollard commemoration, a woman named Frances, who gave birth in the institution, told me she cared for someone else's baby while pregnant, a boy named Dominic who was pale and gaunt. For three weeks she tried to look after him, but he couldn't keep milk down. She told the nuns he wasn't feeding and asked them to get him medical attention, but no doctor was called in to see him. 'Persevere, he'll be grand,' she was told. He died one night, and when she asked the nuns where he was buried they wouldn't tell her.

Every year, survivors gather on the grounds of Castlepollard for a commemoration. Paul Jude Redmond, who organizes the gathering, was born in Castlepollard in 1964, and through his own research obtained death registers. These showed a steep fall in the institution's death rate following the introduction of legal adoption in 1953. Redmond saw a clear causal connection: once adoption became legal, the Sacred Hearts realized that 'illegitimate' children were now worth something. The drop in the infant mortality rate at Castlepollard from a reported 13 per cent average in its early years to 0.5 per cent in its final two decades was dramatic – perhaps too dramatic to be explained by improvements in hygiene or medical care. 'When we illegitimate Irish bastards were suddenly worth more than the cows on the farms, we stopped dying by the thousands,' Redmond wrote.

At a commemoration at Glasnevin for survivors of the St Patrick's mother-and-baby home, around thirty people gathered around a grassy field in the cemetery. An historian who worked at Glasnevin told the small crowd that up to 60,000 bodies were buried in this field, from stillborn babies to children up to the age of eight. It was a 'poor ground' that became known as the Old Angels' Plot because of the number of infants and children buried there. The Glasnevin historian emphasized that the name of every person buried in the cemetery was recorded, 'from the great O'Connell to the meekest and least important person'.

There is a grey stone watchtower at the edge of Glasnevin's roadside wall, with a turret at the top. It formed the far corner of the Old Angels' Plot, overlooking the unmarked stretch of ground. A plaque informed visitors that the watchtower was constructed in 1842 to 'prevent bodies being snatched' from the cemetery for 'use in medical schools'. Some of the children whose remains were buried there had been born in Dublin's mother-and-baby homes; by the time they were buried, their bodies had already been used as anatomical subjects. In 2011, an RTÉ *Prime Time* investigation found that the remains of more than 400 children were sent from institutions, including St Patrick's on the Navan Road, to Irish medical schools. Up to the 1960s, when a campaign to promote voluntary donation began, it was rare for people to donate their bodies to medical science after death. Medical schools relied largely on 'unclaimed' bodies from workhouses, county homes, psychiatric institutions and mother-and-baby homes. By law, there should be a forty-eight-hour waiting period after death before a body could be considered unclaimed. The Commission's interim report acknowledged that it was unlikely mothers were made aware of this requirement.

The bodies of 950 children who died in Dublin Union institutions, including St Patrick's, were sent to three Dublin medical schools: UCD, Trinity and the Royal College of Surgeons. All but eighteen of the children received as anatomical subjects were 'illegitimate' children, according to the combined register of the Dublin medical schools.

According to the Commission's interim report, the country leader of the Bon Secours, Sister Marie Ryan, told the Commission in 2018 that she didn't know what the burial arrangements were at Tuam, that the Sisters were 'shocked and devastated' by what had come to light about burials in the 'subsurface structure', and that it was the view of the Sisters that the children deserved a 'proper burial and this did not happen', for which they expressed 'deep sorrow and apologise unreservedly'.

The same year, in a letter released through freedom of information by the organization Right To Know, the Bon Secours wrote to Zappone in response to a request for a meeting, saying that they were 'always happy to engage in dialogue' but were surprised at her request to discuss the Tuam institution before the Commission published its report. They curtly reminded her that their nuns had been requested by the local authority to operate the home: 'This was an institution created and operated by the Irish State.' Sister Ryan also wrote that it seemed to them that 'Galway County Council, the Department of Health and the doctor employed by the local authority would have been fully aware of the fact of these deaths and no doubt then would have been aware that burial arrangements would have to be made for the remains.'

The question of what to call the 'subsurface structure' was bitterly contested. The Bon Secours had been given a draft of the burials report ahead of publication and employed an archaeologist to review it. One of the points they argued was that the investigation did not give enough consideration to the possibility 'that the structure could be designed as a burial vault'. But the detailed evidence outlined by the archaeologists, in consultation with an engineer specializing in sewerage installations, and the samples that tested positive for markers of human waste, led the Commission to conclude that the structure in which dead infants and children were deposited was very likely 'sewerage related', and that it was 'likely that the chambers were used for an unspecified duration as sewage tanks'.

The Commission determined that it was unlikely human remains were buried in the structure before 1937, meaning that children who died in the home between 1925 and 1937 might be buried elsewhere on the grounds of the institution, possibly in what were now the back gardens of houses on the Dublin Road estate. Sewerage had been a longstanding problem at the institution. In the 1930s, tenants of houses nearby complained of the 'offensive and unhealthy stench from the sewerage outlet from the Children's Home'. By 1937 there was a residents' petition to remove the cesspool at the back of the home, because it was seen as dangerous to the health of the neighbours. Around the same time, a county engineer who visited recommended new lavatories be built, since those in the institution were dilapidated, without light or ventilation.

The stark conclusion of the Commission's interim report was that many of the 802 children who died at Tuam are buried in these chambers. The Commission thought it was unlikely that the Bon Secours conducted the burials of children themselves; people employed by the County Council and its members and staff 'must have known' about them. The report also observed that 'there must be people in Tuam and the surrounding area who know more about the burial arrangements and who did not come forward with the information'.

Before the interim report on burials was published, I spoke with Niamh McCullagh, the forensic archaeologist who carried out the test excavation at Tuam. She told me there was 'no modern comparison' she could think of for the way the children were buried in Tuam. There were examples from ancient times, juvenile remains placed in pots in Greece as far back as 1,000 BC. In the former Yugoslavia, the bodies of people killed during the conflict were sometimes placed in wells. 'They were trying to hide what they were doing there,' she said. Years ago, she had visited a graveyard in Letterfrack, close to where the industrial school used to be. A plaque she read stated that it wasn't known how many children were buried there. 'I couldn't believe it,' she said. 'How is this acceptable? How is this okay? These are children, maybe that's why it was acceptable.'

When bones are exhumed from the burial site in Tuam, Niamh McCullagh told me, it should be possible in some cases to test them to establish the cause of death. When I asked her what causes of death could be found from testing bones, she said: 'Malnutrition.'

The first page of the Commission's interim report on the burials paid tribute to the work of Catherine Corless, as the catalyst for the entire investigation.

I met Corless in person for the first time in Galway, on the university campus, at the launch of an initiative to create an archive of oral histories, safeguarding personal testimonies of the institution.

This was in February 2019, a few weeks before the burials report came out. In Tuam, Corless was sometimes painted as hungry for the limelight, but I had found her somewhat elusive, if anything, and the main impression I got when we met was of someone who just wanted to understand what had happened at the Bon Secours home and in the other institutions.

When I told her about the man I've called Jim, the Knock steward who was searching for blood relations, she was moved. I mentioned that Jim was building up the courage to ask her to help him search for his mother, or at least to find his mother's grave, and she told me she hoped he'd get in touch. 'I do that the whole time,' she said. 'There are an awful lot. Unbelievable. Hundreds of emails, phone calls. People just arrive at the door.' She could tell almost immediately when a person on the phone was trying to trace: there was a hesitancy in their voice, a note of hope but also a sense of shame for having to ask.

'I feel privileged to help them out, it means so much,' she said. 'They don't know who they are.' Sometimes they have only the sparsest of details, such as the mother's age and a county. Just the week before we spoke, a woman came to Corless. Corless realized that she'd met this woman's cousin, also searching, a couple of years earlier, and she was able to put them in touch with each other. 'I never knew all these people existed until they started coming to me,' she told me. She felt that the growing understanding of how many people are affected had made Tuam residents more compassionate towards survivors of the institution and their descendants, and changed the way she was viewed: 'I'm not the baddie who opened a can of worms.' A sudden loud ringing interrupted her and she pulled a block of a mobile phone out of her bag, an old brick with spongey buttons and a yellowish square screen. 'I insist on having this old-fashioned phone,' she said. 'It's a mighty phone.'

Until she started her research, she had no idea what had gone on behind the walls of the institution or how children were separated from their mothers for adoption. She had gone to school with children from the home, but it wasn't a place you asked questions about. 'I thought they were orphans,' she told me. 'Kind nuns looking after orphans.'

One fact that has often become lost in the story that is told about Corless is that in the beginning she made strong efforts to allow the religious Sisters, the Church and the County Council to take the initiative. She brought them the information she'd compiled, thinking they would want to know. 'Nobody cared,' she said. 'That really got to me.'

When she asked the Bon Secours nuns if they had further records, they wrote her a 'lovely letter', she told me, 'delighted I was doing history on the home, but [they] had no records'. The County Council told her to go to the health board, and the health board said it only had private registers from the home. The Archdiocese of Tuam claimed it had no records at all. In the beginning, she said, the local town council agreed to meet the graves committee, offering around €300 towards the cost of memorial plaques. 'They didn't want it at all at first,' she said. 'They nearly went berserk when they heard we were naming all the children.' They suggested that mothers would be offended by the children's names being made public, or that there might be legal concerns; but Corless felt it was because they didn't want anyone investigating further. 'We were up against it.'

Corless and another local woman – Mary Moriarty, who had stumbled upon bones behind the former Tuam institution in 1975 – met with the Archbishop of Tuam, Michael Neary, and his secretary at the time, a Father Waldron. Corless asked the Archbishop to write to the Bon Secours order and the council, to use his influence compassionately for the sake of people impacted by the institutions. 'He didn't say yes or no,' she said. 'Completely complacent.'

The morning after Corless's findings were aired in a story by Alison O'Reilly in the *Irish Mail on Sunday*, Corless received a call from the head of the Bon Secours, Sister Marie Ryan, asking to meet. The meeting was in a hotel in Galway. Sister Marie was accompanied by another nun; Corless was accompanied by her husband and by two other members of the graves committee. 'They were stiff upper,' Corless told me. Corless presented the facts she had found and expressed her belief that a significant number of the roughly 800 dead children she'd identified were buried in the disused tank within the old walls of the institution.

The message from the Bon Secours was that they had no records and that all the Sisters who'd worked in the Tuam home were dead or incapable of talking. 'Did I realize the pain I was causing their Sisters and the hurt and distress, and what was all this about anyway?' Corless remembered telling them that survivors of the home had been suffering all their lives. 'There was no offer of help, only denial,' she told me. 'Only consideration for themselves and what they stood for. They more or less asked me to stop it.' It was made clear to Corless that henceforth she would be expected to deal with Terry Prone, their public relations representative at the time. Corless never did speak with Terry Prone.

I asked her why she thought the Bon Secours might have buried babies in a tank. 'Money, money, money, money, money, money,' she said carefully. 'What else? Bother, expense, and having to get someone in to dig holes.'

I told her then about my encounter with some of the Bon Secours Sisters in Cork at their Christmas gathering. Corless wanted to know about the women I'd spoken with. Her voice became animated and there was a yearning in her questions. I explained that one of the Sisters said she wanted people to have answers and that she thought about it every day. 'She's probably not allowed to speak,' Corless shook her head. 'If you see that nun again, ask her would she talk to me? Not for the press, but just to know, just a one-to-one.'

If any of the Bon Secours Sisters were willing to meet with her, Corless assured me, she would go to Cork in an instant to speak with them. 'I need it for myself, just to know there's one compassionate person down there,' she explained. 'Just to hear it, it will be healing for myself. I'm hurt and disappointed. I'm absolutely shocked at the reaction of the nuns and the Church. I keep saying that, there has to be some compassionate woman there that knows. I know they're bound by obedience or whatever but it'd be healing for myself.' At school and when she was a young woman, she admired the nuns and the religious, because she felt they taught the students good things: 'How to treat people and how to live.' She remembered them as genuinely nice people. But she no longer attends Mass or takes part in other Church activities, because it would make her feel complicit. She walks the fields with her dogs, fills her mind with new thoughts or lets her pent-up mental energy disperse. 'There's definitely something guiding me.'

Catherine Corless had what seemed to be a straightforward answer to the question of why Tuam children were buried in a sewerage tank: money. But it also cost money to provide proper burials to the members of their own congregation; and the order had even gone to the trouble and expense of exhuming the remains of nuns buried on the grounds of the Grove Hospital and reinterring them in Knock.

Willie Walsh, the former Bishop of Killaloe, had put forward a very different theory: that because the children had been baptized, 'there was a certain attitude that their remains didn't matter'. This, too, didn't quite work as an explanation, because the baptized children of married parents were buried with customary ritual and respect; their remains did matter.

Another theory I'd heard was that the burials on the grounds of the homes were never individually marked because the sight of hundreds of little crosses would put off visiting adoptive parents. But there was no necessity to bury children on the grounds of the institutions; if the Sisters had wished to bury them with dignity and discretion, that could have been achieved.

Most babies born in the mother-and-baby homes were quickly baptized – and yet, their bodies still carried the stigma of sin. The bodies of mothers were no different. A 2018 RTÉ documentary by Conor Keane and Liam O'Brien told the story of Peggy McCarthy, an unmarried woman in Co. Kerry who died of eclampsia after giving birth in 1946. While in labour, she was driven from hospital to hospital by her neighbour, a hackney driver, but no one would take her in as a patient because she was not married. Then, when it was time for her body to be buried, the local priest refused. That night, a group of men broke open the gates of the church. She was eventually buried in the family plot, without a funeral Mass. Her baby survived and was raised by her grandparents until the grandmother died. At the age of eighteen, a priest sent Peggy's daughter to a Magdalen laundry for the rest of her life.

Stories like Peggy's, and all the evidence of how the home babies were buried, indicated that those who were viewed as stained by sexual sin occupied a moral category all their own. When illegitimacy and sexual transgression needed to be hidden even in death, when the institution of the family was more venerated and protected than the human beings who constituted it, when superficial respectability outweighed compassion, the result was mass graves. The standard rituals – whereby baptized Catholics were buried and visibly memorialized in consecrated ground – were not applicable. Upon the deaths of priests who were serial abusers, the Church went to great lengths to bury their bodies in consecrated ground; but children who had done nothing wrong received no such respect. The logic of secrecy and shame that underpinned the institutions may also explain why the religious orders did not keep good records of burials. And the slowly dawning realization that great wrongs had been done might explain why the orders have been so consistently unhelpful to those seeking the truth.

In the first week in June 2019, more than a month after the Commission's interim report on burials was released, Carmel Cantwell's mother Bridget received a document from Tusla confirming that William was buried at Carr's Hill. It was a letter dated 12 December 1994, written by an administrator named J. Devery at St Finbarr's Hospital in Cork and addressed to a Sister Eleanor Redican in the hospital's Chaplaincy Department. 'I refer to the request for information which you have received from the Sacred Heart Home,' it began. 'I have checked my records and found the entry in the "burial book" for 1960.'

Infant William Gerald Walsh died on the second day of

December in 1960 and was buried in Carr's Hill on the 13th, a month after being admitted to St Anthony's Ward. The burial was carried out by the hospital. His mother's domicile was recorded as the Sacred Hearts Home.

After decades of searching for proof of where her son was buried, Bridget held the record in her hand. The letter contained what might have been a clue as to why she was never told the truth about where her son was buried. 'If you are involved in imparting information on the place of burial, I would advise a very sensitive approach,' the hospital administrator warned. Carr's Hill, he wrote, 'was the original work-house burial ground and was a place that most would prefer not to know!!'

There is a significant ambiguity in the Commission's account of the 1994 correspondence. The interim report notes that the administrator of the hospital 'provided a full overview of the child's stay in St Finbarr's including the cause of death and the place of burial'. It would be natural to assume that this overview was provided to the Sacred Hearts at Bessborough; but the letter that Carmel finally saw in June 2019 was internal hospital correspondence. Though the Commission casts doubt on the Sacred Hearts' claims that they do not know anything about where these children were buried, it doesn't provide evidence that the information contained in this letter was passed on to Bessborough. The lack of such evidence, and the hospital administrator's advice to take 'a very sensitive approach', leaves open the possibility that the nuns were never informed that William was buried in Carr's Hill. The likelier scenario, of course, is that the Sacred Hearts were told the truth by St Finbarr's, and then lied to Bridget about William's burial place – perhaps out of a belief that she'd prefer to think of her son resting in a demarcated nuns' plot, or out of a fear of legal action, or both. Carmel is in no doubt that the nuns knew the truth, and lied.

Now that Bridget and Carmel knew the date on which William was buried, they knew that there had been another lie. The nun who told Bridget of William's death had also told her that he was already buried. Now, it was clear that William's corpse was still in the hospital, presumably in the morgue, when Bridget left Bessborough. If she had known the truth, she could have visited the hospital morgue, to say goodbye, and she could have attended the burial.

The years Bridget and Carmel spent searching for answers about where William was buried weighed heavily now on Carmel's mind. The truth had been known for twenty-five years and none of their inquiries had managed to unearth it. But they also held on to the idea that the truth probably never would have come to light if Bridget had not made her inquiry to the nuns back in 1994.

I spoke to Bridget for the first time in June 2019, several weeks after the publication of the burials report. Her voice broke as she said, 'I could have afforded to bring him out and bury him.'

Her son was still in the mortuary at St Finbarr's Hospital when she was put in a cab at Bessborough and sent to the boat. It would have been a short detour. She could have had a brief moment with William before he was buried. But those things had not happened, and instead she had spent decades preoccupied with the question of how and where her son was buried.

She first noticed William was sick three days after he was born. She was made to sit on a stool in a cold corridor outside the nursery to breastfeed him. 'I said to Sister that he wasn't eating,' she recalled. 'She snatched him from my arms and said I wasn't feeding him properly. She rammed the bottle down his little throat.' His medical record said he had difficulty swallowing. Bridget had abscesses on her breasts, but the Sister would push his little mouth to Bridget's nipple until he struggled to breathe. The harshness with which the children were treated horrified her. 'They weren't fit to look after children,' she said of the nuns.

There was another young woman in Bessborough whose baby was sick with a rash. She confessed to Bridget that she was praying to God that the rash didn't heal so that he wouldn't be adopted. Some of the women would sneak out of the dormitory and try to visit the nursery in secret at night to see their babies, but doors were often locked. The nuns sometimes brought the women for a walk in big groups around the grounds. Bridget felt they were being marched like prisoners. She was caught standing on a bed once, looking out of the window at crows nesting in the trees, and as punishment she had to stand in a corner, seven months pregnant, until the nun returned. A priest would come every morning for Mass, but she remembered him standing far back to administer Communion, as if the women were untouchable. He ate eggs, bacon and a grapefruit for breakfast. They never got food like it.

When they wrote their letters home, a nun would look over their shoulder. Bridget's letters were sent to the Crusade of Rescue in London and redirected 'to mammy' so that she could maintain the pretence that she was over there working. Bridget was working as a cook with a family who bred horses when she realized she was pregnant. Despite all her experience with babies at home, she never knew where they came from. She had no idea of birth control, except for stories she heard about women being sentenced to death for carrying out illegal abortions. She never told her boyfriend, who was the father. If anyone knew the truth, she thought, she would never get a job again, and nor would any member of her family, due to the shame. She feared they would end up homeless.

The course of her life had already been altered because of shame. At thirteen, while working at a convent, the Sisters of Charity encouraged her to become a postulant because she knew her prayers so well. She agreed, believing it would be a reward to her grandmother, who raised her. 'It was a great joy for her,' she said. When her sixteenth birthday came, they were going to send her out to the foreign missions. Her birth certificate was sent for, and then everything was cancelled: 'They absolutely disowned me once they knew I was illegitimate myself.' Bridget was seventeen when she became pregnant and was in Bessborough by her eighteenth birthday.

It was a summer evening, still bright out, when she was brought to the nuns' graveyard in Bessborough and told William was buried there, decades after she left the place. She remembered a short nun called Sister Mary telling Sister Sarto where to go in the cemetery. 'Three-quarters down, the right-hand side, she tapped her foot,' she said. When they told her she could not place a plaque with his name, it made her feel the culture of secrecy had not changed.

'It's human nature,' she said. 'To want to know where our babies are buried.' She wanted her baby to be buried with her. Soon she would be in Ireland, visiting Carr's Hill. She would go out and buy a pair of baby shoes to hang somewhere in the cemetery. She would keep asking questions.

'We were told so many times in Bessborough it was the will of God,' she said. 'Everything was the will of God. William was dying because of the will of God.'

Now people wanted the truth.

Afterword

In June 2019, just as I was finishing this book, the annual Bessborough survivors' commemoration was held indoors, away from the folly, on a day of unrelenting rain. For the first time, the people gathered were able to speak the number of the Bessborough dead, thanks to the Commission's interim report on burials. Ann O'Gorman sat amongst the survivors. The report had left her without any answers about where her baby daughter Evelyn was buried. Shortly after the report was published, she had gone to Bessborough and removed the ornaments she'd left to remember her daughter in the nuns' graveyard.

Carmel Cantwell's mother, Bridget, was also there, having travelled over from the UK. The day before, she had gone to Carr's Hill and stood in the overgrown field where the records say her son William is buried.

I was reminded yet again of how much unfinished business the shame-industrial complex has left – for individuals and for Irish society. In 2016, the government had published a bill intended to liberalize access to information for adoptees and birth parents. Three years on, shortly before the Bessborough commemoration, the bill was 'paused'. People I spoke to were pleased: they believed that adoptees deserved an absolute right to their birth information, and the legislation fell a fair distance short of that. But the suspension of the bill left Ireland's unusually restrictive adoption-information regime in place.

The final report of the Commission of Investigation, having been delayed twice, was now due to be published in February 2020. Ageing survivors worried they might die before getting answers, or redress. Although the Commission did not have a role in redress, survivors worried that the government would not even consider redress until the report was published.

Early on in the research for this book, I spoke with the former head of special projects at the National Archives, Catriona Crowe. She has called for the opening of the Church's archives as a form of redress. The Commission did not allow people to give public testimony, as some wanted to, and past redress schemes have often involved gag orders or indemnity clauses, further silencing people. There were plans for the records of the Ryan commission on child abuse to be sealed within the National Archives for seventy-five years. Lawyer and advocate Maeve O'Rourke has argued that the State's continuing obsession with secrecy shows that we are 'still capable of silencing and keeping out of sight those who are not us, who we have marginalized, who we have stigmatized'.

With adoption information restricted and the religious orders' archives closed, some survivors are making use of the Freedom of Information Act. Clodagh Hourigan, who works in the European Parliament in Brussels, was adopted through Temple Hill. After her two sisters from her birth mother's marriage found her, the three of them applied for the records. Clodagh and her siblings all gave consent for each other to access the documents and so were able to argue for access to the records in full. They received correspondence between the nuns and her mother, detailing her mother's struggle to pay the fees.

The State is finally being forced to reckon with the implications of the illegal-adoption scandal at St Patrick's Guild. By June 2019, the known number of falsified birth certificates had grown from 126 to 148. Many of the people implicated have yet to be located and informed. While some of the people whose birth certificates were falsified were already aware that they'd been adopted, some – middle-aged or elderly now – are receiving identity-altering information, and others still have no idea.

Fergus Finlay, the former CEO of Barnardos, spoke at the 2019 Bessborough commemoration. Afterwards, he told me about working in the Department of Foreign Affairs and being among the first people to see the evidence of the large-scale export of Irish babies for adoption in America. He said that not one of the adoption forms that he saw had the signature of a mother; they were usually signed by someone from the Church. He believed thousands of children could have been illegally registered and adopted abroad.

Sister Eileen McLaughlin, a Sacred Hearts nun with whom I'd been in contact about interviewing other members of the order, was present at the Bessborough commemoration, moving around plates of biscuits but never seeming to speak to anyone. A few days earlier, I'd spoken on the phone with Thomas Quigley, director of the Bessborough Centre, about the Commission's view that the religious orders, including the Sacred Hearts, knew more about burials than they were revealing. Quigley said that one of the Sacred Hearts nuns, a Sister Mary McManus, had worked in Bessborough since the 1940s and still lived in the modern convent on the grounds. Sister Mary was the named witness, 'present at death' on death registrations for children in Bessborough in the late 1950s.

With that conversation in mind, I approached Sister Eileen and asked her how the order could explain that none of the Sisters was able to provide any information on the burials. She said she couldn't explain it. When I mentioned the Sister Mary whose name was signed as a witness to deaths, she suggested it could be a different woman of the same name, who was dead.

Note on Sources

This book is a work of journalism, and its most important sources are the people who shared their stories with me. But I have also drawn on the published work of pioneering historians, journalists and memoirists; on research published by the State and by advocacy groups; and on State and ecclesiastical papers, some of which are available in public archives and some of which I accessed via the Freedom of Information Act. I have tried, in the writing of this book, to 'show my work' as far as possible, and many of my key sources are named in the text – but some are not. What follows is not a comprehensive listing of every non-human source I consulted, but it is an attempt to give credit where credit is due.

There are a number of survivors' organizations whose research has been useful to me. These include the Adoption Rights Alliance, the Coalition of Mother and Baby Home Survivors, First Mothers, CLANN Project, Justice for Magdalenes Research, Beyond Adoption, Know My Own, the Tuam Home Survivors Network, the Tuam Babies Family Group, and the many Facebook community groups devoted to individual institutions.

Christine Buckley, a survivor of the industrial school at Goldenbridge in Dublin, spoke of her experiences on Gay Byrne's radio programme in 1992, and later collaborated with the director Louis Lentin on his documentary *Dear Daughter*, which aired on RTÉ in 1996. Buckley's testimony and activism exposed systematic abuse within religious-run carceral institutions in Ireland, and Mary Raftery's 1999 RTÉ documentary *States of Fear* had a huge impact in forcing the public and the State to reckon with the institutions' legacy. I have written in these pages about the role of Catherine Corless in researching the Tuam dead, and of Alison O'Reilly in reporting Corless's findings in the *Irish Mail on Sunday*. A number of other journalists have done valuable work on the mother-and-baby homes and Magdalen laundries over the years, and no other newspaper journalist has been as deeply committed to investigating these institutions, or has broken as many stories about them, as Conall Ó Fátharta of the *Irish Examiner*. As long ago as 2010, his reporting on the experiences of Tressa Reeves showed that the Adoption Board and state authorities were officially aware of illegal adoptions at least since the 1990s. His dogged reporting – most notably on Bessborough – has expanded our understanding of the institutions and their legacy.

As Ó Fátharta and others have documented, and as I discovered for myself in researching this book, there are many obstacles to accessing essential documentation. But some public archival sources are full of fascinating and revelatory information about the institutions.

The transcripts of Dáil and the Seanad debates, dating back to the early years of the Free State, were an extremely valuable resource in my research. The transcripts are available online and easily searchable. Another very useful source was irishgenealogy.ie, which contains civil records of deaths from 1864 to 1968, births from 1864 to 1918 and marriages from 1845 to 1943.

Local Government Reports (LGRs) compiled by the Department of Local Government and Public Health from 1922 to 1945 detailed numbers in the mother-and-baby homes as well as children boarded out.

Department of Health files at the National Archives include references for records relating to the mother-and-baby homes, unmarried mothers and boarded-out children. Some have been removed, including records relating to 'Unmarried Mothers'. The references to St Patrick's/Pelletstown come from A8/331 Proposals for Reform of St Kevin's Institutions.

I found the details of institutional closures in the minutes of Eastern Health Board meetings on 9 January 1986 and 6 February 1986.

My account of the operations and eventual closure of the mother-and-baby home at Tuam was crucially informed by material from the Galway County Council Archives:

    – Finance / Estimate of Expenses, 1905–1967, with gaps, GC/F/1
    – Finance / Abstracts of Accounts, 1920–1975, GC/F/2
    – Finance / General Ledgers, 1947–1987, GC/F/3
    – Board of Health, Abstract of Accounts, 1926-1942 (GC5/22) & 1929–1942 (GC5/23)
    – Homes & Home Assistance Committee, Financial & Statistical Abstract, 1923–1944 (GC5/28 & 28b)

The Dublin Diocesan Archives was another valuable source:

    – Adoption Papers of Archbishop McQuaid
    – Adoption L11/A/1-122
    – Folder L11/A/1-6 'Homes'
    – L11/A/4 – Bessborough death rates 1939–1944
    – Folder L11/C/8/1-26 Baptism Certs

At the time of writing, the work of the Commission of Investigation into Mother and Baby Homes is ongoing, and its final report is due to be published in February 2020. I have made use of the Commission's interim reports, most notably the fifth, on burial arrangements in the institutions.

Select Bibliography

Books

Cecil J. Barrett, *Adoption: The Parent, The Child, The Home* (Clonmore & Reynold: 1952).

William Binchy, *A Casebook on Irish Family Law* (Professional Books: 1984).

Sister M. Emmanuel Browne, *A Tale of Two Hospitals: St Finbarr's Hospital – Regional Hospital* (D&A O'Leary: 1989).

Sister Rosemary Clerkin, *A Heart for Others* (Sisters of the Sacred Hearts of Jesus and Mary: 1983).

Mary Creighton, *The Baby Snatchers* (Blink Publishing: 2017).

James Deeny, *To Cure and to Care* (Glendale Press: 1989).

Lindsey Earner-Byrne, *Mother and Child: Maternity and Child Welfare in Dublin, 1922–60* (Manchester University Press: 2007).

Diarmaid Ferriter, *Occasions of Sin: Sex and Society in Modern Ireland* (Profile Books: 2009).

Frances Finnegan, *Do Penance or Perish* (Oxford University Press: 2001).

June Goulding, *The Light in the Window* (Poolbeg Press Ltd: 1998).

Phyllis Hamilton, *Secret Love* (Mainstream: 1995).

Sharon Lawless, *Adoption Stories* (Carnegie Hill Publishing: 2016).

Derek Leinster, FIRST edition: *Hannah's Shame* (2005).

Maria Luddy, *Prostitution and Irish Society, 1800–1940* (Cambridge University Press: 2007).

Angus McIntyre, *The Liberator: Daniel O'Connell and the Irish Party 1830–47* (Hamish Hamilton: 1965).

Mike Milotte, *Banished Babies* (New Island: 1997).

Annie Murphy, *Forbidden Fruit* (Little, Brown: 1993).

Alison O'Reilly, *My Name Is Bridget* (Gill: 2018).

Caitríona Palmer, *An Affair with My Mother* (Penguin: 2016).

Jacinta Prunty, *Our Lady of Charity in Ireland, 1853–1973* (Columba Press: 2017).

Mary Raftery and Eoin O'Sullivan, *Suffer the Little Children* (New Island: 1999).

Paul Jude Redmond, *The Adoption Machine* (Merrion Press: 2018).

Maura Richards O'Dea, *Single Issue* (Poolbeg: 1998).

Martin Sixsmith, *The Lost Child of Philomena Lee* (Pan: 2010).

James M. Smith, *Ireland's Magdalen Laundries and the Nation's Architecture of Containment* (University of Notre Dame Press: 2007).

J.H. Whyte, *Church and State in Modern Ireland, 1923–1979* (Gill and Macmillan: 1980).

Published reports and articles

Dan Barry, 'The Lost Children of Tuam', *New York Times*, 28 October 2017.

Aidan Beatty, 'Where Does the State End and the Church Begin?': The Strange Career of Richard S. Devane', *Studi Irlandesi* no. 9 (2019).

Finn Delaney, Jacinta Kiely and Linda Lynch, 'Archaeological Excavation Report, Toberjarlath, Tuam', *Eachtra Journal*, no. 17, April 2014.

Richard Devane, 'The unmarried mother: some legal aspects of the problem', *The Irish Ecclesiastical Record* (series 5, vol. XXIII, January–February 1924).

Pamela Duncan, 'Extent of child deaths in Dublin home revealed', *Irish Times*, 21 June 2014.

Maria Luddy, 'Sex and the Single Girl in 1920s and 1930s Ireland', *The Irish Review* no. 35 (Summer 2007).

Niall Meehan, 'Church and State and the Bethany Home', supplement to *History Ireland*, vol. 18, no. 5, September–October 2010.

Peter Murray, 'A Militant Among the Magdalens – Mary Ellen Murphy's Incarceration in High Park Convent During the 1913 Lockout', *Saothar* (Journal of the Irish Labour History Society), vol. 20, 1995.

Conall Ó Fátharta, 'Focus of Mother and Baby Homes Investigation has Moved onto Headline-Generating Institutions', *Irish Examiner*, 17 April 2019.

Maeve O'Rourke, Claire McGettrick, Rod Baker, Raymond Hill et al., *CLANN: Ireland's Unmarried Mothers and their Children: Gathering the Data: Principal Submission to the Commission of Investigation into Mother and Baby Homes.* Dublin: Justice For Magdalenes Research, Adoption Rights Alliance, Hogan Lovells, 15 October 2018.

Geoffrey Shannon, 'Human Rights issues at the former site of the Mother and Baby Home, Tuam, Co. Galway', Department of Children and Youth Affairs, 26 October 2018.

Ann Sheridan, 'Irish Bishop Was Accused of Raping His Own Niece', *Daily Mail*, 24 March 2019.

Joseph Summerville, 'Tuam Diocesan Assembly Bundoran, 23–29 October 1983', *The Furrow*, vol. 35, no.1 (January 1984).

Barbara Walshe and Catherine O'Connell, 'Consultation on the Options and Appropriate Courses of Action available to Government in relation to the site of the former Mother & Baby Home, Tuam, Co. Galway', 16 April 2018.

Film documentaries

Steve Humphries, director, *Sex in a Cold Climate*, Channel 4, 1998.

Note on Sources

Mia Mullarkey, director, *Mother & Baby*, Ishka Films, 2017.
Tanya Sillem and Katie Hannon, producers, 'Anatomy of a Scandal', RTÉ
   Prime Time, October 2011.

Radio documentary

Becky Milligan, producer, *The Home Babies*, BBC Radio 4.

Acknowledgements

I owe this book to the people who shared their stories with me. Many people in Ireland are breaking a silence for the first time, whether publicly or within their own lives. Women were called 'offenders', 'penitents' and worse for becoming pregnant out of wedlock. They often felt they had no choice and no say. It requires a deep resilience and determination to break through the shame bred by the culture and the institutions. No one can give anyone a voice. Space must be made for voices to be heard.

A friend of one of the mothers I met during the writing of this book had a tattoo on her back that read: 'There is no greater agony than keeping an untold story inside you.' There are still people bearing untold stories, including those who worked in the institutions and within the wider system that concealed the pregnancies of unmarried women and facilitated the adoption of their children. Ireland has experienced a time of radical change. The foundations of this change were laid by people speaking out when it felt impossible to do so. There are systems still in place that continue our history of institutionalization. The people affected by the institutional system of the very recent past should be listened to and learned from.

I was able to speak with only a fraction of the living survivors; and I was able to tell the stories of only a fraction of those I did speak with. My profound thanks to the people who appear in the preceding pages, whether under their own names or under pseudonyms. And my equal thanks to the many, many people whose stories are not told directly in this book, but who generously took time to talk with me and who deepened my understanding of the subject: Sheila O'Byrne, Laura and Mary Collins, Anna Corrigan, Terri Harrison, Francis Timmons, Beth Wallace, Carmel Larkin, Catherine Coffey, Theresa Hiney Tinggal, Ann Crowe, Gerry Corbett, Michael Donovan, Edel

Furlong, Marie Barry, Mary Smith, Noleen Belton, Kathleen Byrne, Joanne Byrne, Maureen O'Sullivan, Carol Cosgrove, Clodagh Hourigan, Elaine Mackey, Jane Conlon, Alice Young, Fiona Mills, Susan Dunne, Coleen Anderson, Kevin Battle, Peter Mulryan, Margaret McKinney, Deidre Wadding, Jarvia Foxter, Conrad Bryan, Damien O'Hare, Rita Collins, Siobhan Harman and many more. Rest in peace, Kathy McMahon and Dennis McKenney.

For their insights and advice, my thanks to: Catriona Crowe, Mary McAuliffe, Patricia White, Margaret Dromey, Donal O'Keeffe, Margot Doherty, Caitríona Palmer, Alison O'Reilly, Phil Garland, Charles Delap, Conor Dodd, Ruairí McKiernan, Helio Leon, Mia Mullarky, Sylvia Tighe Murphy, Jill Dinsdale, Paul Rouse, James M. Smith, Ailbhe Smyth, Frank Crummey, Maeve O'Rourke, Clodagh Malone, James Gallen, Ursula Halligan, Lisa Connell, Annmarie Kennedy, Susan Lohan, Lorraine Quinn and Sharon Lawless.

I am grateful to archivist Patria McWalter for facilitating research at the Galway County Council Archives and also to archivist Noelle Dowling for her help conducting research in the Dublin Diocesan Archives. Thanks also to the staff of the National Archives, Cork City and County Archives, the National Library of Ireland, Trinity College Library and the General Registration Office. Also to Theresa Friel and Loraine McGrattan for facilitating Freedom of Information requests to Tusla.

I would not be the writer I am without having worked with Brendan Barrington. As an editor he has provided a mentorship that is rare and invaluable. From the first story I pitched him for the *Dublin Review* as a young freelancer reporting on Syria, his insightful editing helped me to both hone my writing and to experiment. He believed a book needed to be written on Ireland's shame-industrial complex. This work would not exist without his vision and trust. Thanks also to Michael McLoughlin, Shân Morley-Jones and to everyone at Penguin Random House who helped make the book a reality.

The Irish Writers Centre, which has given me the wonderful opportunity to teach creative non-fiction to emerging writers, generously supported me to attend their Cill Rialaig writers' residency in 2018, a unique escape to a pre-Famine cottage on the edge of a cliff in a remote and breathtaking stretch of Kerry coast. Those were precious days and I met a wonderful group of writers.

Thanks to Simon, Ana, Ariane, Maryam, Aoife, John, Ruth, Niamh, Matt, Amy, Dave, Hugo, Olivia, Nicky and Orla for all their support. Thanks to Caitríona Daly for being one of the first pair of outside eyes to read this book.

I am grateful for my granddad Bill, who told the most incredible stories and who encouraged me to be a writer. For my nana Mary, who died when I was young but whose deeply thoughtful response to my mum's pregnancy with me tells me everything I need to know about the kind and independent woman she was. For my granny Máire, whose tight-knit group of friends was legendary. For my granddad Joe, who had an epic memory, who sang 'Tit Willow' and who told me proudly about refusing to shake de Valera's hand as a boy. Joe passed away peacefully at the age of ninety-three last year. This book is dedicated to them, in spirit.

This book is dedicated to my defiant parents, with all my love. For my mum, Róisín, who believes everything is possible. For my dad, Dermot, who is always in my corner. And for my brother, Rory, whose solid advice and big heart are a lifeline.